How to Observe Face – to – Face Communication: A Sociological Introduction

Matthew Speier
University of British Columbia

How to Observe Face-to-Face Communication: A Sociological Introduction

Goodyear Publishing Company, Inc.,
Pacific Palisades, California

Copyright © 1973 by Goodyear Publishing Company, Inc.
Pacific Palisades, California

Current printing (last digit):
10 9 8 7 6 5 4 3 2 1

ISBN: 0-87620-390-X
Library of Congress Catalog Card Number: 72-88567
Y-390X-6
Printed in the United States of America

To Jeremy and Michael,
and to all those who live at the edge of knowledge
and know the pleasure of its uncertain terrain.

The primary goal of the social sciences is to obtain organized knowledge of social reality. By the term "social reality" I wish to be understood the sum total of objects and occurrences within the social cultural world as experienced by the common-sense thinking of men living their daily lives among their fellow men, connected with them in manifold relations of interaction. It is the world of cultural objects and social institutions into which we are all born, within which we have to find our bearings, and with which we have to come to terms. From the outset, we, the actors on the social scene, experience the world we live in as a world both of nature and of culture, not as a private but as an intersubjective one, that is, as a world common to all of us, either actually given or potentially accessible to everyone; and this involves intercommunication and language.

All forms of naturalism and logical empiricism simply take for granted this social reality, which is the proper object of the social sciences. Intersubjectivity, interaction, intercommunication, and language are simply presupposed as the unclarified foundation of these theories. They assume, as it were, that the social scientist has already solved his fundamental problem, before scientific inquiry starts.

Alfred Schutz, 1953

Contents

x

Contents

Author's Foreword

This text is dedicated to the hope that a whole new generation of beginners in sociology and other social sciences will find here a means to build a new and more relevant and therefore more solidly based foundation for the study of man as a social animal. The strength of this foundation will have to be judged by the validity and usefulness of the edifice of knowledge that workers build up from it. This strength can only come about if students are willing to grant the credibility of the foundation in the first place as possibly leading to the kind of knowledge they are willing to devote their labors toward. The foundation must seem to provide an opportunity to increase human understanding, and by understanding we mean not only how we get on with our fellow men in the most mundane circumstances first but, also, how we strive to improve human conditions and how we can live with crises—if human understanding of these sorts cannot grow out of the foundation offered in this book, then it will most likely be ignored by the present and coming generations of beginning social science students.

I am absolutely convinced, however, that students will consider the new foundation some sociologists—particularly the ethnomethodologists —have been developing in recent years a very promising beginning. One of the most exciting developments I have witnessed in my teaching has been the receptiveness of beginning students to the invitation I have made to them to be co-workers in building that foundation together. To them, it is unprecedented that they should be asked to participate equally with an "expert" and a professor in forging new conceptual knowledge and collecting hitherto ungathered materials from social life. I have not asked them, as is too often the case in social science, to participate in formalistic intellectual ventures or imitative exercises. Instead I have asked them to take the phenomenological principle seriously: go and see for yourself what human activities consist of and how they are routinely organized; do not start with theory or even trust the theories of authorities, but use your own sensory apparatus and your own inferential capacities—just as you always do to make sense of the world you are asked to participate in outside the university, every day. Bring back information and figure out how to translate it into fertile conceptual terms that tell us how to account for the structure and process of that information, but always in a way that preserves the original integrity of the information.

This text is written in the same spirit. It allows me to share a type of sociological reasoning and the factual and conceptual outgrowths of that reasoning. I have tried to put that reasoning into its simplest and most straightforward form. The measure of success I will look for, is whether you learn how to formulate a sociological problem on your own and can do the work needed to develop it into a newsworthy finding. This measure may sound far too ambitious a goal for a beginner's text, and perhaps I will be criticized for giving the student too much credit. I do not think I do so, however.

I will also be criticized, I am sure, for not instilling in you the respect or reverence for high level theory, what C. Wright Mills has called "Grand Theory." In this regard I must frankly confess that highly elevated theorizing is a luxury available only to those disciplines that have worked for it—and sociology has not. I regard the learning situation I am recommending in this text as a necessary stage in early science.

I therefore present to you a highly unorthodox framework for an introductory textbook. It is a position that I am thoroughly committed to in my teaching and research and it has indeed earned me some disfavor in the academic world. However, my optimism springs from the enthusiastic responses of many students who have thanked me for the opportunity given them to study the social organization of their own communities directly through their own senses, which I recognized to be a far more enriching intellectual experience than merely being expected to learn what some sociologists have written in response to other sociologists.

I owe a great debt to various persons who have in one way or another led me to the writing of this book. My earliest teacher in these matters was Alfred Schutz, with whom I briefly studied in 1958 in New York City. But it was not until later in 1965 in California that I discovered the relevance of Schutz's work for changing the course of modern sociology. I encountered two men who opened doorways to a new sociology. At that time I came across the work of Harold Garfinkel and then a little later at Berkeley I studied with Aaron Cicourel. Both these men have written extensively on what is now known as "ethnomethodology";* their most basic assumptions about sociological method and reasoning, as well as their critiques of modern sociology owe much to the writings of Schutz. Their work has been a powerful influence on my thinking.

At Berkeley I also was introduced to the unpublished writings of Harvey Sacks. To him I owe perhaps the largest debt because of my decision to concentrate on the special field of conversational analysis he has pioneered. I am very grateful to him for providing me numerous unpublished drafts of his work over the past five years. I have often taken the liberty of referring to them in this text and in my work in general. I hope that he will not be too offended by the many simplifications I have made of his analyses for the sake of an effective general introduction to studying the natural history of conversational interaction.

I must also thank Professors Roy Turner, Henry Elliot, Don Zimmerman, and John Gumperz; and Bruce Katz, Stan Persky, Rudiger Krause, and the many other students who have worked with me, with all of whom I have personally discussed at one time or another some aspects of the material that has taken its present form in this text. I am also indebted to the writings of Emmanuel Schegloff and especially to the widely published work of Erving Goffman, whose conceptual richness and inventiveness has been a continuing source of illumination and an indispensable resource for me.

Some readers may wonder why I have not adopted the term "ethnomethodology" in the title of this brief text. It is because I believe the term is best applied as a professional label to a diverse group of practitioners who are not uniformly working along the same lines of analysis or who would not even all agree that this text is an ethnomethodological one. Also, this text is not intended to develop an esoteric speciality within professional programs of advanced sociological training but to reorient the discipline as a whole at an introductory level.

Matthew Speier
Vancouver, B.C., 1971

---

*See Hans Peter Dreitzel, *Recent Sociology, Vol. II: Patterns of Communicative Behavior* (New York: Macmillan Co., 1970), which devotes itself to presenting works in the "ethnomethodological paradigm," of which Cicourel and Garfinkel are leading exponents.

Preface

The purpose of an introductory course is to acquaint the beginning student with basic issues and materials of a discipline of knowledge. Normally, there are two methods of approaching an introductory course. The first, a survey of the discipline as a whole, presents the broadest scope of issues and materials. This method is essentially a review of the literature and as such it aims for literacy of materials in a particular field. A second method deliberately restricts its scope in favor of a deeper examination of a particular point of view toward a whole discipline. The aim of this method, in contrast to the first, is to be more creative by constraining both the materials and the analysis of those materials, in such a manner that the student will hopefully develop a greater mastery of one way of doing sociology, for example.

The educative advantage of the second approach, the one taken by this text, is the promotion of thoughtfulness through intellectual commitment, a feature normally absent from the first method because of the stress it places on literacy for its own sake. Survey outlines have always been the predominant form of introductory texts. It is often believed that the beginning student can make useful comparisons if presented with a smorgasbord of authoritative source materials from which he will be able to select those parts of the fare most interesting and congenial for future study or use.

It is my conviction, however, that the traditional survey method has not proven to be successful in undergraduate education, and that educators are increasingly turning away from this method and from the large survey textbook that usually accompanies it. They are seeking to replace it with more meaningful introductory formats and are either organizing courses around a single point of view, or combining several points of view with the aid of representative written materials.

It is also my belief that when the beginning student of sociology is confronted with the survey course at the worst he comes away bewildered and dissatisfied and at the best only achieves a superficial smattering of understanding. Those students who decide to major in the discipline soon find that they must make more intensive commitments to particular points of view, anyway, in order to achieve some workable degree of intellectual competence or professional training. But those who do not desire or get an opportunity to develop an interest of this magnitude are left with a fragmented knowledge which, however useful in limited ways, leaves them in a weak position to relate the survey course to themselves and to their daily lives, and to incorporate course material into their intellectual perception of the social world.

This text adopts a point of view on sociological reasoning. *It emphasizes a how-to-do-it approach to one type of sociology for the beginning student.* Normally, introductory sociology courses teach what sociology is by pointing out what sociologists have done, rather than by instructing the beginner in how to go about doing it for himself. This volume, then, may be conveniently thought of as a do-it-yourself manual; its aim is to provide you, the student, with a practical framework of sociological reasoning within which you can strike out to develop problems inventively and originally.

Although the text provides a set of readings to go with each chapter —those works that contribute to an understanding of the text's general perspective and which supply the student with conceptual tools related to that perspective—it emphasizes the role of firsthand observation in doing sociology. You will be encouraged to observe for yourself the ongoing events of everyday interactions. You will be called upon to develop observational and conceptual skills in seeing what others are doing when they communicate to each other in routine social environments. You will also be encouraged to draw upon your own resources of social knowledge and social experience. You will be asked to do simple field work in your own communities. Suggested field assignments, at the end of various chapters, will ask you to make and analyze observational records of social activities accessible to you. One way to think of the approach in the text is that it asks you to move out from the library into the natural environmental laboratory of your own social world and discover the methods used to communicate within it. How do everyday social participants organize their face-to-face communicative behaviors when they do activities together? This is the text's central question and guiding orientation.

The text focuses almost entirely on conversational communication, and only briefly mentions the nonverbal elements of interaction. This limitation is intentional, because it is felt that the visual and spatial elements of communicative behaviors are best left for a separate treatment, given the scope of this introduction.* However, it also appears a perfectly sensible and logical place to start a consideration of human communication activity with the ubiquitous phenomenon called "talk." It is virtually everywhere in the social world and no culture is free from it. Talk also allows for certain rigors of analysis because of everyone's familiarity with standard speech notational systems. Furthermore, much of what is understood by participants in a social environment gets communicated via talk, and perhaps even structured by it. Finally, it is a strange fact of intellectual history, in the face of the seeming importance of talk in social life, that sociology has virtually ignored its analysis.

The overall educative aim of the text, which should appeal to students of disciplines outside of sociology proper, is to enable the student to develop skills in seeing and understanding how the interactional fabric of everyday life works and to develop an awareness of the communicative order he is actively engaged in constructing—with his own contributory behavior in the social environment.

---

*I am presently planning a volume on the study of visual communications in society and social interaction.

How to Observe Face – to – Face Communication: A Sociological Introduction

Chapter One

The Natural History Approach
to the Sociology of Everyday Life

This course proposes that the student of social life adopt a very simple working method for his investigations. It is a method we might call naturalistic, in the same sense that biologists use that term for the study of natural history. The objects of study in a natural history approach to the sociology of everyday life consist of social phenomena that are amenable to naturalistic observations, i.e., the ongoing stream of naturally occurring social activities. Traditionally, sociological investigations have not developed out of nor aimed toward the model of investigation established by biology as far back as 1665, when Robert Hooke, first curator of the Royal Society of London, described cork and other tissues and introduced the term "cell." Sociology has grown up, instead, out of orientations within other areas of human intellectual fields, such as philosophy, political theory, history, and social criticism. It will not be possible in this course to trace these developments in the discipline, but in its early history sociological orientations were founded that remain strongly with us to the present day and which have to do with such basic notions as society, community, class, nation, race, culture, kinship, economy, and so on, all of which are deeply imbedded in our sociological as well as in our ordinary language.

These basic notions have so deeply entered into sociological thinking, that they have become conventional guides to formulating problems in the discipline. Following Thomas S. Kuhn, author of *The Structure of Scientific Revolutions,*[1] we might say that these notions have been the ingredients of a working paradigm for sociologists, or so it would seem. A paradigm, or "normal science," as Kuhn refers to it, defines legitimate problems and methods for a generation of scientific practitioners and their successors. These practitioners are able to enforce these definitions because they share two basic characteristics:

Their achievement was sufficiently unprecedented to attract an enduring group of adherents away from competing modes of scientific activity. Simultaneously, it was sufficiently open-ended to leave all sorts of problems for the redefined group of practitioners to resolve.[2]

Where social science is concerned, however, and in particular sociology, commitment to shared rules and standards of scientific practice is not evident in the same way as it is in the natural and physical sciences. If this commitment and apparent consensus are prerequisites for normal science, i.e., for the birth and development of a particular tradition of research, as Kuhn claims, then what appears on the surface to be a working paradigm for traditional sociology, with regard to the formulation of sociological problems, is in reality only one competing mode of scientific activity. Sociology, then, does not constitute a paradigm in terms of the two basic achieved characteristics of normal science. That is, there is wide disagreement among sociological practitioners as to what their working methods are and ought to be. Terms such as "society," "class," "culture," etc., are not treated as equivalent in meaning from one type of research to another in the discipline, and have become sources of continuing debate among practitioners who are seeking to clarify, specify, operationalize, and otherwise define these terms in research contexts. Indeed, some practitioners do not even regard such terms as relevant for their research. Much sociological writing is in fact devoted to resolving these debates over classic terms originating in the early works of political theorists, philosophers, historians, social critics, and so on.

There are, of course, many new terms and notions that have been added to the intellectual activity of the discipline, not all of which are relatives of the ancestral terms we have noted. But they have come into play in much the same manner as these terms: namely, they have been generated through initial theoretical interests rather than by derivation from naturalistic observations of everyday life.

Another aspect to the development of sociological problems through initial theoretical interests pertains to the practical demands of everyday life itself. Toward the end of his book, Kuhn says:

Unlike the engineer, and many doctors, and most theologians, the scientist need not choose problems because they urgently need solution and without regard for the tools available to solve them. In this respect, also, the contrast between natural scientists and many social scientists proves instructive. The latter often tend, as the former almost never do, to defend their choice of a research problem—e.g., the effects of racial discrimination or the causes of the business cycle—chiefly in terms of the social importance of achieving a solution.[3]

Sociology has paid considerable attention to developing theories about the social problems of our society, as any glance at publishers' catalogs will show. This is not the place to investigate the reasons for the predominantly theoretical stance taken by workers in sociology. In contrast, an orientation that is closer to early biological science will be proposed here that is decidedly empirical in its emphasis on using a natural history technique to study social life. But one clue to sociology's theoretical predicament is found in a well-known book by Philip Selznick (coauthor of perhaps the most widely distributed introductory sociology textbook in the world). In his study, *TVA and the Grass Roots,*[4] Selznick argues that the notion of "unanticipated consequences," where human actions are concerned, may be regarded as the "key analytical tool" for sociological inquiry. Selznick says, "the meaning of an act may be spelled out in its consequences and these are not the same as the factors which called it into being."[5]

This predominant focus of sociological reasoning on antecedent and consequential conditions surrounding social events has led to a disregard for conditions of the moment and for inquiries into the ongoing stream of observable behavior. This focus has practically precluded empirical observation from the problem-formation phase of analysis and has led to the prevailing theoretical interest in formulating sociological problems about the cause-and-effect relationships of social events, rather than first setting out to describe social events by direct empirical observation. The overall result of this abiding habit of theorizing social events into existence has been a marked disinterest in describing the mundane occurrences in the everyday social world.

More seriously, perhaps, generations of students have been trained to talk about the social world without ever taking the trouble to actually look at it as a necessary first step in talking about what exists in it. It has become commonplace for students to develop very elaborate and highly abstract ways to talk or write about society or class without making concrete observations. Moreover, when some concrete observations are brought into the discussion, they are normally treated as examples of underlying forces or causes at work and reckoned in terms of initial theoretical positions.

The hypothetical method, which has become highly successful over the centuries in the deductive analyses of the physical sciences, for example, has been promoted in the standard methodological approaches to social data. Students are encouraged to form and test hypotheses and after doing so will be asked to check them out against findings in the real world of social events. Typically, a sociological problem is decided on before the students look at social events and consider how they might best be described and understood in themselves. *The approach proposed by this text asks the student to derive problems from inspection of social data itself. The formulation of sociological problems has to be responsive to the data of observation.* In fact the noted paleontologist, George Gaylord Simpson, argues that, if there is any one basic feature to the so-called scientific method, it is observation.[6]

Let me give an example of what I mean. A short time ago a group of students came to see me for advice on a project for an introductory sociology course. They were studying children's behavior and were told they had to form a hypothesis about it. They presumably recalled from experience that children play together in groups. They also presumably recalled that on occasion a child can be noticed breaking away from the group. They hypothesized that, if a child is from a higher social class, then he would be more likely to break away than a child from a lower class background. My response to this project was to ask a simple question: Had any of the students actually observed children on a school ground, the setting they had chosen to consider? Their answer was no.

Obviously, then, it is conceivable to formulate a sociological problem around the theoretical issue of causality: i.e., what causes children to break away from other children when they play? One can find the underlying agents that determine this sort of behavior, the students reasoned, by forming an hypothesis about a characteristic of children's social backgrounds which presumably does the job of explaining the behavior. If checked out with the children (by interviewing their parents perhaps), one could discover whether those that broke away were indeed of one or the other class. If higher, then the hypothesis is confirmed and, if lower, it is disconfirmed.

What can we make of this procedure? Obviously, the problem was informed by a notion of social-class influence on one's behavior. That is, the problem was theoretically conceived from a traditional concept in sociological inquiry and as such it was imported (bootlegged would be a better term) into the specific context under study, children's behavior in school yards. To propose an alternative procedure would be to ask, What do the children's behavioral events consist of, in and of themselves and as topics of inquiry in their own right? That is, what is the behavioral context of children at play in a school yard? What do their activities look like and what is their structure and organization? How do the children organize their interactions as orientations to each other and to the ongoing sequence of activity as a whole? Can the sequential flow of activity be analyzed in terms of the children's methods of orienting to that flow and to each child's participation in it? And so on.

While it is possible for us to describe a child's actions as "breaking away," do we have any empirical warrant to do so without consulting the data itself? It may be the case that we are witnessing leave-taking events among children and as such there may be numerous methods children use to leave each other's presence. And what is the relation of a child's leaving the arena of action to what he is about to do next or to the part he played in the activity? Are the children playing a game or just conversing on some topic of mutual interest? Are they preparing to go home or talking routinely about the school day with each other? These questions are just some that one could ask. But in each case one would have to ask questions based on some concrete observations. To suggest that children's activity can be described in terms of class-determining forces that govern how they leave each other's presence is an irrelevant orthodoxy that leaves aside the vital formulations needed to describe the events themselves.

What does a simple biological model of investigation look like? Keep in mind I am speaking of eighteenth-century biology, although the model still holds for some biological research, even in the present day of advanced electron microscopy. Consider the branches of biology known as ecology and ethology. The following is an excerpt from a recent issue of *Time* and it pertains to recent attempts to study the adaptability of animals to their natural environments.

> Among the odder jobs in the U.S. these days is one held by a man in northern Colorado who spends hours following a pronghorn antelope, watching it feed, and then whispering into a tape recorder. Absurd? Hardly. By such surveillance, ecologists are learning the animal's precise relationship to its environment—the grasslands of the American West.[7]

In such a manner the ecologist gathers many hours of observations on the habits of the creature. It is a painstaking enterprise and cannot be done by any theoretical shortcuts. Either there will be a highly detailed record from which to derive facts and crucial analytic problems (although many problems worked out or originated elsewhere may be applied later to the data) or else there simply will not be any advances in understanding the life of the creature in its environment.

What we mean by a natural history approach to everyday life, then, is a sociology which begins with a collection of data gathered from the natural habitats of humans who are doing things together in a shared environment. In this manner, sociology begins as primitive science and trains itself on the events of everyday activities. The sister discipline of sociology, anthropology, has indeed been practicing this direct observational method for a long time and has given to it the name "ethnography." The problems anthropologists have faced in their work are many but, pertinent to our discussion, an outstanding one has been the organization of observational data into traditional categories dealing with the classic functions of social life, e.g., the family, religion, political activity, subsistence activity, the forms of art and music, etc. Like the sociologists, the anthropologists have been oriented to the traditional notions of social institutions found within societies and cultures. On the pitfalls of retaining the traditional institutional labels of society, the anthropologist Moerman, in a paper on the Lue of Thailand, says the following:

Contemporary ethnography contains no explicit and consistent procedures for relating actual on-going interactions to the abstract roles, norms, rules, institutional labels, etc., which the interactions are supposed to somehow represent. There is characteristically no reason other than professional orthodoxy for supposing that what transpires between two individuals is, for example, relevantly genealogical and not sexual, political, economic, etc. . . . The reader who encounters the observation that, "of the fifteen plots acquired by gift, most were given by brother to brother or by father to son" . . . is seduced by anthropological concern with kinship into supposing that genealogical connections motivated and explain the transactions. Only an overpowering faith in the omni-relevance of one's professional scheme of classification could recommend editing away the undoubtedly large number of social scenes which must have transpired between one event and "the next stage of this social drama [which] followed the month of the Chipenji gathering" . . . [8]

Notice the similarity of this discussion to the one about the children in the school yard. Both discussions ask what the investigator intends to take as the objects of study and *both suggest that traditional classifica-tions and notions of how to study the relevance of social data, any concrete instance of it, must be reconsidered in the light of what the instance itself can be made to be relevant for, from the point of view of social participants themselves, and how we can render that point of view, using analytic concepts suitable to understand it.*

We take up this need to connect our own conceptual abstractions to the social data under scrutiny—participants' knowledge of their own activities and the methods they use to organize them—in the next chapter. Suffice it to present an example to clarify the foregoing remarks at this point.

Suppose you select a particular setting in everyday life that for one reason or another appeals to your interests. Let us say you chose to study a bus. You might not find this mundane setting very exciting at first glance, yet, from your own experience, you may have noticed the kind of social patterning that occurs there very regularly and an interesting fact about that fascinates you: riders are temporarily confronted with others who share their "quarters" in close proximity (think of elevators as similar environments). They must engage in very uniform behavior as riders. But at times you notice that apparent strangers who occupy adjacent seats enter into a state of talk with each other. You note that, more often than not, unacquainted parties do not engage each other conversationally. They sit in fixed positions and most of their activity consists of the working of their eyes and the movements of their head.

A structure of communications presents itself to your observing eye. You see that a set of methodical behaviors organizes the structure into recognizable patterns: attentions and involvements are differentially allocated among the riders. The actions of the driver stand in special relation to that of the riders and the forms of social intercourse between driver and rider are regulated by methodical orientations and by enforced rules of communication that differ from those existing between one rider and another. In this manner you begin to discover a small rule-governed world of methodical actions and appearances, practical activities, and regulated conversation.

In an analysis of this world, using the data of your observations, you find that you must build a conceptual machinery to account for the concrete events you have recorded. For the most part it must be built out of specific details of the naturalistic activity in the bus, and it serves to do just that job, if nothing else. What it avoids is the necessity of junking many concepts and notions that were imported into the analysis by theoretical fiat, one might say, e.g., by irrelevant orthodoxies. On the other hand, it will prove very likely that your findings about this particular environment will be usable for other environments, not just other buses of course, but settings that look quite different at first glance. People are brought together in close proximity in many different kinds of public places and presumably they get to know how to organize their actions towards others, within them. In many settings people who were previously unacquainted engage in conversation quite naturally. In situations where persons either know each other or are strangers to each other the events of talk and of exchanged looks and gestures may have very uniform features from one setting to the next.

In the study of naturalistic activity the search for the invariant properties of cultural patterning takes precedence over other aims, in the same way that the whole science of biology appears to rest on the recognition of an invariant organizing principle for all life forms, the cell. The systematic development of sociology—the science of everyday life —can progress successfully only insofar as it seeks to discover the invariant properties of culturally organized activities. The social objects under study must yield discoveries about how they work as naturalistic events.

Summary

Traditional sociological analysis has not employed a naturalistic approach to the study of man in his social environment. Instead, it has grown up within a prevailing atmosphere of speculative theorizing about the relation of man to society and culture. It has sought to map this relation out in essentially theoretical terms, without initially formulating sociological problems in which conceptual terms clearly correspond to actual events in the social stream of life and are in fact responsive to those empirical events. It is perhaps an overused cliché, but the science of sociology sprang up out of sophisticated armchair theorizing by individuals whose sensitivity, intelligence, and social conscience led them to posit grand problems in society as they saw them in the context of common-sense issues relevant for and shared by others in their time and culture. From the beginning, sociological problems were often formulated in response to "the social importance of achieving a solution," to quote Kuhn again. From a citizen's point of view this response makes good common sense.

    However, the relation between common-sense thinking about society and the science called sociology is not properly understood (it is discussed in the next chapter). It is very important to understand the role of this relationship in deciding what the objects of sociological study ought to be and, consequently, how problems are to be formulated about these objects. *We shall propose a way to study how men's communicative actions and activities occur within an organization of daily practices guided by common-sense understandings.* In the next chapter, we will discuss the meaning of human organization in terms of the following statement made by Schutz:

> Thus, the exploration of the general principles according to which man in daily life organizes his experiences, and especially those of the social world, is the first task of the methodology of the social sciences.[9]

Our most important goal, then, is to consider how we can construct precise and valid natural histories of the social organization of everyday life experiences.

Now this goal is not original, since it can be found spelled out in 1895 in the writing of the father of modern sociology, Emil Durkheim, who was himself trying to overcome the theoretical bias of traditional sociologists before him:

> And in truth, up to the present, sociology has dealt more or less exclusively with concepts and not with things. Comte, it is true, declared that social phenomena are natural facts, subject to natural laws. He thereby implicitly recognized their character as things, for in nature there are only things. But when he passes beyond these philosophical generalities and attempts to apply his principle and develop from it the science implied in it, he, too, takes ideas for the subject matter of study. It is the course of human progress that forms the chief subject of his sociology.[10]

As Durkheim pointed out, science ought not to proceed from ideas to things, but from things to ideas. The theoretical bias of early sociologists prevented them from adopting the correct method used in natural history and from acquiring objective results. Ideas or concepts, Durkheim emphasizes, "are not legitimate substitutes for things," and he asserts that the "first and most fundamental rule" of sociological observation is: "Consider social facts as things."[11]

If Durkheim has indeed spelled out this goal, why is it being raised again in this text more than 75 years later? It is simply because that goal has never been realized. Durkheim's proposal had a very serious flaw in it, one that precluded the accomplishment of a natural history of social experience. It involves his mis-assessment of the role of ideas or concepts in human organization and everyday social activity. Desirous of liberating sociological science from commonplace ideas, he also unwittingly threw out the subject matter for that science, namely, the social organization of those commonplace ideas. He failed to distinguish between the organization of science and the organization of society of which science is a very specialized and uncommon part. This point will form the main subject for the next chapter.

Notes

[1] Thomas S. Kuhn, *The Structure of Scientific Revolutions* (Chicago: University of Chicago Press, 1962).

[2] Ibid., p. 2.

[3] Ibid., p. 163.

[4] Philip Selznick, *TVA and the Grass Roots: A study in the Sociology of Formal Organization* (New York: Harper & Row Torchbook, 1966).

[5] Ibid., p. 253.

[6] George Gaylord Simpson, "Biology and the Nature of Science," *Science* 139, No. 3550 (Jan. 11, 1963): 81.

[7] *Time,* March 23, 1970, p. 72.

[8] Michael Moerman, "Analysis of Lue Conversation: Providing Accounts, Finding Breaches, and Taking Sides," in *Studies in Interaction,* ed. David Sudnow (New York: Free Press, 1971), pp. 170–228.

[9] Alfred Schutz, *Collected Papers, I: The Problem of Social Reality* (The Hague: Martinus Nijhoff, 1962), p. 59.

[10] Emil Durkheim, *The Rules of Sociological Method,* trans. S. A. Solovay and J. H. Mueller and ed. George E. G. Catlin (New York: Free Press, 1962), pp. 18–19.

[11] Ibid., pp. 14–15.

Suggested Readings and Study Questions

1. Thomas S. Kuhn, *The Structure of Scientific Revolutions* (Chicago: University of Chicago Press, 1962), chapters 1 through 4.

What is a scientific revolution and how does it compare to the popular idea that science is continually evolving in a given direction? Do you think that sociology has ever had the period of natural history investigations that all physical and natural sciences presumably began with? Can you locate some source books on the history of social science to find out whether there has ever been the "normal science" that Kuhn speaks of in reference to other sciences? Can you make a list of sociological discoveries since the discipline first began, using the list provided in Norman S. Cohn, *Elements of Cytology* (New York: Harcourt, Brace, & World, 1964), pp. xi-xvi, as an example of a summary of historical events? What do you think might constitute a sociological "specimen"?

2. Emil Durkheim, *The Rules of Sociological Method,* trans. S. A. Solovay and J. H. Mueller and ed. George E. G. Catlin (New York: Free Press, 1962), chapters 1 and 2.

In his chapters, "What is a Social Fact?" and "Rules for the Observation of Social Facts," Emil Durkheim presents his views on the relation of sociology to the norms of natural science. How do his views provide for the possibility of building a natural history of social phenomena? How does he distinguish between the social and the psychological, between individual and collective forms of behavior?

3. Raymond Firth, *Elements of Social Organization* (New York: Philosophical Library, 1951).

Firth is a renowned anthropologist whose famous study of Tikopia has merited him as a leading ethnographer of world cultures. In this general book he discusses the role of firsthand observation in studying human activity. Can you find any clues to the problem of relating the making of natural histories (social descriptions) to the making of social interpretations by the field worker?

4. Roger G. Barker, *The Stream of Behavior* (New York: Appleton-Century-Crofts, 1963), pp. 1–22.

Without getting into too great detail at this point, do you see any value to the author's concept of "behavioral units" in terms of making natural histories of human activity? Consider the role of taxonomy in scientific work. What would constitute a social taxonomy? Relate this question to your answers to study question number 1. How does time enter as an element in making natural histories of social activities?

5. Select a recent book on animal behavior or primate behavior and attempt to get a picture of how natural activities of nonhuman animals are described and analytically reconstructed.

Chapter Two

Necessary Suppositions for the Naturalistic Study of Social Organization

In chapter 1 the objects of study were classified as naturalistic everyday life events, namely, the social actions and activities of members who share understandings of how to organize their actions and activities into a common culture. It is to this central fact that we now wish to turn our attentions—that everyday life is indeed an organization of events. *Our first necessary supposition may then be stated in accordance with this fact, which itself needs no further proof of its intuitive credibility: The events of everyday life are organized into an ongoing social order.* Your own daily experience attests to the viability of the human organization of which you are a contributing participant. Consider, for example, the organized activity of your participation in a university course. The actions you take to complete the course are built upon your expectation that you will receive the appropriate credit for so doing, which is part of your plan from the start.

Plans are invariant features of the social organization of everyday events. Plans are constitutive of social order. The simplest of decisions to take a course of action, such as to prepare breakfast, is a plan that constitutes the order of all that is normally involved in breakfast preparations. But we must avoid the misunderstanding that we are suggesting that everything is planned out well in advance. When we meet surprising situations that suddenly confront us in the texture of everyday routines, we can organize our actions to confront them; organization of our outward behavior has a planfulness to it fashioned for the contingencies of the moment. Contrary to what you might at first think about plans, as being rigid responses to the social environment, they are in fact far more subtle and intricately flexible than that. This is because they are always taken from alternative possible planful actions open to you.

The consideration of orderliness in socially organized events and its basic feature of planfulness leads us to a second necessary supposition about social life: persons perform actions with respect to others in their environment, who are likewise able to perform actions in return. While it is possible to speak of individual human actions not directed toward others in our environment, e.g., smoking a cigarette in a solitary situation, we are concerned with human actions that are by their very nature social, i.e., directed toward those in our presence. This orientation towards others is quite naturally the basis in substance for what is thought of as the fabric of social life. The classical sociologist, Max Weber, defined social action in terms that have become guideposts to modern sociological thinking about social organization:

> In "action" is included all human behaviour when and in so far as the acting individual attaches a subjective meaning to it. Action in this sense may be either overt or purely inward or subjective; it may consist of positive intervention in a situation, or of deliberately refraining from such intervention or passively acquiescing in the situation. Action is social in so far as, by virtue of the subjective meaning attached to it by the acting individual (or individuals), it takes account of the behaviour of others and is thereby oriented in its course.[1]

This, then, is the third supposition: that human action is based on subjective interpretations on the part of the social actor.

The feature of human actions we are calling "subjective interpretation" is important enough to be elaborated in our discussion. On its proper understanding hinge vital issues in the spelling out of how social organization works. The notion of plans adverted to previously must make reference to a state of intentionality or purposefulness, otherwise it makes no sense. Insofar as persons attach subjective meaning to their actions, they are taking them in accordance with some understanding of how those actions can be accomplished with others who must achieve understanding of them in order to join in their accomplishment. Indeed, to assert that persons fashion their actions with others in mind and to expect that others operate in some reciprocal manner, is to ascribe a form of rationality to human activity. It is by no means a perfect form of rationality, since that would amount to precise knowledge of the predictable relation between means and ends, but neither is it ever expected to be perfect in some scientific sense of rationality.

In everyday life, rationality takes on a practical shape, it is what people think of as reasonable, in the same sense as one finds that idea built into the practical administration of the legal system, for example. Another term for this reasonableness is common sense. *Everyday rationality in social situations, then, is the exercise of the subjective interpretations that are possible within a common-sense frame of reference in thinking, or knowledge, and which enter into the construction of everyday discourse.*

Keep in mind that we are not using the idea of subjective interpretation in a popular sense. Subjective interpretations in everyday actions are not degraded or defective ones, or poor relatives of scientific and objective interpretations, as some logicians and philosophers have tended to treat them. That is, as typical schemes that orient persons' actions they are not normally defective by their fellow man's standards of reasonableness. When persons do indeed take courses of action that get them to appear unreasonable—and that occurs regularly, too—they come to be noticed only because the typically appropriate subjective interpretations for given social circumstances are being breached. The supposition of human action based on subjective interpretations of the actor and a fourth correlative supposition—that of common-sense rationality in everyday human conduct—taken together, provide us with a key topic for this chapter.

This topic is the relation between a conception of social organization and the suppositions we have spelled out here. Another way to conceive of this relationship is simply to put it into a question we might try to answer: What is the consequence of the suppositions we hold for an understanding of how those affairs are socially organized? In other words, how is common-sense experience socially organized? As Alfred Schutz puts it:

There will be hardly any issue among social scientists that the object of the social sciences is human behaviour, its forms, its organization, and its products. There will be, however, different opinions about whether this behaviour should be studied in the same manner in which the natural scientist studies his object or whether the goal of the social sciences is the explanation of the "social reality" as experienced by the man living his everyday life within the social world. ... *we take the position that the social sciences have to deal with human conduct and its common sense interpretation in the social reality, involving the analysis of the whole system of projects and motives, of relevances and constructs (in common sense experience).* ... Such an analysis refers by necessity to the subjective point of view, namely to the interpretation of the action and its settings in terms of the actor. Since this postulate of the subjective interpretation is . . . a general principle of constructing course-of-action types in common sense experience, any social science aspiring to grasp "social reality" has to adopt this principle also.[2]

Compare this view on the role of common-sense experience in everyday life, and its place in sociological analysis, with the following passages by Emil Durkheim, recalling our remarks at the end of the last chapter:

The sociologist ought, . . . whether at the moment of the determination of his research objectives or in the course of his demonstrations, to repudiate resolutely the use of concepts originating outside of science for totally unscientific needs. He must emancipate himself from the fallacious ideas that dominate the mind of the layman; he must throw off, once and for all, the yoke of these empirical categories, which from long continued habit have become tyrannical. At the very least, if at times he is obliged to resort to them, he ought to do so fully conscious of their trifling value, so that he will not assign to them a role out of proportion to their real importance.[3]

And again:

. . . it is not our aim simply to discover a method for identifying with sufficient accuracy the facts to which the words of ordinary language refer and the ideas they convey. We need, rather, to formulate entirely new concepts, appropriate to the requirements of science and expressed in an appropriate terminology. Of course, lay concepts are not entirely useless to the scholar; they serve as suggestions and guides. They inform us of the existence, somewhere, of an aggregation of phenomena, which, bearing the same name, must, in consequence, probably have certain characteristics in common. . . . But, as they have been crudely formed, they quite naturally do not coincide exactly with the scientific concepts, which have been established for a set purpose.[4]

Durkheim makes his position unequivocally clear, if not altogether convincing. (In the footnote to the second passage above, he says, "In actual practice one always starts with the lay concept and the lay term.")

Durkheim clearly treats lay conceptions or common-sense interpretations of social organization as defective, as though he looked upon them as poor rivals of science. Under what conditions for viewing human actions would a sociologist ascribe a scientific expectation to everyday discourse? That is, although Durkheim is perfectly correct in proposing that a science must have its own plausibility for a set of special problems and special terms of reference for them, he does not see that *lay conceptions themselves constitute an organization of social experience that provide us with a topic of analysis worthy of scientific study, indeed necessary to study if social experience is what we propose to be sciencing in the first place.* Moreover, Durkheim freely concedes in his footnote that the scientist must always start with a lay conception.

What role does Durkheim ascribe to common sense? Clearly he does not give to it the status of a key topic in the study of human life, but chooses instead to treat it as a rival or unacceptable competitor for scientific knowledge. He recognizes all too well that its presence and influence on human behavior is powerful, but likens it to a veil or an illusion that stands between things and ourselves. Pull it away and we will discover scientific truth. To Durkheim, then, common-sense knowledge is responsible for ideological analysis and could not therefore be expected to lead to science, as if that were its purpose. For some very strange reason he did not see that sociology might be developed into a science of common sense, that the elements of common sense could themselves be studied as proper subject matter for scientific and naturalistic treatments, and that the aim of a science ought to be the understanding rather than the replacement of the phenomena it studies.

In his paper entitled "The Concept of Organization," Egon Bittner makes a point that confirms Durkheim's argument about the separation of lay from scientific concepts as a basic rule for scientific analysis:

In general, there is nothing wrong with borrowing a common sense concept for the purposes of sociological inquiry. Up to a certain point it is, indeed, unavoidable. *The warrant for this procedure is the sociologist's interest in exploring the common sense perspective.* The point at which the use of common sense concepts becomes a transgression is where such concepts are expected to do the analytical work of theoretical concepts. When the actor is treated as a permanent auxiliary to the enterprise of sociological inquiry at the same time he is the object of its inquiry, there arise ambiguities that defy clarification.[5]

Bittner, unlike Durkheim however, insists that the common-sense perspective be explored as an area of dominant sociological concern. In his critique of the traditional approach to the study of social organization, Bittner assails the long-sustained convention of conceptually distinguishing formal and informal social structures. He does so on the grounds that to treat human organizations as normative idealizations and to interpret them literally as formal structures, is to do violence to the facts of every-day rational conduct that organization members engage in, i.e., how they construct their actions from day to day. (Notice that we are talking at this point about *an* organization, a particular one.) Criticizing Max Weber's famous study of bureaucratic organization as failing to live up to its objective of reconstructing bureaucratic organization from the actor's perspective, Bittner says:

He failed to grasp that the meaning and warrant of the inventory of the properties of bureaucracy are inextricably embedded in what Alfred Schutz called the attitudes of everyday life and in socially sanctioned common sense typifications.[6]

To summarize the discussion so far, we have been trying to see what import common-sense interpretations have for the study of social organi-zations. It should be clear by now that what cannot be avoided, and indeed ought to be used to its fullest advantage, is that the sociologist's own use of common sense as a resource ought not to obscure his main purpose—to study the forms of common-sense experiences themselves as they are manifested in social actions and activities. In this regard, organization is a concept which presupposes that everyday actors have at their normal disposal common sense schemes of interpretation as powerful resources for organizing their own daily activities. The proper-ties of organization, therefore, cannot be decided without reference to these methodical organizing activities constructed by social actors them-selves. By the word "reference" we mean quite simply their importation into analysis in the form of data on those methodical organizing activities.

So far, our list of necessary suppositions includes:

1. The events of everyday life are organized into an ongoing order of appearances.
2. Human action is oriented to others in the social environment.
3. Human action is based on the social actor's subjective interpretation of social reality.
4. Everyday conduct employs common-sense rationality.

We now add a further necessary supposition to this list. Implied throughout the previous discussion, it can now be stated explicitly: *All forms of human organization are based on the joint lines of action of participants, that is to say, they are brought together by their own concerted behaviors. We shall henceforth refer to this condition as the interactional arena.*

This course gets its point of view from our preoccupation with the arena of human interaction. The focus of our analyses and discussions is on the organization of interactional events. It should be pointed out, however, that not all studies of interactional events are based on a prevailing supposition of common-sense experience as the source of humanly organized interactions. There is another school of thought interested in interactions, but it conspicuously avoids the investigation of the common-sense principle in organizing such interactions. Instead it employs an approach akin to that expounded by Durkheim quoted earlier. It makes implicit use of common-sense resources in its interpretations of what interactions consist of—it could not do otherwise of course—but it does not treat these resources as topics of inquiry in their own right. An example will distinguish this approach from the one we propose here.

I chose this example from a reader entitled *Interaction Analysis: Theory, Research, and Application,*[7] which has a number of papers on various subjects from the study of aggressive behavior to teacher influence in classrooms. Let us consider the classroom environment for a moment. In one of the studies reported in this volume, observers watched various routine classroom activities in twenty-five classrooms at each grade level in an elementary school. The observers were trained to watch behavior and code or categorize what they saw according to a set of standardized items already known as generally applicable to human group behaviors. The author of this observational system states that a set of items was prepared for the analysis of classroom instructional activity and consisted of an observational system of 16 categories that was developed in order to test various hypotheses about classroom teaching generated from learning theory. These categories were grouped into four major subdivisions:

1. teacher indirect verbal behavior;
2. teacher direct verbal behavior;
3. student verbal behavior;
4. silence, or nonfunctional verbal behavior.

The observer tallies the behaviors that are recorded within each of these subdivisions for comparative purposes to aid him in his hypothesis testing about classroom behavior. For example, the total number of indirect tallies can be compared with the number of direct tallies recorded in a given observation period, or teacher talk can be compared with student talk, etc. By compiling a summary of such tallies into a statistical chart, a matrix, one can see at a glance the different statistical results for each of these categories in the observation system, and then be in a position to study certain patterns of teacher influence, the authors of this paper assert.

What behaviors are recognized by the observers as instances of this or that type of categorized behavior? What enables them to make decisions about coding the teacher-student interactions into the categories of the system they are trained to apply to what they see? Take "teacher direct verbal behavior," also called "teacher direct influence," for example. The following are offered as choices for the observer in coding teacher-student interactions:

Initiates information or opinion: Includes all statements regarding content or process that give information or opinion. Also included in this category are rhetorical questions.

Corrective feedback: Includes statements that are designed to indicate the incorrectness or inappropriateness of behavior, so that the student sees that his behavior is incorrect or inappropriate. . . .

Requests and commands: Includes directions, requests, and commands to which compliance is expected. Also included are questions preceded by a student's name after a question has been asked which the student has not indicated a readiness to answer.

Criticism and rejection: Includes statements that criticize or reject student ideas or behavior without reference to clearly identifiable authority. . . . Also included in this category are sarcasm and rejection or denial of student feelings.[8]

These, then, are the things observers are supposed to recognize so as to be able to score the appropriate categories when coding the classroom activity. That they can indeed recognize such behavioral categories is no surprise or wonder, since they are members of society who have the competence to make such judgments about the appearances of social activity before their eyes—if they could not in fact make such tallies, it would suggest they have not the means to culturally participate in everyday life as normal societal members. Although different observers may not always agree in their judgments about which piece of behavior goes under which category, they nevertheless can make interpretive selections of one kind or another *using some describable procedure* which they may be called on to report about should wide disagreement arise.

Now what is there about this observational method that does not meet with the approach proposed in this chapter? Why doesn't this method carry within it the acknowledgment of those suppositions we have called the suppositions of rationality, or common sense, and of the subjective interpretation of human actions? It fails to take these suppositions into its analysis as scientifically important topics and problems in their own right, but uses them instead as undisclosed or hidden resources in doing what looks like a very objective set of observations. That is, the patterned and structured features of talk that teachers and students organize together in the classroom are not examined for those properties that make them socially organized achievements by the talkers themselves. This is so because the analysis never takes up the methods the observers use to go about their recognition of specially coded behaviors in the first place. These methods are the undisclosed common-sense experiences and competences that observers possess, which enables them: to know a rhetorical question when they see one, to decide about inappropriate behavior in that setting when they see it happen, to recognize a request or a command when they hear it, to see a student indicating an unreadiness to answer when called upon to do so, and so forth. All of these abilities are indeed the subject matter, or the objects of study, for an interactional analysis, but nowhere are they investigated. Here, for example, is a paragraph from the findings of E. Amidon and J. Hough:

> The relationship of indirect to direct influence. The first important overall statistical description is the I/D ratio which is the total number of indirect teacher statements divided by the total number of direct teacher statements. In grades one and two the I/D ratio for all subject areas is between 1 and 1.4, indicating that the teacher uses more indirect statements than direct statements.[9]

Further on, they give the findings that teacher talk comprises 50 percent of talk in the first grade, 45 percent in the second grade, etc., and that student talk makes up 34–39 percent of the total interaction in the first and second grades, 33–36 percent in third and fourth, etc. Finally, we note that they call attention to the "percentage of silence" in their findings, 15 percent of the total lesson for first and second grades, etc.[10]

Can these statistical descriptions aid us in understanding the social organization of classrooms? Can we recover from these quantitative abstractions the way in which teachers and students organized their ongoing routines in the classroom setting? The entire research product presupposes a common-sense understanding of the features of classroom activity—who talks to whom, in what manner; who has special rights to talk, to be heard, to get others to be heard, to get others to be silent, to run the order of events; who can be appealed to, sanctioned, called on, expected to take turns; and so forth—without, however, giving us an interactional analysis of these events and their formal or structural features as organized by the participants of this environment.

Instead, the research cited above is informed by theories of learning which become rationales for studying the environment of the classroom and provide the researchers with theoretical purposes and the means of generating hypotheses out of these purposes. *What is treated as a relevant problem of study—the types of teacher influence used in the classroom—is solved by a quantitative inspection of the amount a teacher talks, a student talks, or the amount of silence of both. But what is amount of talk?* The number of words per minute? The number of sentences? Is a teacher's silence equivalent to a student's silence, and what is a silence? Is it merely an interval of time between two uttered sounds? Or might it be something far more subtle, such as unwillingness to speak when called upon to do so, or a pause in the middle of one's remark that clearly belongs to that person and to that remark?

We take up issues such as these in coming chapters. It is clear that such issues are at the heart of interactional analysis and must be explored if we are to discover how cultural participants organize their everyday events together. It is not enough to be able to code a sarcasm or a rejection in order to test hypotheses about classroom learning. The way in which participants organize their interactions so as to systematically produce sarcasm or rejection, or whatever else was noted in the classroom study cited above, becomes the object of study in a naturalistic investigation of the school setting. *Therefore, the question we take to be most relevant for a naturalistic science of sociology is: How do members of the society methodically construct interactions into mutually organized social activity?*

A sixth supposition can now be entertained in light of the foregoing discussion. *This is the supposition of a grammar of interaction and, with it, the rules for using that grammar.* To answer our question about how members of a society go about constructing interactions into organized activities, we must suppose that they have at their disposal some means to do so in the nature of a grammar of rules, or procedures, or methods, or principles, call them what you will—any of these terms is at present interchangeable. Such rules are used by everyday participants to organize lines of action taken with others, who presumably are able to recognize and use the rules as well. Organized social activity requires the mutual participation of persons who are in possession of a corpus of rules and who can use them intelligibly, recognize their misuse, invoke them when dealing with others in socially situated circumstances, and otherwise treat others as competent rule users. The rules of interaction can be appealed to as enforceable and sanctionable features of everyday life. Every culture has a number of special statuses reserved for those who do not display understanding of interactional rules, who carry on as though ignorant of a grammar of interaction within the culture; for example, fool, retarded, mentally ill, eccentric, child, etc.[11]

Two analogies will be helpful in thinking about the notion of a grammar of interaction and its rules of application.

The first analogy relates to the domain of linguistics. We can speak of a particular language as having a grammar. Any native speaker of that language has the presumed competence to speak recognizable and acceptable sentences in the language. Obviously, lacking that competence he would be unable to perform speech that would qualify him as a native speaker in that language. What he must possess in order to display competence is the "mechanism" that lies behind sentence production, namely, the grammar and its rules. By means of this mechanism he is able to generate sentences ever anew, unique ones that he has never produced before. The grammar provides the speaker with a set of linguistic instruments with which to correctly fashion a sentence out of other units of the language, e.g., words.

The words of a language can be combined into seemingly infinite combinations and permutations of strings of words. Obviously, only some of those strings will make sense; that is, be recognizable as sentences. Yet, even when some strings make no sense on the surface, for example, "colorless green ideas sleep furiously" (to use the often cited one found in the linguist Noam Chomsky's writings on grammar), we can nevertheless discern a grammatically coherent pattern to the string, even if we can make very little sense out of it. It has grammatical if not meaningful sense to it, we might say. This is because the ordering of the words is in accordance with some underlying syntactical structures that the grammar of English generates in systematic fashion, having to do with noun and verb phrases.[12]

We are not engaged in the study of linguistics, of course, but we raise this consideration of the rules of English syntax because we intend to make the analogy between language and interaction insofar as rules governing both are concerned. As the linguist points out, the grammar of a language assigns a structural description to any sentence produced in that language. Where interactions are concerned, if we suppose they are routinely organized in a rule-governed manner analogous to the sentences of a language, what structural description can we assign to any interactional event so as to empirically account for how participants produced it? *To put this more simply, what kind of analysis do we have to make to account for how interactional events happen? How do interactional events work?*

The second analogy pertains to playing certain games. Take chess, for example. The syntax of chess would include the known rules of chess. Any events that transpire between players of the game, the moves they take with respect to each other as competing players, would presumably be describable by the basic rules of chess; e.g., player *A* moved his pawn to Queen's Knight 3, and whatever his strategy or the outcome of his move, it had to be made in accordance with the rules governing how pawns move. But the rule regulating how pawns move obviously does not account for the reason behind the move—the strategic interaction of the player who seeks to capture the King of his opponent. Nevertheless, to investigate chess strategies the moves must be part of the terms of reference of the description of the strategies, and by laying out a string of moves one is in a position to study the planfulness of the series constituting a strategic activity.

To study the game of chess as a sequence of moves taking chess partners' moves into account, one would require the corpus of rules of chess as an interpretive schema for recognizing and distinguishing legitimate from illegitimate moves. To each and every move observed, one could assign a structural description in terms of the particular named pieces moving from one locatable square to the next. Any references to strategies in the description of the progressive moves, e.g., move eventuating in Queen's Rook 6 placing opponent's King in check, would require structural descriptions all along the way to show how a strategy was organized.

In other words, the rules for proper play are powerful constraints on how players can organize game interactions with respect to the move-by-move progress of the game and its logical outcomes. While the rules do not cover all the actions surrounding a game, such as talking, eating while playing, deciding where to play or when to start, etc.,[13] none of these normal human conditions need be present for a game to be played. Computers can be programmed to play chess and they presumably do not have to attend to these other conditions present when normal interactants play chess. Yet, it can be said that two computers played a game of chess and one beat the other. It is sometimes the practice for chess players to play by mail, merely writing out the next move, mailing it to an opponent, and waiting for his reply. Surely, everything that transpires in the lives of the separated players between moves cannot be made necessary terms of reference in order to describe the moves and outcomes of the game. In this respect, the moves and the rules regulating the moves fully constitute the essential activity called chess. Whatever we might need to describe all other interactional events that occur while chess is played by two confronting players, we would at least need the knowledge of chess rules and their regulative power over strategic moves organized in the players' service.

We have been making an analogy between language and interactions on the one hand, and games and interactions on the other, for the purpose of arguing that a grammar or syntax presupposes that participants are oriented to the rule-governed character of language or game activity. Likewise, interactional activity, whatever its substantive nature, has a syntax of rule-governed behavior to which interactants are continually oriented.

Given all the stated suppositions, what would we require as a working method for a sociological inquiry that would incorporate them? In going about our examination of social phenomena in everyday life within a naturalistic perspective, *we seem to require a method with at least the following two conditions:*

(1) A piece or segment of human interaction (the meaning of "piece" or "segment" is problematic, as compared to the meaning of "sentence" or "move" in a game—which we discuss later on).
(2) An analysis of the piece (1) that accounts for the manner in which it took place, i.e., an analysis that stands as an empirically valid structural description of it.

We can see from these conditions that the minimal requirements of the method proposed is that there always be a segment of interaction and some structural description of the segment. The analytic machinery constructed for each segment aims at seeing precisely how that segment works as a piece of organized human interaction. Some parts of this machinery might be borrowed from other analyses of other interactions; the machinery might serve again in a new context of empirical material. To the extent that it does, that part of the analysis is generalizable. But new machinery will always have to be fashioned, to some extent, to deal with the new empirical material. In this fashion the student will find he makes discoveries steadily and does not have to scrap some theoretical apparatus that does not apply, where he started out with the hope or expectation that it would apply, e.g., some hypothesis.

Naturally, what we decide is a satisfactory solution to (2) above, an analysis that accounts for the segment, is the crux of the enterprise. To start with, we cannot expect more than the simplest or crudest end products, whose empirical validity hopefully will be demonstrated, but which are really more of a start and a promise of what might follow than a conclusively final treatment.[14]

Quite often our analysis will produce spin-offs, things that will suggest other analytic problems, related but not central to the initial problem the data exposes.

One way to characterize this method of approaching human behavior is to say that it is the method of instances. We look at interactional events as instantial cases and we try to account for their workings in each concrete case, always showing the tie between our abstract conceptions and conclusions and the concrete data on which they are based.

To conclude this chapter, the distinction between analytic and normal knowledge is stressed. Analytic knowledge originates when scientific problems about human activity are posed. These problems are not a direct product of the practicalities of everyday common-sense living and its special forms of knowledge, but constitute an inquiry into these forms of common-sense knowledge and experience. The kind of knowledge that this course strives for as a scientific task in understanding everyday life is not required for participation in everyday life, as though we could not carry on our daily business well enough without valid scientific knowledge about how we do in fact carry on. Rather, the course seeks to discover the structure and processes of such everyday participation. Unlike much traditional sociology, the point of view presented in this course does not look upon everyday social participants as protoscientists or poor scientists, who look to, or need, a scientific analysis of social life in order to live it better.

The point of departure we propose does not initially seek to remedy everyday life of whatever defects participants find in it. Not because we do not find defects—what one normally thinks of as social problems—but because of a firm commitment to the priority of characterizing how human interactions take place. Humanistically speaking, however, if one were in possession of characterizations of everyday life that were true, one would gain deeper insight into the workings of that life, and its clarification might be profitably used in many ways. It may be a little too early to say exactly how that might be achieved, as much as we might want to rush in that direction. A prognosis is offered later in the text.

The next chapter takes up some of the aspects of building analytic machinery for an understanding of interactional events.

Notes

¹Max Weber, *The Theory of Social and Economic Organization,* trans. A. M. Henderson and Talcott Parsons, and ed. Talcott Parsons (New York: Free Press, 1965), p. 88. The suppositions of common-sense rationality and of the subjective interpretation of human action are both derived from the phenomenological analysis of everyday life by Alfred Schutz. For the importance of intersubjectivity, interaction, intercommunication, and language as undefined yet implicitly used elements of sociological reasoning, see Schutz's paper "Common-Sense and Scientific Interpretation of Human Action," in his *Collected Papers, I: The Problem of Social Reality* (The Hague: Martinus Nijhoff, 1962), pp. 3-47, as well as his paper "On Multiple Realities" in the same volume, pp. 207-259. In his second volume of *Collected Papers* see also "The Problem of Rationality in the Social World," pp. 64-90. Taking many of his ideas from the latter paper of Schutz, Harold Garfinkel has developed his own treatment on common-sense rationality in "The Rational Properties of Scientific and Common Sense Activities," in his volume of papers, *Studies in Ethnomethodology* (Englewood Cliffs, New Jersey: Prentice-Hall, 1967), pp. 262-284.

²Schutz, *Collected Papers,* p. 34.

³Durkheim, *Rules of Sociological Method,* p. 32.

⁴Ibid., pp. 36-37.

⁵Egon Bittner, "The Concept of Organization," *Social Research* 32 (1965):241. Italics added.

⁶Ibid., p. 246.

⁷E. Amidon and J. Hough, eds., *Interaction Analysis: Theory, Research, and Application* (Reading, Mass.: Addison-Wesley, 1967).

⁸Ibid.

⁹Ibid.

¹⁰Ibid.

¹¹The notion of rule-governed interaction is basic to the so-called ethnomethodological sociologists. An outstanding exponent of this perspective, and one to whom I owe my understanding of practical actions and the properties of everyday practical reasoning, is Harold Garfinkel. A key paper among his writings is "Studies of the Routine Grounds of Everyday Activities," found in his collected papers, *Studies in Ethnomethodology* (Englewood Cliffs, New Jersey: Prentice-Hall, 1967), pp. 35-75. I also owe much to Aaron Cicourel's discussions of practical rationality in his *Method and Measurement in Sociology* (New York: Free Press, 1964), pp. 189-224, and his volume, *The Social Organization of Juvenile Justice* (New York: John Wiley, 1968), pp. 45-57.

¹²My first exposure to this analogy with linguistics was in the lectures of Aaron Cicourel delivered at Berkeley in 1966. He introduced me to the current trends in linguistics (e.g., Chomsky's transformational grammar), anthropological linguistics (componential analysis) and socio- and psycho-linguistics, including studies in the child's acquisition of grammar. See for example Cicourel's paper "The Acquisition of Social Structure: Towards a Developmental Sociology of Language and Meaning," in *Understanding Everyday Life,* ed. Jack D. Douglas (Chicago: Aldine Press, 1970), pp. 136-168.

¹³For a description of those aspects of game interactions that fall outside of what Garfinkel refers to as "basic rules," see Garfinkel, "A Conception of, and Experiments with, 'Trust' as a Condition of Stable Concerted Actions," in *Motivation and Social Interaction,* ed. O. J. Harvey (New York: Ronald Press, 1963), pp. 187-238. Also see Goff-

man's discussions of "gaming" behavior in his *Encounters* (Indianapolis: Bobbs-Merrill, 1961).

[14]A final treatment would in fact be an advanced state of theory which would allow us to generate or reproduce those behaviors that were originally accounted for in a piece of methodically produced behavior. That is, precise ability to duplicate a set of behaviors from a formal set of instructions derived from an analysis of these kinds of original behaviors would constitute scientific understanding.

For example, if one could build a machine that could converse with a human, based on a successful simulation of the formal properties of human speech, that accomplishment would show advanced understanding of the phenomenon of conversation, i.e., would demonstrate a theory of it in practice. A competent machine speaker could carry on fluent conversation with a human speaker. The interesting thing to note in this example is that what may indeed come about is that, in aiming for a conversation of this sort by a machine, linguistic competence might be achieved first, rather than interactional competence. To achieve the latter a machine would have to be programmed to act as a normal member of the society, which may not be possible given it would always be a machine-member, no matter what interactional skills were programmed into it. It would have to have an experiental life of its own and a relationship with other humans. It would more likely become a member of a machine-intelligent culture, quite different from a human culture, that is, unless it were disguised to pass as man.

Suggested Readings and Study Questions

1. Schutz, *Collected Papers,* pp. 3-47, pp. 207-259.

Distinguish between the two types of interpretation described by Schutz that pertain to very distinct forms of rationality. What role in common-sense thinking does Schutz attribute to constructs of typicality? What is the reciprocity of perspectives used by everyday participants and what is its relation to intersubjectivity? How does Schutz conceive of a project of action and its relation to time? Which layer of reality is the "paramount" reality and in what sense is it so? What does Schutz mean by the *epoché* of the natural attitude in everyday life?

2. Cicourel, *Method and Measurement,* pp. 172-224.

What is the significance of language for the suppositions of this chapter, insofar as you are able to relate Cicourel's eighth chapter to this one? How does he treat the relation between norms and social meaning, and what criticisms does he make of traditional sociological conceptions of norms for social behavior?

3. Garfinkel, *Ethnomethodology,* pp. 35-75, 262-284.

What does Garfinkel mean by "background understandings" and what are some of its features? What "experiments" are reported on the investigation into breaching expectancies in normal environments? How would you begin to define a "normal environment?" Choose any of the items in the inventory of the properties of practical reasoning and supply some data from your own experience to document their existence. Attempt minor breaches of background expectancies in your daily activities and make a record of the results. Do they confirm the existence of an implicit set of common-sense rationalities in interactional circumstances?

4. Herbert Blumer, *Symbolic Interactionism: Perspective and Method* (Englewood Cliffs, N.J.: Prentice-Hall, 1969), pp. 127-152.

How is traditional sociological analysis neglecting the supposition that interaction is the basis for human group life? What are Blumer's criticisms of the relation of theory to fact in much of sociological reasoning? What is the concept of social organization in Blumer's orientation to human action? Does the supposition of subjective interpretation find a central place in a symbolic interaction perspective?

5. Jack D. Douglas, ed., *Understanding Everyday Life* (Chicago: Aldine Press, 1970), Chapter 1 (the title chapter by Douglas).

Trace the main argument Douglas makes in criticizing Durkheim's sociological reasoning as being in the service of an "as-if science of man." What basic flaws does Douglas expose in Durkheim's position vis-à-vis the role of subjective interpretations in everyday life? Does Douglas show that Durkheim was himself motivated by an ideological position about natural science?

6. Don Zimmerman and Melvin Pollner, "The Everyday World as a Phenomenon," in Douglas, *Everyday Life,* pp. 80-104.

What do the authors say about differentiating a sociological resource from a sociological topic? Compare their argument to the one presented in this chapter on the failure of Durkheim to take account of the role of common-sense understandings in human behavior. Are there any additional suppositions expressed in this paper that modify the perspective put forth in the first two chapters of this text? Is there a different slant to their conception of ethnomethodological analysis of interaction and, if so, can you describe it? Do you think that they would concur with our usage here of the term "natural history"?

7. Emil Durkheim, *Suicide, a Study in Sociology,* trans. J. A. Spaulding and G. Simpson and ed. George Simpson (New York: Free Press, 1951), pp. 41-53.

Study the opening statement by Durkheim on the common-sense concept of suicide and consider how it exemplifies treatment of subjective meanings in social life within his own perspective on the role of science in a common-sense world. For a detailed analysis of this question consult Jack D. Douglas, *The Social Meaning of Suicide* (Princeton: Princeton University Press, 1967).

Chapter Three

Some Formal Elements of Interactional Events: an Overview

This chapter introduces a method by which the student can go about making interesting and useful formal descriptions of everyday interactional events. Out of these descriptions he can begin to build viable natural histories of social interactions, social occasions, and social settings. Keep in mind the minimal requirements we have set ourselves: a piece of interaction and some formal analysis to account for its workings.

One might very well ask, where do we begin with such a wealth of opportunities around us? Is there some systematic way to decide what to look at first? Why describe this part over that part of the social organization and culture we live in? One recommendation for a start is almost Zenlike in its simplicity: Select any piece of interaction that is accessible and within your immediate grasp, and do so because it is there. Your own personal interests and biographical experience will determine to a large extent those things you choose to observe and record; that plus the element of chance, since you might find something to look at purely because you happened to be at the right spot at the right time. If, for example, you are a student-teacher, you have special access to a school as a place to observe; or if you are a student-nurse, then selected spots in a hospital, doctor's office, or medical building might be open to your inspection. The various problems that surround your job of looking at some piece of the social world—the problems you take on as a field-worker of everyday activity—will have to be worked out on your own as unique situational contingencies arise. Some of these problems are discussed in a different section later on, in connection with the substantive materials presented in the last chapter of the text.

In this chapter our task is to set out some guidelines for making the kind of formal descriptions of interactions that lead to an understanding of the natural properties of everyday activities and how the participants go about organizing those activities for each other. To do this, we will trace out an overview of the more important issues dealing with elements of interaction that we have to bring into our formal descriptions. To start our discussion off, read the following passage by an outstanding modern novelist, André Gide:*

... The gravity of her look was made charming by her childlike smile; I recall that gently and tenderly enquiring look as she raised her eyes, and can understand how my uncle, in his distress, sought support and counsel and comfort from his elder daughter. In the summer that followed, I often saw him talking to her. His grief had greatly aged him; he spoke little at meals or sometimes displayed a kind of forced gaiety more painful than his silence. He remained smoking in his study until the hour of the evening when Alissa would go to fetch him. He had to be persuaded to go out; she led him off to the garden like a child. Together they would go down the flower-walk toward the place where we had put out a few chairs at the head of the steps leading down to the kitchen garden.

One evening, I was lingering out of doors reading, and as I lay on the grass in the shade of one of the big copper beeches, separated from the flower-walk only by the laurel hedge, which prevented me from being seen but not from hearing, Alissa's and my uncle's voices reached me. They had no doubt been talking of Robert; then I heard my name uttered by Alissa, and I was just beginning to make out their words, when my uncle exclaimed: "He! Oh, he will always be fond of work."

An involuntary listener, at first I had the impulse to go away or at any rate to make some movement to show them that I was there; but what was I to do? Cough? Call out, "I am here; I can hear you?" It was much more awkwardness and shyness than curiosity to hear more which kept me quiet. And besides, they were only passing by, and I heard what they said only very indistinctly. But they came on slowly. Alissa, no doubt, as was her habit, with a light basket on her arm, was cutting off the heads of faded flowers and picking up from under the espaliers the unripe fruit that the frequent sea-mists used so often to bring down. I heard her clear

*From *Strait is the Gate,* by André Gide and translated by Dorothy Bussy. Copyright 1924 and renewed 1952 by Alfred A. Knopf, Inc. Reprinted by permission of Alfred A. Knopf and Martin Secker & Warburg Limited.

voice: "Papa, was Uncle Palasier a remarkable man?"

My uncle's voice was low and indistinct; I could not make out his answer.

Alissa insisted: "Very remarkable, do you think?"

Again an inaudible answer and again Alissa's voice: "Jerome is clever, isn't he?"

How could I help straining to hear? But no! I could make out nothing.

She went on: "Do you think he will become a remarkable man?"

Here, my uncle raised his voice: "First my dear, I should like to understand what you mean by 'remarkable.' One can be very remarkable without its showing—at any rate in the eyes of men— very remarkable in the eyes of God."

"Yes, that is what I mean," Alissa said.

"And then, one can't tell yet. He's too young. Yes, certainly, he's very promising, but that's not enough for success."

"What more must there be?"

"Oh, my child! I can hardly tell. There must be confidence, support, love—"

"What do you mean by support?" interrupted Alissa.

"The affection and esteem that have been lacking to me," answered my uncle sadly; and then their voices finally died away.

When I said my prayers that evening, I felt remorse for my unintentional eavesdropping and resolved to confess it to my cousin. Perhaps this time there *was* a mixture of curiosity in my resolution.

At my first words the next day, she said: "But, Jerome, it's very wrong to listen like that. You ought to have told us you were there or else to have gone away."

"Really, I didn't listen—I just overheard you without meaning to. And you were only passing by."

"We were walking slowly."

"Yes, but I hardly heard anything. I stopped hearing almost at once. What did uncle answer when you asked him what was necessary for success?"

"Jerome," she said, laughing, "you heard perfectly well. You are just making me repeat it for your amusement."

"I really heard only the beginning—when he spoke of confidence and love."

"He said, afterwards, that a great many other things were necessary."

"And you, what did you answer?"

She suddenly became very serious. "When I spoke of support in life, I answered that you had your mother."

"Oh, Alissa, you know I shan't always have her—and then, it's not the same thing—"

She bent her head: "That's what he said too."

I took her hand, trembling. "Whatever I hope to become later is for you."

• "But, Jerome, I may leave you too."

My soul went into my words: "*I shall never leave you.*"[1]

Now, what is there about this passage that, although it is from a work of fiction written in 1909 in France, offers a convenient opportunity to open our discussion of formal interactional description? Because this is a piece of constructed interaction by the novelist, whose purposes for constructing it this particular way are connected to his purposes for writing the novel, we cannot treat the passage as a piece of actual data, of course. But we can conveniently get many clues from it about elements that are needed by the novelist to construct an interaction scene, which presumably mirrors typical everyday scenes whose understanding the author expects his readers to share. We shall try to use the passage to spell out some of the basic elements Gide uses in its construction and which correspond roughly to those elements found in naturally occurring, everyday scenes.

The first element is the *setting*. We recognize the type of setting for this set of interactions—a home, or residential household, with a garden outside of it. It is the home of a member of the narrator's family, his uncle and his uncle's daughter, where the narrator has certain rights to be present because of the particular relationship he has to those who live in it; he does not live there, but visits frequently. He actually lives close by with his mother in another house, though we cannot extract this fact from this passage alone.

All interactions, whatever their nature, occur within the domain of some describable setting. Try to think of interactions without settings, and you will see it cannot be done.[2] Setting is as natural a fact of social life as day and night. It is always possible to describe the features of a setting, but the relation between a setting and the interactions occurring within it is not a simple one-to-one phenomenon. That is, the very same kind of interactions can take place in very different settings.

People can greet each other in households or in supermarkets and the greetings remain the same, except for the important fact that settings presumably have different conditions under which such things as greetings can be performed. The particular characteristics of a setting, as a place where persons do things together, provide participants with mutual orientations towards how they can come into and stay within each other's presence, and, if necessary, take leave of their presence. What is normal and appropriate for one setting may be quite out of place and negatively sanctionable in another. Social sanctions can be either positive or negative—the term "sanction" refers to the controlling power of some agent in social action.

A setting supplies its participants with an interpretive basis as they routinely interact, a frame of understandings shared and enforced by them. To give a crude example, we know that persons in our own culture orient to the interpretive basis of settings such as restaurants, because they will prepare to participate in a restaurant in variously different ways depending upon whether they know, or expect, the place to be fancy or expensive, for family dining or to grab a bite, an institutional cafeteria, and so forth. It is not simply a case of preparing oneself by dressing a certain way, but it involves a myriad of fine details for conducting oneself in the setting. Interpretive orientations in the setting are key elements in accomplishing socially appropriate action. Thus, we see that the notion of setting is not a simple physical one, but one which can take into account the whole range of normal occurrences pertaining to the where, the what, the how, and the who of the normal environment.

The notion of setting is at the very heart of human actions and their interpretive basis. To make sense of alternative, and equally important, notions such as situation, occasion, episode, and so forth, one must treat them as events within a setting. Setting always stands there as a fact that supplies continual clarification when describing interactional events. It is an omniprevalent background consideration to any and all interactions. However, we want to pay attention to the ways in which persons go about their interactions, whatever the settings, so as to provide each other with the interpretive clarifications required to carry on what they are doing together. And we do not mean to use the word "clarification" in the strong sense here, as when one calls upon another to clarify what he has said or done—although there are certainly frequent enough instances when that is in fact done. By clarification we mean to point to *the methods of orienting* others, and vice versa, whenever action and activity are mutually entered upon and developed by participants. Through the use of methods of orienting, ongoing behavior gets organized in continually clarified ways.

While we might think of the notion of setting in its most general sense as another term for context, meaning a totality of human experience at any given social moment, we want to specify aspects of this general meaning in more restricted analytic terms. To return to the where, what, how, and who of any setting, what distinctions of a useful sort can we make?

Let us begin with the "what." It seems safe to say that persons routinely organize their behavior into recognizable activities for which they normally can produce names. These activities, as nameable ones, usually consist of a core of practical events that participants achieve on a daily basis. By practical we do not necessarily mean an achievement of economic production, such as an automobile assembly line (and the practical activities of the world of work are made up of just such achievements for the larger part). But *we do mean by practical any achievement involving what Goffman calls main involvements,[3] those involvements that participants are committed to sustaining when in each other's presence.* Interactions are events that may center around such practical involvements that are taken by participants to comprise some recognizable central activity. If you work somewhere and someone asks you to give an account of what your job consists of, you would normally include the things that get done by those in the work setting that constitute the main activity and the involvements of those who accomplish it. If you were to report that you were paid to "sit at a desk and look busy," it would be heard as a kind of occupational joke that would not stand as a serious job description, though you might in fact spend a lot of time seated at your desk looking busy.

To clarify the point that practical activities are sustained by mutual involvements look at the passage by Gide again. Consider the kind of activity that is described there. It consists of taking a walk, an evening promenade in the garden, which terminates in a conversation held in some garden chairs. The narrator is engaged in a solitary activity, reading outdoors, and because of his placement in the setting he becomes involved, almost unavoidably as he later reports, with the activity of his uncle and cousin walking and talking together in the garden near where he is lying in the grass. He tells us that this promenade is a routine event in the lives of these two people, because it is relevant to how he came to hear their otherwise private conversation. We may even be led to wonder if Jerome had not prearranged his placement knowing the routines of those around him quite well. But that is not the immediate issue for us here.

Their activity is a simple practical arrangement: they walk and talk together. Persons so engaged could later report they were walking with so-and-so in the garden and having a conversation. It would seem sufficient in some cases to describe an interactional occasion as "just talking" or "taking a walk and talking." These words, then, would constitute an adequate common sense description of the main involvement in the practical activity, however simple it is; in such cases, we would expect to find that the things talked about were the central events of the activity. Compare this kind of walking as a conversational occasion with that which normally takes place when hikers on a trail walk single file quite far apart, thus precluding sustained conversation for the most part—on such occasions persons might stop to point out objects in the surrounding environment.

Our point is simply that talk itself can constitute a main involvement and main activity, whatever its setting. Indeed, we find it is a fact of life that persons can and do seek each other out for the predominant purpose of talking. Work settings, for example, provide opportunities for talk in a different way, because the participants assemble themselves for practical purposes and involvements other than just conversation for its own sake, i.e., their talk is tied into the nature of the organizational purposes of the work setting.

In constructing his description of the scene, Gide provides us with terms of reference or labels for the characters, which we recognize as going together within a family of like terms that define for participants how they are socially related to each other. For example, you can be called "students" and I, the author of this text, can so address you. That 'is, for the practical activity of enrolling in a course you can be called and treated as students. You stand in relation to the author as a reader, but you also stand in relation to him as a student. Were I to review your answers to the study questions, I would look upon them as a student's work.

Now of course, you know that you are not just students; under other circumstances many other terms, quite unrelated to students, could be applied to you, depending upon the nature of the activity and the persons who would refer to or address you within certain relationships. So, some of you may be freshmen or sophomores, males or females, Blacks or Whites, or baseball fans or music-lovers or senators, or student government representatives, etc. The range of such terms applicable to you is probably vast, but you recognize the applications when they are applied, either as you or others around you make the applications.

There are, however, many such terms that never apply to you, and which you might never apply to others. You also recognize that some terms seem to go together, whereas others do not. One such well-known collection of terms pertains to familial relations. For example, this collection would contain mother, father, child, baby, son, daughter, etc. These terms are not found in one and only one collection, but each may be used in quite different collections. For example, another collection might be called stage of life, in which the terms would be: baby, child, boy, adolescent, man, middle-aged, old man, etc. Most important to notice is the fact that the same person can have more than one term applied to him depending upon the social circumstances. That is, in interactions we find now this person is a father and now again he is a man, or now she is a wife and now again she is a clerk, etc.

The key issue to keep in mind, then, about terms that label persons into social positions is that the manner in which such terms are used by cultural participants is decided in each and every case of human interaction. The relevance of this term over that particular term is always enforced by participants when doing things together. It is never simply an issue of which is the one and only correct term, *but rather it is always an issue of which, among many competing terms, is the relevantly correct one for the occasion.*

The sociologist who has devoted the most effort to studying the problem of referential procedures is Harvey Sacks.[4] Sacks refers to these labeling terms as categories and because they are deeply involved in how persons interactionally treat each other in groups, Sacks calls them *membership categories.* The families of such categories that participants recognize as going together Sacks calls *membership category devices,* or simply *MCDs*. One of the basic rules for using MCDs, says Sacks, is called the consistency rule. This may be stated: Once you choose an MCD, stick to it in order to make your classification of a person coherent to yourself and to those for whom such classifications matter. This is a rule for interactional use, not for abstract, theoretical playing around, sociologically speaking. That is, you might argue that one could enter into a real human situation with the idea not to use the consistency rule, e.g., you willfully classify the persons you meet according to different MCDs every 20 seconds: now he is a teacher, now he is a father, now he is a Giant fan, now a Pontiac owner, etc. And the person may indeed be all these things, but to impose these possible categories on him without respect to recognized particulars of the interaction on that occasion, would produce a bizarre social situation, a kind of a game that would qualify as a breaching experiment.*

The feeling of a breach occurs because there appears to be an inertia about the way persons relate to each other and do things together. For example, the way we normally go about talking on a coherent topic. If you want to talk about cars and categorize me as a fellow car owner, car buyer, car driver, etc., for the conversation at hand, and I permit you to get talk going that way, then the consistency rule is in operation, because you assume that I will be categorizable that way as long as we continue talking about cars. This does not mean, of course, that only that particular category can be mobilized for the conversation as a whole, or that other categories cannot enter in, but presumably one can have more than one category going at one time and consistently use it over the course of the conversation. It is most certainly not the case that persons normally go through some activity by switching categories and MCDs in a random, haphazard fashion. There appears to be considerable stability in using membership categories in interaction.

Membership categories, then, are the "who" part of the cultural apparatus available to persons when interacting with each other. Gide brings this part of the cultural apparatus to bear upon the actions of his characters. They are depicted as taking particular courses of action that are intimately tied to the categories Gide applies to them. That is, we see the interaction proceeding along lines natural for persons in those cate-

---

*By this term we refer to those experiments with the social order described by Harold Garfinkel,[5] whereby the ordinary appearances of everyday actions are called into question and made the object of special attention in the manner of a puzzle, in short, i.e., making problematic the taken-for-granted world.

gorical relationships, namely, father to daughter, daughter to father, old man to young girl, young girl to old man, young boy to young girl and vice versa, and so on. To some extent, the power of the narrative is due to Gide's skillful construction of characters who act in relevantly clear ways with respect to the categories they are assigned. (Perhaps the power of the novelist lies in his skill at manipulating relevancies of this kind.)

From the start of the passage, Gide employs contrastive devices to show the categorical appropriateness of actions and the categorical basis for interpretive description. Although Alissa was a young girl, 16, she was not quite an adult and most certainly not a child, and Gide shows this middle period of youth between childhood and adulthood by giving her a look of "gravity" and yet a "childlike smile." Again, he uses a contrastive device dependent upon categorical characteristics when he constructs a father, an older man, who seeks support, counsel, and comfort from his young daughter. His daughter needed to persuade him to go out and when she fetched him, much as a parent might fetch a youngster, she "led him off," as Gide tells us, "like a child." Gide alludes to the position of responsibility of an elder daughter who has the obligation to look after her grief-stricken father and replace her mother who a short while ago ran away with another man. That is, in this situation it is the adult, contrary to normal conditions, who is dependent on his own child to watch out for his welfare and offer understanding and support. Social circumstances have created this reversal of categorical relationships in the family.

In other words, the author relies on the reader's sense of social structure and his knowledge of normal family arrangements: membership categories and the rights and responsibilities that are attached to those categories. Without this common-sense understanding of the culture's workings, the reader could not follow Gide's purpose for telling the story as he does. There are, then, conditions for understanding interactions that involve the describable positions of persons who stand in social relationships to each other via those positions. For example, to Jerome, Alissa's father is uncle, and to Alissa, he is Papa. The same person gets to be referred to and addressed in two different ways interactionally. Using terms of reference and address in this way is informative about the social organization, with respect to how social relationships provide certain possibilities of calling someone this or that name.

Let us move on to a consideration of the "how." It is true, of course, that main involvements, practical orientations, and the use of membership categories, all constitute aspects of how interactions take place. But thus far we have not really said very much about the way in which the scene is a scene at all; that is, the way it develops as a progression of interactional events. What in fact takes place in this conversational activity? *We now see what the recognizable activity is, who is involved with whom, but we have yet to see how it unfolds as a piece of concerted interaction—and that after all is the crux of making adequate formal descriptions.*

Why does Gide provide us with a description of the old man's evening routine? He sets it up so we can see how it is that Jerome becomes an unwitting party to the talk between his uncle and Alissa, with whom Jerome is very intensely involved and in love. He places Jerome in a position to hear others talk without their knowing it and, moreover, talk about him in particular. Jerome is aware that he is shielded from sight and describes his connection to the conversation as that of "involuntary listener." How does he handle the situation that arises?

He is not simply a stranger (as in a park where one might find such situations arising). He is closely related to the speakers. He knows they are talking about him, something they would not likely do in his presence. He knows, furthermore, that if he continues to hear their talk, information will be disclosed to him that might be quite consequential and fateful for his future interactions with Alissa. He considers some methods for disclosing his presence, which he believes is the proper action to take, since remaining an undisclosed hearer would amount to an impropriety. Should he move conspicuously? Should he cough, or otherwise announce his presence? It is a moment of social awkwardness for Jerome. He chooses to remain unnoticed.

In this manner, Jerome becomes a party to a conversation that the other conversationalists are building without his participation. This subverted position suggests some interesting features of conversational interactions. It means that one can monitor others' interaction and interpret their meaning by both looking at and hearing what they are doing and saying. We find this to be a general fact of everyday life, insofar as our interactions with others are open to observation by those around us who are not in fact active participants in the interaction. This is true of all settings, but most especially those that are public or semipublic in nature. We cannot always control our interactions in ways that effectively seal them off from the monitoring of others. In fact, we learn how to take systematic account of such monitoring to maintain our bearings as we make our way through daily activity.

In the case of Jerome, the interactional conditions are special, but by no means unique. He is in a position to have the interactions of others available to him, accessible to his scrutiny, where the conversation directly involves him as a talked-about party. It is somewhat similar to picking up the extension telephone at home or at the office, expecting it to be free, and finding instead that persons you know are conversing, perhaps about you. The issue to consider is this: if you are an unwitting party to a conversation in your proximity, how do you govern your own conduct with respect to it; that is, how can you enter, if you should wish to? This is not the only interesting issue here, of course, but we can see that for Jerome it becomes crucial to how he handles supposedly secret knowledge when he confronts Alissa the next time he encounters her. From this we find another interesting issue: how does one conduct future interactions with those who have been unknowingly monitored by us, so that one either lets them know they have been monitored or refrains from disclosing it?

The whole phenomenon of monitoring is very central to sociological business, because we do not go through our daily lives unaware of the actions of others around us. We make a study, if you will, of others' actions, sometimes quite casually, other times quite intensively. By study I mean that we are common-sensically taking others' actions into account, those who we have direct dealings with and those who are complete and uninvolved strangers to us in the surrounding environment. It is a natural fact of everyday life that we are able, we have the remarkable competence, to decide in a glance what others seem to be up to. This is not a matter, normally speaking, for verifying whether our observations are true or false (as in a court of law, for example), but simply attests to our methodical ability in scrutinizing and making judgments about everyday activities we see around us. For example, you drive by a gas station and *in less than one second you are able to detect at a fleeting glance what the courses of action of others at that station appear to be—you use an inferential apparatus about the world which warrants your conclusion, unless otherwise contested,* that there was a station attendant filling up a man's car, or that a woman was standing in front of a dress shop, an elderly lady with graying hair, looking at the merchandise, window-shopping, and then she walked into the shop. There is nothing surprising about this ability, of course, but it is one that has never been adequately explicated in science.

Returning to Jerome's predicament, Gide shows us how he goes about hearing the conversation between Alissa and her father. The scene is constructed to show how the interactional arrangement makes it hard for

Jerome to maintain his access to the conversation: the voices are low and indistinct, answers are inaudible, hearing is strained, the voices finally die away, etc. What Gide does is construct a situation of eavesdropping. Then he next goes about constructing another scene between the eavesdropper and Alissa, one which must, of course, be built on the garden scene. This is an interesting sequence of events, for it shows how two interaction scenes are sequentially relevant to each other, from the point of view of the author, of course, since we can naturally assume that many things took place between the time Jerome overheard the talk in the garden and the time he encounters Alissa again the next day. (Once again the power of the novelist lies in his skill at manipulating sequential relevances.)

It is this element of sequentiality that we wish to consider next in the making of interactional descriptions.

Interactional events take shape over the course of time, immediate time and historical time. Immediate time refers to the instant occasion, the social situation at hand, which develops by the concerted activities of participants. Social events transpire in units as small as seconds; the time it takes, for example, to say hello and get hello back. Temporal orientations are omnipresent in human interactions.[6] Interactants attend to time not merely as an abstraction referring to the unending flow of human events, but more concretely to the orderly flow of those events. As participants construct activity together they attend to the order of that activity over the course of time.

Temporal flow is not only measured in clock-time units of measurement. There are calendrical notions of temporal flow: the day of the week, the month, the year, the seasons, etc. Then there are days, nights, mornings, afternoons, holidays, vacations, and a whole range of periods, phases, or eras dealing with past, present, and future orientations, such as yesterday, tomorrow, now, then, later, soon, and so on. *Interactions proceed with orientations to what we might think of as the temporal parameters of common-sense experience.* The most basic lay conceptions of human development, biography and history, are grounded in the use of temporal parameters. Time is shared by coparticipants in activities and in life situations in general—the fabric of human relationships is understood in part by temporal orientations within which the relationships come into being, are sustained, and are eventually terminated. Birth and death are perhaps the most notably crucial time-bound events which either create new human relationships or cancel old ones.

Correlative to the element of temporality in human interactions is a feature that is quite subtle and very central to our studies. It is time-bound in nature, but involves the property of orderliness, of which we have spoken already. *As events occur in time, they are organized by participants into sequences. Sequentiality involves the serial ordering of actions into an arrangement of events that might follow one another according to describable ordering principles.* As Jerome describes his next encounter with Alissa, he has his "first words" with her to inform her that he overheard the conversation in the garden—that is the way he opens the encounter with her. And upon hearing them, Alissa informs him that he has acted with impropriety and tells him what action he ought to have taken in the garden.

In this paragraph Gide constructs an interaction between the two young people that is in itself a reconstruction of their events on the previous day. It stands in relation to those events as an account of what took place, and, of course, it involves the questions of culpability and responsibility that surround the eavesdropping that Jerome could be charged with by Alissa. In this reconstruction they provide an account of the order, or sequence, in which the garden events occurred. Jerome tells Alissa he heard only the beginning of her father's remark and Alissa reports that her father said certain things afterwards, to which Jerome inquires, "And you, what did you answer?"

Let us consider for a moment this last remark. What does it suggest about sequentiality in interaction? What Jerome recognizes is that Alissa can have said something in answer to her father; that is, answering to his point, seeing the relevance of a remark in a way that permits her to tie her next remark to it in a particular way. Looking again at Jerome's narration of the garden events, Alissa says, "Papa, was Uncle Palasier a remarkable man?" and Jerome tells us that he could not make out the answer to her question. That is, *hearing a question, one also expects to hear an answer, because a basic rule of conversation is that a question gets an answer.*[7] That is a sequential rule for interaction; interactants use it when organizing their talk.

The reconstructed conversation continues with a series of utterances, many of which proceed as pairs of questions and answers (or expected answers since Jerome cannot actually hear very well). Gide, therefore, adverts to this organizing principle of talk to construct this piece of garden dialogue, and it is made appropriate to the categorical characteristics of the interactants: an elder is asked questions by a youth, and he must answer such naive, yet sincere questions with wisdom and earnestness.

It is only a small part of the organization of a conversation, but the structure called *Question–Answer Pairs* is clearly an important sequential phenomenon in that organization. Notice, however, that Question–Answer Pairs (Q–A Pairs) are very tightly organized structures, despite the possible variations in this contiguity between a Q and an A (which we will not take up here). When Jerome hears Alissa answering to a point of her father's, this is not a Q–A Pair, but it makes reference to the manner in which conversationalists can build their remarks to tie to previous ones. I say something and then you say something next that clearly shows you heard and understood what I said, and in one of many ways your remark may incorporate something that I said or implied in mine. We can recognize, then, that conversations develop in a part-by-part fashion because speakers are attending to who is saying what at any given moment during the course of the talk. They are equipped to show understanding and thereby build a conversational sequence with the subjective phenomenon of understanding.[8]

Let us try to spell out this sequencing phenomenon of conversation a bit more clearly, if only briefly for now. Speaking of a conversation as an interactional arrangement of talk, what we mean when we say that it displays a part-by-part order is that for a single conversation participants are engaged in hearing each other speak in relation to their own speech. That is, they appear to be fitting their speech in with those around them in anything but a haphazard and random way. There are constraints on who talks when.

Normally, we do not find persons conducting a conversation by talking all at once. On the contrary, in a single (as opposed to a multiple) conversation we find that participants take turns at speaking in accordance with a simple rule of sequencing: *One person speaks at a time.*[9] The also observable facts that talkers sometimes overlap or start up together, etc., does not mitigate the adherence to this general rule of conversational sequencing, as we show later in another chapter in more detail. Another simple rule that is observed by talkers pertains to the distribution of speech in a conversation and how persons take another turn at talking: *Speaker-change reoccurs.*[10] Participants have methods for taking turns and recognizing when others have taken them; they also have methods for relinquishing turns to others, taking turns away from others, and so forth.

When Alissa's father is saying, ". . . There must be confidence, support, love . . .," Alissa breaks in with, "What do you mean by support?" As Gide describes it, Alissa has *interrupted* her father. One feature of a conversation's sequential organization to which speakers are attuned is how turns belong to their speakers; it is as though a speaker owned a piece of the conversation for the duration of his turn, a slot that others treat as properly his. When another speaker starts up while one is still talking in turn, that can be constructed and interpreted as an interruption. Naturally, we know that every time speaker-change occurs an interruption is not being done, but that more often than not participants have methods for watching out for proper junctures in which to fit their own turn. How is this done? It is indeed a major accomplishment of conversations that such fitting-in is regularly managed by speakers.

The discussion of proper junctures in single conversations is central to understanding how participants watch out for or attend to, what makes a conversation a viable unit of activity. But our remarks must also take into consideration activities that are not primarily conversations, "just talking" as opposed to ongoing activities that have practical orientations toward other kinds of involvements such as building boats, or running department stores, or playing hockey, or teaching third grade, for example. Although many settings within our culture have a lot of concerted talk activity, our formal descriptions must see what that talk primarily orients to with respect to practical, main activities that are being pursued, and similarly with respect to side activities.[11]

It should be clear by now that we have the following as invariant features of interactional events: main activities with practical orientations (within which mutual involvements are built up into situations and occasions), local settings, a cultural apparatus of labels or calling terms for selective identifications of interactants, temporal orientations, and conversational structuring and sequencing rules.

Another element to take into consideration when making formal descriptions of interactional events is *the invariant feature of spatial orientations.* We may think of this feature as ecological. *It pertains to the proximate elements of interaction,*[12] such things as physical spacing and distancing and bodily positioning, those aspects not properly part of speech but which nevertheless enter into the domain of conversational activity and which are always present as resources for controlling interactions and making interpretations of social events. In the passage from Gide, you saw how central ecological features became in constructing an eavesdropping scene consequential for the ongoing love relationship of the narrator to Alissa.

A final invariant feature is the domain of actions that fall into the classification of nonverbal communicative behaviors, e.g., gestures, facial organization, body movements, etc. In this text, we concentrate heavily on verbal behaviors.

We emphasize acquiring skills in the making of formal interactional descriptions as a basic work-method for studying the sociology of everyday life. You will be expected to select environments around you and describe invariant features of interactional events happening in them. Those invariants outlined in this chapter are by no means the only ones, but would be expected to appear on a basic list of such features. Each may have numerous subfeatures capable of considerable elaboration as invariants. You are encouraged to seek out and discover on your own these and other features with which you can construct formal descriptions of social activities.

We spoke earlier of one major analytic problem of locating proper junctures—as understood by interactants themselves—in ongoing activity. With respect to conversational structure we noted the methodicalness with which talkers can fit their speech together in single conversations so as to regulate a conversation internally in terms of who speaks when. In this respect junctures would occur during persons' utterances, or between them. Now, there is also the problem of recognizing junctures, we may call them natural junctures, in ongoing activities with multiple as opposed to single conversations.

What we have in mind are those affairs of everyday life that involve large groups of participants doing jobs and household things, recreation, education, and so forth. In the course of these activities practical involvements require attention to temporal, sequential, and spatial organization —all of which comprise an interlocking set of orientations to activity units: i.e., when and how an activity begins, gets developed into mutually sustained involvements, and terminates.

The traditional ethnographic descriptions of anthropologists observing participants in other cultures show that they have always had to deal with decisions about the relevant activity units of the cultures. For example, persons are seen to assemble for some kind of ceremony connected with religious rites and food preparation. They are described as getting into a state of readiness for the activity and at some point they get underway. Things are observed as interactional events within the frame of reference of that unit of activity. That is, in an apparently religious ceremony, all that is said and done is naturally assumed to be understood in terms of religious practices and beliefs. But, one must stop to ask, were we to consider our own culture's activities, in which we are participants of some competence, would we assume that all the events that transpire at a church meeting are understandable strictly by reference to the religious text and talk of the service? We will inquire into this kind of problem in later chapters. It is introduced now as a problem for you to keep in mind as you attempt to construct formal descriptions of interactional events.

The next two chapters deal specifically with talk and what we have called "conversational structure." This is a major focus of the text for the simple reason that of all the elements in formal interactional description, talk is the most amenable data for precise and intensive analysis.

By contrast, you will find that the analysis of ecological and nonverbal features such as spacing, body movement, facial work, gestures, etc., will be much more difficult because of the problems involved in using words to represent communicative actions of this sort. What one needs in fact is visual data, such as films or videotapes, and some means of notation to technically refer to observables in these visual media. For the present we will have to rely on ordinary language to convey observations drawn from these media deemed important for interactional analysis.

This is not to say that visual data is less important than speech data, but only that we begin with talk because it is more tractable for analysis —we can get further as a start. Moreover, one should keep in mind that it is not possible to give interpretations of visually perceptive actions without recourse to language and the linguistic properties of descriptions. Even if we should develop an abstract system of notation for describing visual events, the recognition of these events would always have to originate with ordinary language procedures before coding into the notational system could then be accomplished.[13] The resource of common-sense knowledge must always remain intact.

Notes

[1] André Gide, *Strait is the Gate* (New York: Alfred A. Knopf, 1956), pp. 21-23.

[2] For an ethnomethodological argument to this effect, see Harold Garfinkel and Harvey Sacks, "On Setting in Conversation," presented to the Annual Meetings of the American Sociological Association, Section on Sociolinguistics, San Francisco, August, 1967.

[3] For the explanation of the concept of "involvement" and its allocation in social interactions, see Goffman's *Behavior in Public Places* (New York: The Free Press, 1963), pp. 33-79.

[4] For a detailed analysis of membership category procedures see Sacks "The Search for Help," in *Studies in Interaction,* ed. David Sudnow (New York: Free Press, 1971). I take the liberty here of giving a very crude sketch of the operation of categorization procedures described by Sacks in his general findings on these procedures based on intensive conversational analysis of callers to a suicide prevention center. For a fuller

description see Speier, "The Everyday World of the Child," in Douglas, *Everyday Life,* pp. 199-209.

[5] Harold Garfinkel, *Ethnomethodology,* pp. 35-75.

[6] For one of the earliest sociological inquiries into the temporal element of social behavior see the little-known volume, Pitrim A. Sorokin and Clarence Q. Berger, *Time-Budgets of Human Behavior* (Cambridge, Mass.: Harvard University Press, 1939). As the authors state, "Seldom has anyone bothered to make a detailed examination of all the activities with which people fill their time and to keep a record of them day after day for twenty-four hour periods." Although they are committed to a very positivistic approach to behavior they note that the "daily minutiae of existence" have not been given the attention they deserve. Unfortunately they are not concerned with the procedural basis of temporal behavior, but are influenced instead by psychological theorists on human motivations, such as E. L. Thorndike, "How We Spend Our Time and What We Spend It For," *Scientific Monthly,* May 1937.

A paper more relevant for our concerns in natural histories of social activities is Howard N. Boughey, Jr., "Time, Space Occasion: An Analytic Scheme for the Study of Timing and Spacing Acts," presented at the Annual Meetings of the Canadian Sociology and Anthropology Association, St. John's, Newfoundland, June 1971. Schutz, "Multiple Realities," offers a phenomenological analysis of social and psychological time derived from Bergson and Husserl. In this discussion on making natural histories of everyday events, we are focusing on time as an element of sequencing in ongoing activities and on members' procedures for orienting to and formulating talk about temporal phenomena.

[7] I borrow this from Sacks, "UCLA Lectures," No. 2, Spring quarter, 1966. Sacks points out that one finds various paired phenomena in conversational structures and one predominant one is the Q-A pair. The import of paired phenomena for analysis of recursive features of conversation is its apparent demonstration of what might be regarded as very strong tying behavior, i.e., given a speaker takes one action called a question, the next speaker has his action already selected for him, i.e., an answer; and if he should not perform this tying operation, its absence would be very noticeable, in some circumstances sanctionable, and almost always accountable.

[8] Sacks has elucidated the concept of "understanding" in precise terms with respect to understanding syntax, action, and topic, in a lecture delivered at the University of California at Santa Barbara, Department of Sociology, Feb. 29, 1968. I use "understanding" in the senses described in this lecture. The main thrust of this contribution, I take it, is Sacks' attempt to expose empirically the nature of an otherwise purportedly elusive phenomenon, and to transform a metaphysical concept into a set of recognizable behaviors. In another sense he has given empirical warrant to Schutz's postulate of intersubjectivity by asking simply, how do we understand what we say and mean in conversation?

[9] This basic rule of conversation is stated throughout Sacks's lectures on conversational analysis and restated in a joint paper with Emmanuel Schegloff, "Opening Up Closings," paper delivered at the Annual Meeting of American Sociological Association, San Francisco, September, 1969, p. 1.

[10] This basic rule also appears in restated form in Sacks and Schegloff, "Opening Up Closings," p. 1. The authors state that a conversational machinery operates these rules for ordering speaker turns, utterance by utterance. When one speaker completes his

turn, this serves as an occasion for making a transition to the next speaker's turn, or provides a "transition relevance" for speakers.

[11]Goffman, *Public Places,* distinguishes main from side involvements, the latter being an activity that a person can do at the same time as the main one so long as it does not threaten the continuation of it, and thus will often appear to have a distinguishable abstracted character from it.

[12]The study of proximate elements of interaction has been the concern of very recent workers in environmental psychology, human ecology, and nonverbal sociology. See the works of Edward Hall, *The Silent Language* (New York: Doubleday, 1959) and *The Hidden Dimension* (New York: Doubleday, 1966); and Ray Birdwhistell, *Kinesics and Context: Essays on Body Motion Communication* (Philadelphia: University of Pennsylvania Press, 1970) University of Pennsylvania Series in Conduct and Communication, No. 2, which are the most notable of recent studies of proximate elements. Works arising in psychiatric contexts are Robert E. Pittenger et al., *The First Five Minutes* (Ithaca, New York: Paul Martineau, 1960) and Albert Scheflen, *Body Language and the Social Order* (Englewood Cliffs, N.J.: Prentice-Hall, 1972). Very recently, a volume of papers has appeared dealing with the subject of space and behavior, Harold M. Proshansky et al., eds., *Environmental Psychology: Man and His Physical Setting* (New York: Holt, Rinehart, and Winston, 1970).

[13]See the paper on the subject of interpreting and describing behavioral episodes by visual inspection of cartoons, in Sheldon Twer, "Persons' Structures for Making Sense Out of Behavioral Episodes: Examinations of Persons' Descriptions of Behavioral Episodes," in *Studies in Interaction,* ed. David Sudnow (New York: Free Press, 1971). I have often used photos, e.g., from the *Family of Man* collection, as a device to exercise students' categorization practices by asking them to look at and interpret the pictures, their social figures, social scenes, social activities, etc. I have done the same with films, with special reference to both the behaviors being deliberately displayed for the camera by the subjects and those recognized behaviors as interpreted by filmmakers and film audience. I am currently doing video research on children's nonverbal behaviors in an experimental elementary classroom and preparing a more general report on the uses and techniques of visual documentation in social sciences.

Categorization. What social membership categories can you select for these individuals? Do certain categories go together and define the relationship of the persons to each other as a group? (photo by Marian Penner Bancroft.)

What are some possible categorizations for these two people and what is their
social relationship? (photo by William Darrough.)

How does body contact enter into your selection of categories for these three persons? (photo by William Darrough.)

What is the first class of categories that springs to mind for this grouping? (photo by Marian Penner Bancroft.)

Suggested Readings and Study Questions

1. Erving Goffman, *The Presentation of Self in Everyday Life* (New York: Doubleday, 1959), chapters 1, 2, and 3.

Erving Goffman, *Interaction Ritual: Essays on Face-to-Face Behavior* (New York: Doubleday, 1967), pp. 1-45.

Erving Goffman, *Behavior in Public Places: Notes on The Social Organization of Gatherings* (New York: Free Press, 1963), chapters 1-5.

a. What does Goffman mean by "front" and "misrepresentation" as features of performance?

b. How does Goffman employ the concept of "team" as a fundamental point of reference and as a basic unit of analysis for the study of performances that differentiates the concept from that of "individual performer"? Relate teams to activities of a specific nature.

c. What is the relevance of Goffman's concept of "region" for an understanding of ecological arrangements in interaction? Go to public places and observe "regions" of behavior.

d. What is the distinction made by Goffman between "main" and "subordinate involvements," using your own social experience to document the concepts?

e. Using a setting familiar to you, locate involvement shields and note how they enter into interactions of the participants.

f. Using your own social experience, illustrate what Goffman calls the "corrective process," one of the two basic types of "face work" in everyday life. Does your example fit the sequential phrasing of Goffman's typical process?

g. What significance might Goffman's discussion of "spoken interaction" have for studying routine sequencing rules in interactions? What specific features of conversational structure does Goffman allude to?

2. Hall, *Hidden Dimension,* chapters 8, 9, and 10.

Do you find Hall's discussion of the four distance zones for interactional spacing useful? Can you see any shortcomings of this classification system? Make a simple observation of a piece of interaction to see how Hall's system might apply to what you see. Can you see spacing rules at work?

3. Sacks, "Search for Help."

In a setting of your choice make a simple observation of a piece of interaction in which some talk is exchanged that contains social catego-

Social Spacing. What does this spatial organization tell you about the communication between the two persons? (photo by Marian Penner Bancroft.)

Social Spacing. How does the body language used here show a different state of communication from the opposite photo? (photo by Marian Penner Bancroft.)

Involvement Shields. How does the physical environment structure communicate in this setting? (photo by Marian Penner Bancroft.)

How do hands or held objects provide communication shields from the camera? (photo by William Darrough.)

ries. Using this simple observation, what can you conclude about the procedures participants might be using to select the categories? Draw on categorization rules specified by Sacks. What MCDs are operative? Can you identify category-bound actions and activities?

4. Twer, "Structures for Making Sense."

Using Twer's method, select some photos from magazines and make alternating categorizational descriptions of each. What visual cues do you use to make inferences about projected courses of action and settings in the scenes shown in the photos? Try this first without, then with, the aid of the photo captions. Compare analyzing still photos in this manner with film. Can you construct a pictorial natural history of a social activity using still photos to capture stages of sequential development?

Chapter Four

The Element of Talk

As an observer of social life you will readily grant a natural fact that stands as firm as the Rock of Gibraltar: People normally go about their daily activities talking to each other. Talk is as pervasive as the air we breathe. It is one of the most powerful resources human groups have at their disposal for organizing social life and communicative behavior. Cultural settings that organize practical activity without talking are few and far between. Moreover, in social life the world over, we know of no cultural group that lacks the communicative competence of talk or that goes about its daily business without the patterned speech of its members.

Textbooks of anthropology invariably introduce the subject of cultural study by pointing to language as an essential defining feature of human culture. Indeed, one of the first routes of access an anthropologist must secure to a culture he wishes to study, normally not his own, is that of acquiring linguistic competence sufficient to understand the members of that culture. It would be nothing less than utter absurdity to attempt understanding in depth of cultural activities of a human group without a working knowledge of the language its members use when going about their daily business. As observers of your own culture, of course, you are fully equipped with a linguistic competence sufficient to make the subtlest interpretations of everyday social events. But is the competence necessary for such interpretations purely linguistic? When you talk with others and listen to their talk, is it correct to assume you are culturally competent merely because you are able to use a language?

Let us for a moment think of this ability to use a language in terms that are important to a linguist. A linguist would consider linguistic competence to be essentially the ability of a native speaker of a language to speak recognizable and acceptable sentences in that language. We might say, then, that a linguist studies language by employing a model of competent language use or, in terms of native speakers, he employs a model of a language user.

In contrast to this method of the linguist, consider how we might want to study talk. We are not making the object of our study the ability of a speaker to produce sentences in his native language, although we recognize that persons acquire and require that ability, to be sure. But instead of language being the focus of our interests, we are concerned with the phenomenon called "talk." This concern has to do with the fact that talk is not merely sentence production, it is social exchange and social coordination. Talk is interactional. Instead of a model of language use and of a language user, we need to develop a model of interaction and of the use of interactional abilities. Our concern, therefore, is with interactional skills rather than linguistic ones. How is talk an interactional skill, one that enters into the organization of everyday activities? How is it a regulative and a constitutive feature of that organization?

A moment ago we pointed to the task an anthropologist faces when seeking to understand the activities of a culture. We have not pointed to the sociologist's task in the same regard, simply because it is the anthropologist who has faced the problem of language in relation to human action when seeking to study cultures other than his own. The orientation to linguistic use has been a traditional part of the development of the discipline of anthropology. This has not been the case of sociologists, who have chosen almost without exception to study their own cultures. For this reason the problem of the relation between language and human action has not posed itself as a basic practical requirement for doing sociological investigations. The sociologist has had a presupposed competence in using his own language in taken-for-granted ways also shared by most of those persons he is studying in his own society. He has virtually the same resources of language and talk that are available to his subjects and, like them, he is able to use interactional skills consonant with their own use of them.

Thus from the very start, the sociologist has had the seeming advantage of within-the-culture interpretive ability. Yet sociologists have also suffered from the disadvantages of being in this position because they have not had to question the basis for their own interactional competence and interpretive abilities. It is therefore not surprising to find that whenever the question of the relation between language and human action, or between speech and interaction, does indeed emerge in sociological inquiry, the subject matter involves so-called subcultures and ethnic groups within our culture. Despite such opportunities, however, the whole sociological discipline has shown a very sluggish interest toward problems in talk and interaction. The basic aim of this text is to correct this course for future sociology.

We have said that talk is a central communicative activity in organizing cultural life. Suppose for a moment that you were doubtful of the claim we are making, that it would be a hopeless enterprise to understand cultural activities without a working knowledge of the language participants use when they talk and do things together. Consider the following situation:

Suppose you are traveling on holiday, or in pursuit of sport and adventure such as one finds presented on television programs or in travel films. You are in the South Pacific, on a foreign island culture, say the Trobriand Islands off the coast of New Guinea. You observe some men of the community, who spend time fishing in the sea and building their boats. You do not know the language of the people. As you watch, an inferential machinery from your own cultural background is at work. It tells you that the men are fishermen and that they need to build boats to sustain their fishing industry, an important source of sustenance for the community. You watch them building a boat and, although you cannot understand their language and therefore what they are saying at any given moment, you can nevertheless describe their activity using your own linguistic and common-sense resources: Now they are heating the wood to bend it, now they are putting it into place, and now they are doing such-and-such to fit it together, etc. The activity proceeds in this manner until the boat is built.

Now, suppose you wrote down in your own words what the men were doing as they were building their boat and, when you finished your description, you used it to supplement the film you had also made of the activity. When you show that film to your friends or others in your own culture back home, your cultural partners interpret your description of the activity in terms of their own common-sense notions and experience about boat building and fishing as an economic enterprise, plus ideas they had about the strange culture of the South Sea Islanders.

All this work could be done without knowing the language of the boat builders and the details of cultural meanings they share in their activity and common culture. When you attempt to do this task, you find that the adequacy of your description to your friends at home is built on a system of shared relevances with them, and not on one that is shared by Trobrianders. To successfully understand the activity *as a cultural activity,* however, you would have to understand the Trobriander's system of relevances surrounding the building of boats. And so your description needs to include all aspects of Trobriander interaction when building boats, naturally including any talk that takes place.

Suppose, for instance, they have a way of building that takes into account beliefs about supernatural forces in nature which come into play when men risk grave danger on the high sea in small outrigger-type canoes. It may be a very important part of their activity to follow magical practices, have ceremonial rituals, make incantations, etc., as constitutive features of the boat-building activity. Such features are not organized by speech alone, of course, but are also organized into a sequence of a physically accomplished set of actions. For example, to use another culture, the ritualized sand paintings of the American Navajo Indian are painted according to a strictly followed sequence. In your description of the Trobrianders to your friends, you might have noted that certain actions caught on the film looked like meaningful physical gestures of the hands, or that the builders painted certain pictures or signs on the finished hull of the boat, etc. You might guess these to be primarily for decoration; but if the sequence of the boat building was carefully regulated to conform to a ritual procedure tied to magical and religious beliefs, you might not detect this fact—particularly if talk indicative of it, or even peformative of the procedure, were present but left out of your description.

Suppose finally that you wanted to actually make a scientific description of Trobriander boat building. Could you put it to a test? If you were scientifically adequate in your description you would presumably be able to instruct anyone in performing the activity successfully. By successful we mean according to standards applied and recognized by Trobrianders themselves. Presumably your instructions would even be adequate enough to teach a Trobriand child the art of boat building sufficient to meet the standards of the adults of the community. The elements of your formal interactional description would do this job: you could reproduce the behaviors of the culture because you had a firm empirical grasp of its natural history and interactional workings.

This firm grasp of empirical workings of a culture's daily interactions can only be achieved if the elements of interactions are adequately represented in an analysis. This means, then, that one must have a specimen of interaction which makes elements of its constitution available for analysis. And talk certainly is a major element in interactions, as we have already noted.

You will probably wonder if anthropology and sociology have really failed to take talk into account when studying human group life. Naturally, they cannot fail to take it into account when they are observing some behavior—when they do indeed observe at all—or even when they theorize about what cultural participants do in hypothetical circumstances. They must always rely either on what participants actually say to each other or on what they hypothetically would say in such-and-such social circumstances. We are not arguing that the social scientist does not take talk into account in his studies of social life, but only that *he does not show how he takes it into account when making analytic abstractions based on it.* To illustrate this point here are a number of passages selected from well-known sources. See for yourself how the authors rely on the speech activity of those they observe in making conclusions or inferences about their daily activities or about those they interview.

Excerpt One

Margaret Mead describes the daily activities of children in *Growing Up in New Guinea:*

Argumentative conversations sometimes ending in fisticuffs were very common. They had an enormous passion for accuracy, a passion in which they imitated their elders, who would keep the village awake all night over an argument as to whether a child, dead ten years, had been younger or older than some person still living. In arguments over size or number, attempts at verification were made . . .

This interest in the truth is shown in adult life in various ways. . . .

So the form of children's conversation is very like their elders'—from them they take the delight in teaching and repetitious games, the tendency to boasting and recrimination, and the violent argument over facts. But whereas the adults' conversation turns about feats and finances, spirits, magic, sin, and confession, the children's, ignoring these subjects, is bare and dull, preserving the form only, without any interesting content.

The Manus have also a pattern of desultory, formal conversation, comparable to our talk about the weather. They have no careful etiquette, no series of formal pleasantries with which to bridge over awkward situations; instead meaningless, effortful chatter, is used. I participated in such a conversation in the house of Tchanan, where the runaway wife of Mutchin had taken refuge. Mutchin had broken his wife's arm, and she had left him and fled to her aunt's. Twice he had sent women of his household to fetch her and twice she had refused to return to him. On this occasion I accompanied her sister-in-law. The members of her aunt's family received us; the runaway remained in the back of the house, cooking over a fire. For an hour they sat and talked, about conditions at the land market, fishing, when certain feasts were to be held, when some relatives were coming from Mok. Not once was the purpose of the visit mentioned. Finally a young man adroitly introduced the question of physical strength. Someone added how much stronger men were than women; from this the conversation shifted to men's bones and women's bones, how easily broken the latter were, how an unintentional blow from a well-meaning man might shatter a woman's frail bone. Then the sister-in-law rose. The wife spoke no word, but after we had climbed down into the canoe, she came slowly down the ladder and sat in the stern. This oblique conversational style is followed by some children when talking with adults. They make prim little statements which apply to any topic under discussion. So Masa, when her mother mentions a pregnant woman in Patusi, remarks, "The pregnant woman who was at our house has gone home." She is then silent again until some other topic gives her a chance to make a brisk comment.[1]

Excerpt Two

A passage from "Tarong: An Ilocos Barrio in the Philippines," by William and Corinne Nydegger, in Beatrice Whiting's *Six Cultures*.
Although much attention is paid to young children within the family circle, once infancy is past they are expected to "be ashamed" before visitors. This means the child must never pass in front of a guest, must never unnecessarily interrupt a conversation, should be seen but not heard, at least in the immediate vicinity of a visitor. Theoretically these rules include all non-family guests but are enforced only when the guest is a person of importance or a stranger to the household. Young children are very shy before strangers, whose appearance is relatively infrequent and associated with a shaming technique which will be discussed shortly. . . .

During this period, then, a child is gradually trained to accept responsibility, to curb some of his impulses and to be obedient. But the training is coaxing rather than demanding and is taken lightly by the adults; mild scoldings or teasings are sufficient for most lapses, praise, the usual reward for accomplishment. . . .

The child quickly learns that, as in adult life, intention is not so important as action and its results. For example, if two children quarrel, both are assumed at fault, and punishment is evenly distributed unless one is much older. "He started it" is almost never heard from a Tarongan child. . . .

But there is a positive side to this lack of concern with motives. Discontent can be expressed openly as long as there is compliance. For the child the benefits are obvious: he can grumble, complain, procrastinate, yet still be rewarded for his eventual completion of a chore. He is not called upon to "want to help mother"; he is only asked to help when she catches him.[2]

Excerpt Three

From the article by John and Ann Fischer, "The New Englanders of Orchard Town, U.S.A." we cite the following, also in Beatrice Whiting's *Six Cultures*.

These children are highly aware that they have graduated from the rank of "baby" and are likely to exhibit considerable scorn of babies, whether a neighbor's child or a younger sibling. This feeling of superiority is the residue of the parent's praise for advanced behaviour and their inciting the child by remarks like "Only *babies* do that. *You're not a baby."* The frequency of these remarks at this age, however, suggests that in adult minds, at least, there is concern lest the children lapse into babyish ways.

Proper discipline is felt to be especially important for a pre-school child, and physical punishment is used more often in this period. . . . Negatives become more common in the parents' speech with the child: "No! No!"

A typical mother shows some worry about others learning the full extent of her troubles in controlling her child. In public she may tell him to stop doing something quite sweetly, addressing him as "dear," "darling," and so forth; when at home she might spank or speak more peremptorily for the same offense. . . .

Standards for table manners vary from family to family but all families have some behaviour on which they insist. These apply especially to the evening meal when the whole family is together. Proper table manners are seen as making the child more acceptable socially. This is clearly illustrated by one mother:

I don't often praise them but when children are here who don't have good table manners, I'll say "Now, you see, you don't like that. Now you know what other people think when you go out in public and don't eat right."

Some of the activities which are socially unacceptable at the table are listed in this manner:

Now I have been beginning to give her a little salad . . . and I let her pick out the onion. I say, "Well, just put it to one side and don't speak about it. I'll beat the brains out of the next one that makes one of those disgusting noises" (laughing). I try to keep control over the conversation. Of course, they do forget . . . I feel that I should give way a little bit, but I don't because I feel that if they're going to sit at the table with us, I have to insist for my sake. . . . I think they do want to imitate too, don't you know, and they do like to go out occasionally too, and I'll say, "Well, I don't see how you expect us to take you out to a restaurant if you can't do so and so . . ." I just ask her to do it.[3]

Excerpt Four

Harold Conklin describes the daily life of Maling, a seven-year-old Hanunoo girl in the Philippines. See J. B. Casagrande, *In the Company of Man.**

Sukub now handed the afterbirth to Panday who placed it in the bamboo container, filled the tube with earth, and then went off into the forest. . . . The bamboo floor in front of Sukub was cleared and spread with an unused homespun cloth on which the infant

*"Maling, A Hanunoo Girl from the Philippines," pp. 110–111 by Harold Conklin from *In The Company of Man,* edited by Joseph B. Casagrande. Copyright ©1960 by Joseph B. Casagrande by permission of Harper & Row, Publishers, Inc.

was placed for bathing. While this was Sukub's responsibility, Hanap and Maling helped by heating water and bringing it to their mother's side. Soon Sukub was holding her young son . . . and discussing the events of the past day with her children. Hanap began to winnow rice for the evening meal. Iyang cried for her plaything, and the household gradually settled down to a more normal schedule. When I left, Maling and her mother were still talking about the knot around the turtle's neck.

Maling seemed to be in a talkative mood.

"Mother went down to the stream to bathe today," she began, "and left the baby all alone with Hanap. We are awfully worried that something might happen, but nothing did. He is six days old, and he doesn't have a name yet. Our grandparents are coming up here in a day or two and I suppose we will decide on a name then."

"What do you think would be a good name for your brother?" I queried. "There are a lot of names that are good for boys, but some we don't like because they sound too much like those used by the lowland Christians. Others we can't use because they belonged to relatives who have been dead only a few years. . . .

Our conversation was interrupted at this point by Hanap's call for Maling to go with her to fetch water. As we walked down to the main settlement clearing, Maling asked if girls in America also carry water like the Hanunoo, and whether their brothers ever helped them. Before I had time to answer she had joined Hanap and two other Parina girls on their way to the spring.[4]

Excerpt Five

In *Patterns of Child Rearing*, Sears, Maccoby, and Levin give the following discussion of a mother in the United States.

An excerpt from a third child's mother describes a good deal of dependent behaviour in the form of talking as a means of seeking attention, but the mother evidently did not regard this as much of a problem:

I. How much attention does she seem to want from you?

M. Quite a good deal. She's pretty companionable. In fact, I'm
going through a spell right now where she wants to be pretty much
the center of the stage, and I find that when I have guests she's
inclined to want to come right in and take over. I'm not awfully
smart at handling that. I don't want to shut her up too much. I
want her to feel she is welcome and to join in the conversation,
but she's just apt to take over and she's inclined right now to just
want my attention terribly. I try to give it to her and also try to
explain to her that there are times that you just can't break in like
that. Sometimes I actually distract her by getting her something else
to do, but I find that she likes to follow me around and talk; she's
quite a talker and lots of fun.[5]

Excerpt Six

From Laurence Wylie's *Village in the Vaucluse,* in rural France.
By the time a child in Peyrane is old enough to walk and lisp a few
words, he has learned that 'if you please, Monsieur,' and 'thank
you, Madame' are potent expressions which will bring him what he
wants. He knows they must be said distinctly, directly, and that the
"monsieur" or "madame" may not be left out of the expression.
He has to stand up straight when he says them. And, of course, he
has to shake hands with everyone when he greets him and again
when he takes leave of him. He knows that if he omits any part of
this social ritual anyone present, whether of his family or not, will
remind him of the omission and will withhold favours until the
omission is repaired.[6]

Excerpt Seven

Bossard and Boll, *The Sociology of Child Development,* contains a
description of table talk in the United States.
The family meal often functions as a substitute for classroom
instruction. This happens in several ways. First, there are the
well-known staged conversations—as a rule, for the benefit of the
younger children. Says Mother: "I heard today about a little boy
who ran across the railroad tracks"; to which Father replies
seriously: "I am glad that my children don't do things like that." Or

Mother refers to a visit from Mrs. Terry and her daughter, who was very polite. "Oh yes," says Father, "You can tell that she is going to be quite an attractive young lady."

Again "lessons" for class instruction may be introduced by one of the children. Helen, aged 12, tells of a neighbour's daughter, a proverbial and perennial scapegoat. Father, who is envious of the neighbouring father's business success, expresses himself freely concerning the conduct of his neighbour's daughter. Mother, who dislikes the mother, is equally heated. Without understanding the motives involved Helen is quite impressed. The neighbouring girl's conduct *was* reprehensible.

Finally, many of the lessons learned at family meals are unplanned and spontaneous. "Katie kissed John," pipes up the well-known little brother, and in the wake of this disclosure there may follow either an eloquent silence, or a colorful discussion concerning kissing, John's intentions, John's job, Katie's prospects, and Mother's attitude towards early marriages. Such is perhaps the most common grist in the family round-the-table mill as it grinds, now slowly, now rapidly, but always exceeding fine.[7]

Excerpts such as these seven—and they represent only a few of the household descriptions that are available—all point to one striking fact: *ethnographic and sociological abstractions about family household interaction and activities use the phenomenon of talk as a basic resource.* Time and again observers rely on what cultural members say to each other to make sense of how they interact and how their actions and activities can be described in their natural habitats. It would appear that talk is a feature of social activity *required* for an observer to make some organizational abstractions about the activity, at least those abstractions we normally regard as relevant for studying societies or cultures.

Insofar as talk is a central phenomenon of social activities and is always referred to when we describe activities, our formal descriptions of interactional events must include talk if we are to be adequately equipped to analyze those activities. As we have been pointing out in these chapters, a scientific test of our understanding of how everyday interactional events work is whether our analysis can successfully let us reproduce those events so as to be recognizable and acceptable to members of the culture in which they normally and routinely occur.[8]

The next issue we confront, then, is that of including the element of talk in formal descriptions. How do we do it? What are the composite elements of talk itself? Can that be broken down for detailed inspection? That is, given a stretch of spoken interaction, can we submit it to some penetrating observations that will in effect allow us to "decompose" it? The next chapter will take up this issue.

Notes

[1]Margaret Mead, *Growing Up in New Guinea* (New York: William Morrow and Company, 1953), pp. 78-80. Reprinted by permission of the publisher.

[2]William and Corinne Nydegger, "Tarong: An Illocos Barrio in the Philippines," in *Six Cultures,* ed. Beatrice Whiting (New York: John Wiley & Sons, 1963), pp. 840-841. Reprinted by permission of the publisher.

[3]John and Ann Fischer, "The New Englanders of Orchard Town, U.S.A." in Whiting, *Six Cultures,* pp. 840-841. Reprinted by permission of the publisher.

[4]Harold Conklin, "Maling, A Hanunoo Girl From the Philippines" in *In the Company of Man,* ed. J. B. Casagrande (New York: Harper & Row, Harper Torchbook, 1960), pp. 110-111. Reprinted by permission of the publisher.

[5]R. Sears, E. Maccoby, and H. Levin, *Patterns of Child Rearing* (Evanston, Illinois: Harper & Row, Publishers, 1957), p. 145. Reprinted by permission of the publisher.

[6]Laurence Wylie, *Village in the Vaucluse* 2nd Edition, Enlarged, (Cambridge, Mass.: Harvard University Press, 1957, 1964), p. 43. Reprinted by permission of the publisher.

[7]James Bossard and Eleanor Boll, *The Sociology of Child Development* (New York: Harper & Row, Publishers, 1948), p. 240. Reprinted by permission of the publisher.

[8]By "scientific test" I mean that an understanding of the phenomena we study would be demonstrated by our ability to construct a model of how the phenomena work, using the empirical elements contained in our observations. The test of the adequacy of the model would be whether the conceptual organization of the empirical elements permitted you to reproduce those behaviors that actually occur such that those behaviors would be recognizable and acceptable to members of the culture who normally organize and perform them.

Another way to think of this is the computer concept of "program." The formal elements of interactions can be represented as a set of instructions to program a particular activity, for example, that cultural members routinely perform. If the formal elements are adequately represented as those constitutive of given, naturally occurring interactions, interactional sequences, and social occasions, then the instructions to perform an activity would be an effective program to recreate the behaviors of the activity. With this model of how a portion of cultural behavior is organized one could go to the native culture or to the local cultural setting and know (program himself) how to behave as a normal member.

An analogy would be the student of a language who tests the adequacy of his linguistic competence among the native speakers of the language. Completely acceptable performance would be a display of linguistic competence equivalent to standard competences among native speakers. On the strictly syntactical or grammatical level of language, the rules of grammar provide an organized basis for any user of the rules to reproduce at will the various grammatical forms needed to construct recognizable and acceptable sentences. One does not need to, and indeed could not, know all the sentences (possible ones) of a language that one would construct in speech. The grammatical rules enable you to freshly generate proper sentences in any context. Therefore, knowledge of the rules in a scientific model of a particular language grammar enables you to reproduce linguistic events at will, making explicit the structural features that are implicitly recognized when ordinary persons use the grammar of their language. It would be a model of a language user.

Our aim in interactional and communicational studies is to develop eventually a model of an interactant, showing the structural features and procedural elements of interactional performances and skills. An adequate description of these features and elements would be prerequisite to putting together a model that would be able to reproduce natural behaviors as perceived, organized, and honored by native interactants.

Suggested Readings and Study Questions

1. Douglas, *Everyday Life.*

2. Aaron Cicourel, "The Acquisition of Social Structure: Towards a Developmental Sociology of Language and Meaning," in Douglas, *Everyday Life,* pp. 136-168.

What are some of the properties of interpretive procedures as Cicourel outlines? How central is talk to the operation of interpretive procedures? Locate a statement in Cicourel's discussion of these procedures that relates to our closing discussion on the concept of a program as applied to making a model of interactional events. What special qualification does Cicourel make about how interactional programming occurs insofar as automatic programming of events might be concerned? Do you think that the concept of "program" as used in computer science is misleading or misguided where interactional events are concerned because of the reflexive feature of talk described by Cicourel?

3. Garfinkel, "Studies of the Routine Grounds of Everyday Activities," in *Ethnomethodology,* pp. 35-75.

Using Garfinkel's experiment in clarifying "background expectancies" by asking subjects to read the meaning "between the lines" of their transcripts of natural conversations, produce similar conversational transcripts and show how you interpret the meaning of talk when reading the transcripts. Fill in as much background information and understanding as you require to make interpretations of the talk.

4. Select any anthropological or sociological report published during the last five years and observe how the author makes use of talk as a resource in offering abstractions about the behavior of social groups he studies. Does he treat talk as a subject in its own right?

5. Situate yourself in a setting of your choice and make a simple observation of communicative behavior taking place, but with the stipulation that you do not permit yourself to hear their talk. Write a brief description of what you see. Now do the same thing, only allowing yourself to hear the participants talking. Once again make a description. Compare the two exercises to discover how your interpretive procedures use linguistic and spoken interactional properties. What guides your description if speech is not accessible?

6. John Gumperz and Dell Hymes, eds., "The Ethnography of Communication," Special Publication, *American Anthropologist,* 66, No. 6, Part 2, 1964.

This collection of papers points out the relevance of language and speech in cultural studies. Select from among these papers those most related to your own interests and focus on understanding how the author conceptualizes the data of language and/or speech. For example, how does Hymes use the concept of "speech acts" or how does Ervin-Tripp describe the phenomenon of "topic"?

Chapter Five

Elements of Conversational Structure I: The Interchange

In the previous chapter we saw that talk must be investigated as an element of interaction, and we suggested it could be "decomposed" into distinctive elements of its own, i.e., that the elements can be analytically spelled out, part by part. In this chapter we want to spell out some of the possibilities of such a decomposition. Instead of using the term "talk," we will now substitute the term "conversation."

Not all forms of talk are actually conversational. Talk can be accomplished in certain circumstances without any interaction between the talker and the listener. In fact, a conversation is not normally considered a matter of a talker and his listener(s), as in a public address, but is more normally an affair of alternate talking and listening by all parties to it. The recognition of this distinction tells us that there is a special difference in the relation between a guest speaker and his audience, or the prime minister and his television audience, for example, as compared to the relation among conversationalists. Therefore, we are restricting the term "conversation" to cover only those cases of talking where there is a state of conversational participation open to all parties, where there are shared rights of communication.

The notion central to this conceptual distinction between a conversation and other forms of talk is proposed by Goffman: an interchange. Goffman defines an interchange as "everything conveyed by an actor during a turn at taking action," and indicates that it must therefore involve "two or more moves and two or more participants."[1] We share Goffman's view that

> the interchange seems to be a basic concrete unit of social activity and provides one natural empirical way to study interaction of all kinds.

Conversation, then, shall be treated as one form of naturally sequenced talk that is based on the unit of an interchange, since conversationalists exchange speech (and sometimes accompanying actions of unspoken form). We will make a simple proposal for studying human interactional events:

Treat any observable conversational interaction as a socially organized set of speech events. These events are accomplished, to a large extent, through the participants' knowledge and application of the conventional procedures of conversing. *Conversational competence is based on knowledge of the ongoing procedural basis for talking, which in turn organizes cultural behavior.* To study interaction completely, then, we are proposing that conversational procedures and exchanges be explicated, for they hold a powerful clue to the nature of social organization.

What are some basic features of conversational interchanges? We have discovered (1) conversational participation and availability and (2) utterances, utterance pairs, and turns. Let us take them up in order.

1. Conversational Participation and Availability

First, it is obvious that conversational interchanges take many forms depending upon the composition of the conversational group and the setting and occasion within which it is viable. The first feature we want to consider is a highly general one about the composition of conversational groups. This pertains to *the number of conversationalists in a conversational gathering as that number relates to participation and availability.*

Normally we think of two-party conversations as rather private affairs and those of more than four or five parties as larger types of conversational gatherings. The larger the number gets, it would seem, the more strenuous it becomes to sustain a single interactional focus on a unit of conversation. The tendency of such situations is to develop into multiple conversations going on simultaneously. Two persons alone in a room may engage each other in private conversation that cannot possibly extend to new parties; while, in the confines of a work place, two among a half-dozen workers may at times mutually participate in a single conversational focus, or they may allow it to extend, including others in the activity. It is possible for two-party conversations to develop within a wide range of social settings and within quite disparate kinds of social occasions. The same can be said for three-, four-, and further multi-party talk.

The point here is that there may be rules or procedures for conversing that are built into a conversational event depending on whether the interaction is indeed two- or four-party. There is, of course, always a set of contingent conditions bearing upon these numerical features that emanates from the nature of the occasion and the setting, i.e., two-party talk is more likely to occur in an airplane double seat than at a large round table in a conference room. In the latter setting, side-conversations during an official meeting would normally involve just two adjacent parties, whereas before the meeting had gotten under way, multi-party talk might have taken place across the table. But, despite all these possible contingencies of ecology and occasion, there still appear to be conversational constraints, i.e., limitations imposed on talk by persons or environmental conditions that affect the outcome of a conversation. These constraints are determined solely by the number of conversationalists available for a conversation.

The importance of these constraints of speaker-availability can be appreciated if we consider the speech sequence possible, as a distribution of speech among the participants, when only two parties are conversing. The sequence of talk would run *AB,* and if more than one exchange were made, it would run on in similar structural fashion, *ABA-BAB,* etc.[2] *Two-party talk, as we will define it here, consists of those conversational situations in which two and only two persons are conversationally present.* This is a hard-and-fast definition of two-party talk. Here are the reasons for it.

Adhering simply to a quantitative rule for counting the number of persons in a given conversation amounts to saying: take the number of persons who actually make speech exchanges in that instant of conversation and let that number be the definitive basis for calling it *N*-party conversation—where if two persons make exchanges, *N* equals two, if three persons make exchanges, *N* equals three, and so on. But this rule is wrong because it ignores the structural relevance of speaker-availability of all present interactants and whatever constraints upon that availability might be in a conversation. Therefore, if a group of three is gathered together, but only two of them exchange speech, the third remaining silent from the start to the finish of that occasion, we would not want to call that a two-party conversation, because to do so would be to overlook the structural relevance of the third party as hearer and as a possible legitimate speaker (unless as a special case he were prohibited by the situation from speaking legitimately at all). Silence in such a case would not be simply noted as a negative quantity but as a socially meaningful act of silence. *Refraining from conversational participation in a conversational gathering is a recognized privilege of communication in multiparty groups.*

To consider the phenomenon of silence a bit further, we will not rule out cases of interaction where two persons come into each other's sole presence and one initiates talk with another but gets nothing in return; e.g., as when one reports, "I said hello to him but he didn't say anything, so I said hello again, louder, and he still didn't seem to hear me, so I just dropped the whole thing and walked away." This lack of interaction might be characterized as an attempted two-party conversation where the interval between the first and second speech of the greeter is treated by him as a slot left noticeably unfilled by the party to whom the speech was directed. We might take this up as an interactional encounter that never fully came off; or, had there been an ongoing conversation, the failure of one to keep it going created a premature hiatus, one which went amiss. The latter is a problem in interactional sustainment and the former a problem in interactional starts. Enforced silences can control the development of a conversation, as, for example, when they abort the basic unit of an interchange.

The structural possibilities of a conversation among three persons is notably distinct from one where four persons are gathered, for the following simple reason. When there are four, two persons can focus on each other, leaving an opportunity for the other two to start up a separate stream of interchanges. The availability of speakers provides for different structural patterns of the distribution of speech and speech exchanges.[3] For example, while in two-party talk *ABABAB,* etc., invariably occurs, in three-party talk, *ABCABC,* etc., does not necessarily, in fact rarely, occurs. In four-party speech ABABAB co-occurring with CDCDCD, or we can find two sets of continuous exchanges side by side. But four-party speech always provides for the possibility of a single conversational focus in the gathering such as ACBCBADADB, etc., where the order in which the speakers talk is not based on shared rules for precedence of speakers (i.e., all four parties do not use a rule that orders the precedence of speakers, such as that B can speak only after A, C only after B, and D only after C, then A beginning again—as a round[4] of speech, like a musical round).

To summarize the rather simple point we have been making, one structural property of a conversational interchange is the number of

individual participants *whose conversational presence* is normally sufficient in itself to "count" them as conversationalists: they are available
speakers and legitimate hearers* of all that transpires in the occasion. This
means, in other words, that conversational members are normally always
active as both speakers and hearers and that, further, speaking and hearing are procedurally controlled to achieve a sequence of speakers who
follow one another in turn and alternatively hold or release the floor in
turn. This is so regardless of how disorderly conversationalists seem at
times to be conducting themselves; e.g., overlapping, interrupting, etc.
Even such seeming disorderliness can be produced methodically by conversationalists, because "order" has a common-sense meaning to participants that orients them to interruptions, digressions, etc., as defects or
troubles rather than as intentionally structured behavior.

What we have to start with, then, is a set of minimal conditions for a
conversational interchange: (1) a speaker, (2) others who are hearers of
that speaker and who themselves are available for speakership, and (3)
the speech delivery of each, a finite string of words and parts of words
that are attached to each speaker in the form of his utterance. *Let us
consider the utterance as a central structural unit of conversation.* All
of our remarks will be addressed to the practical problem facing students
of interaction when they observe and record interactions within conversational occasions. Interactional analysts must come to terms with the
problem of making such observation records. The type we are concerned
with particularly is a speech record commonly called a transcript. Transcripts of audiotapes (or video tapes) are the "hard data" without which
sound empirical investigations are not feasible.

2. Utterances, Utterance Pairs, and Turns

The total content of any conversationalist's speech in his share of one
interchange is what he says when it is his turn to speak. At the moment
it appears that nothing more definitive can be said about what constitutes
an utterance beyond the following rule of recognition: *an utterance may
be described as one speaker's turn at talking.* This definition is naturally
quite problematic as it stands, since we would need a means of recognizing a turn when we see one, which conversationalists presumably are

---

*The word "hear" is used throughout as a synonym for listen to or attend to. In the few
instances where physical or acoustical hearing with the ear is meant, qualifying words
(e.g., actually hear, etc.) also appear.

able to do quite regularly without excessive difficulties. Yet, as analysts, we might find it poses a problem in deciding what in fact is a conversationalist's method for determining when he has a turn, how he takes it, how he takes it away from another, how he recognizes when another has completed his turn, etc. Holding to this view of what an utterance is, even minimal grunts or noises would constitute an utterance, as in:

A. Can I have that?

B. Uhm.

A. What's the matter?

We will have more to say later on about the various analytic issues that arise when examining transcripts that contain what look like unfinished utterances, regained turns, etc.

Are utterances to be treated the same as sentences? Offhand, it seems that they cannot be so treated. Utterances are to conversation what sentences are to a language. Like sentences they are produced under the guidance of grammatical rules that assign syntax to their various component parts. Like sentences, they have an internal structure. *But unlike sentences, utterances have structural relationships to the interactional circumstances under which they occur and for which they have important consequences.*

We can imagine a speaker learning a language competently enough to engage in conversations with native speakers of the language and in his lessons reciting simple exchanges such as "Good morning," "How are you?", "I am fine," etc. But when he is confronted with the actualities of making an interchange with a native speaker, the sentences he has rehearsed become the basis for an occasion of social interaction and for possible further conversation. To accomplish the interaction, much more than linguistic skill at producing acceptable and recognizable sentences is needed; when entering the arena of social action one needs to exploit some available procedures for socially organizing his talk into interaction.

The analytic importance of turns that "carry" the utterances of an interchange from one party to another, or others, is that they are indeed the very basis for achieving conversational participation. A turn at talking commits the speaker to social action. It is an event that occurs with respect to other conversational events; e.g., it takes previous ones into account, builds on or alters them in methodical ways, or provides the next speech events. A turn establishes the positional relevance of an utterance in a conversational interchange. It can be seen by participants as following or coming before another speaker's turn. A conversation gets built by means of the flow of turns. In the course of building it, conversationalists must have ways of keeping track of what others have said and tieing their own utterances to them. *By means of turns, conversation becomes a referential activity, not merely in terms of those things in the world that can be named by words, but because what others say in the course of a conversation can be referred to as someone's utterance in the conversation.* That is, speakers can refer to the ongoing parts of the conversation itself.

The unit we can call a conversation, then, must consist of at least one interchange by participants. That is, we can all recognize that some piece of talk among several persons seated about a room, say for a half-hour, amounts to a conversational unit. But are we correct to call the briefest of speech interchanges a conversation? For example, two persons encounter each other on the street. They exchange greetings, then continue on their way. We might not want to say that as far as they were concerned a conversation transpired between them. But for our purposes we want to characterize their talk as a *minimal or single conversational interchange.* One thing we can feel confident about is that those who engage in such an exchange allow an opportunity for further talk to develop in that interactional instance.

We can say that entering into a state of talk[5] involves some kind of preconversational activity. For example, the unit we are calling conversation might follow quite naturally from an initial greeting as a preconversational interchange. (Note: whenever we speak of a single interchange of talk we assume the presence of two utterances.)

Now we can see that the foregoing discussion of the utterance component is problematically tied to the turn-taking phenomenon. The basic unit of the interchange is indeed based on the notion that interaction is fundamentally ordered by orientations to "taking turns at action": Now I do this, now you do that. But the interchange also has as a fundamental assumption that the turns persons take are determinatively interconnected. As neighboring events, they simply are not accidental or chance occurrences without any connection to each other. In fact, we want to see whether interchanges are contiguously organized to happen together.

For example, to use the well-known event called "greetings," it is a natural fact of interaction that when one person greets another he gets a greeting in return. The first greeting gets a return greeting. We cannot quarrel with this empirically established fact. We do not mean to say, however, that a greeting always must get a return greeting as though one had to say hello back automatically whether or not he wanted to. In fact, there are occasions when one might not want to say hello back and this leads to a refraining action to show the first greeter his greeting is unacknowledged. Whatever the reason a person might have for constructing an interchange in this way, he has done so by way of the simple conversational rule that a spoken greeting normally gets a spoken greeting in return. To fail to do so is deliberately (assuming it is actually heard) to make the interchange incomplete. It then becomes a noticeably absent event to the parties involved, i.e., its omission is just as noticeable as its occurrence.

In chapter 3 you will recall that we introduced the notion of paired phenomena with respect to questions and answers. Greetings also appear to be paired phenomena. *What we find, then, is the existence of paired objects*[6] *in conversational interchanges.* Naturally, when we consider some stretch of talk in conversation we see that there is a string of utterances following one upon another in some serial fashion, obviously a sequencing phenomenon. But in studying interchanges we find that some can proceed according to pairing. It is not the case that every interchange is paired or, for that matter, paired in the same way. There appears to be a number of cases in which, so to speak, pairs seem very strong or tight.

One way of describing a strong pairing phenomenon is that both items in the pair are the same. That surely does not happen all the time. In fact, most utterances could not be so duplicated without sounding like echoes or parrotting events. In what way are the items the same? Take greetings as an example.

Greetings come in pairs. The first item of the pair can be "hello" and the return item can be "hello." That is a case of identical items. Now, take the case where the first item is "hello" and the return greeting is "hi." The items are not identical, but they are both greeting terms. That is, we can see that more than one item can do the job of greeting or returning a greeting. There is a class of greeting terms and some of the items in this class can be used identically or alternatively. Thus, even though the terms may not be identical in a pair, they are selected from the same class. For instance, one may find "How are you?" as a greeting term which may get a "How are you?" back, or alternatively, "Hi," "How's life been treating you" "Howyabeen?" etc.

Therefore, we find that another way to describe the strength of the utterance pairing phenomenon is that both items in the pair are not necessarily the same but are drawn from the same class. This fact is essential for the construction of many sorts of utterance interchanges: conversational rules include knowledge of classes from which to select appropriate utterance candidates.

Consider another kind of pair called insult pairs.[7] Here too, we find that both items in the pair can be the same, such as a first insult, "Drop dead!" getting the insult return, "Drop dead!" More often than not, however, insult returns are not the same item, but other items selected from the same class give the return insult its effectiveness. In the case of "Drop dead!" a return might be "Get lost!"

Two regularly found pairs of utterances are question-answer (Q-A) and summons-answer (S-A) pairs.[8] How are these different from the greeting or insult pairs? Basically the items in each pair in Q-A and S-A interchanges are not drawn from the same class, and, in fact, are not selected to return something that is offered at all, but to supply what is a recognizable item in a contrast set. Like the other pairs they link together two utterances, but there seems to be a different kind of constraint placed upon a hearer when he is summoned or asked a question.

The structure of obligation that is produced by Q-A and S-A pairs seems crucial to the outcome of the interchange, in a way that does not seem as evident in the case of greeting or insulting. One can offer a greeting, "Hi," and get some opening comment in exchange that is not a greeting, such as "Have you seen the boss?" It is perhaps correct to say, that greeting interchanges are highly ritualized encounter openings, simple but efficient ways of recognizing another's coming into one's presence—a kind of acknowledgment of presence pure and simple. With Q-A and S-A pairs, however, it is not a simple ritual format that is being used, but a subtle construction of the second item upon the occurrence of the first, under the constraining power of a social obligation. That is, when questioned, one is called upon to answer and normally does answer; and when summoned, one is called upon to give attention and one normally does give attention.

Now in all four types of interchange pairs* we can see, without going into the specific characteristics of each at this point, that simple two-utterance interchanges can constitute speech acts. Conversationalists can construct interactional events by using their speech to produce some specifically recognizable actions. Their words have the power to do things that go beyond linguistic competence. Their words can perform activities. Interactional competence is needed in order to be able to make a relevantly correct selection of the words that perform those activities. To get an idea of how much more complex Q-A interchanges are than the others, for example, imagine trying to learn another language and asking what questions or what answers to questions exist in that language in order to be properly prepared for a conversation. That does not make any sense, of course. While it is conceivable to expect to find a list of greetings in a language learning text, one could not at all expect to find a list of questions as a separately treated category of speech act in the culture of the native speakers. In fact, questions and answers are virtually infinite.

To bring this back again to the empirical relationship between utterances and turns, speech acts that come in pairs are constructed by two speakers whose separate turns are sequenced so that the first speaker's turn is paired with the second speaker's turn to form one complete interchange. Two utterances can, therefore, accomplish a coordinated speech act within a single interchange. This does not mean, of course, that speech acts are always so produced in a single interchange, but it is a testimony to the power of words and their skillful interactional use that they can be so produced.

In this chapter we have considered the importance of the interchange as a fundamental element in conversational structure. The component utterances of a conversation are usually numerous and not restricted to two. Yet, just two can comprise a meaningful interchange of its own—what we have referred to as a recognizable speech act. Clearly it is the case that a conversation proceeds or even opens by means of such speech acts. However many speech acts exist within the course of a single conversation, we nevertheless need a starting place for analyzing conversational interaction, and a good starting place seems to be a single complete interchange. *For within that simple two-part phenomenon we can locate what becomes a crucial issue in analyzing the structure of conversation, namely, the part-by-part sequential organization of talk.* An inspection of these minimal two-part interactions, what a first and then a second speaker says, reveals the startling discovery that well-known, recursive speech acts in everyday life—greetings, insults, questions and their answers, and summonses and their answers (and there may be many more that come in pairs)—are the concerted achievements of the speakers in these minimal interactions. The power of the single interchange is abundantly clear, since so much hinges on it as a social event despite its brevity.

We have considered the utterance as a speaker's turn at talking, but

*(1) Greetings (2) Insults (3) Question-Answer (4) Summons-Answer.

in this chapter we have not said anything about the way turns are succes-
sively taken during the running course of some conversation. An interchange presupposes that two parties have spoken in turn because they
know how to take turns, that they have means for fitting their speech
together into recognizable units. For instance, a greeter produces a greeting that is recognizably adequate and complete as a greeting, and the one
who is greeted hears it that way and then fits his own speech into a turn
by giving back the greeting. Likewise, a questioner offers a complete
question which gets heard as a question and then the hearer proceeds
to answer it, his answer being also recognizably completed by the questioner who may go on to speak again. When one is summoned, his
answer shows he has heard the unit utterance we are calling a summons.

With respect to the methods conversationalists have for determining
what the unit utterance consists of in any given speaker's turn at talking,
the problem of taking turns suggests that *a conversation consists as much
of the phenomenon of hearing as it does of speaking.* In the next
chapter we will explore the role of hearing as a necessary condition for
conversational participation and understanding. To give an answer, one
must know how to hear a question, and how to hear it as a completed
utterance.

Notes

[1]Erving Goffman, *Interaction Ritual* (New York: Doubleday, 1967), pp. 19-20.

[2]On this formulation for the sequencing of two-party talk I am indebted to Sacks's analysis
in "UCLA Lectures," 1-3, Spring Quarter, April 1967.

[3]For an analysis of distribution rules of speech as found in telephone conversation, see
Emmanuel Schegloff, "Sequencing in Conversational Openings," *American Anthropologist* 70, No. 6 (December 1968): 1076.

[4]Sacks's term "round" in this connection may be found in "UCLA Lectures," 1-3, Spring
Quarter, April 1967.

[5]I borrow this idea of entering into a state of talk from Goffman. In the natural history
of an encounter, its initial phase of contact may be regarded as a set of initial adjustments
leading up to a state of talk. See Goffman, "On Face Work" in *Interaction Ritual,* p.
34.

[6]Sacks has devoted much time to analyzing paired objects, as he refers to them, or paired
phenomena, i.e., interchanges that constitute recognizable pairs of speech acts, such as
greetings, questions and answers, and insults. This material is in unpublished form,
mostly lectures. See "UCLA Lectures," 9, Fall 1966, p. 2, and "UCLA Lectures," 6,
October 24, 1967.

[7]See William Labov, "Rules for Ritual Insults" in Sudnow, *Studies,* pp. 120-169. The
insult is the unit of interchange that methodically gets generated by participants in the
gamelike activity among New York Blacks called "playing the dozens," described in
detail in this paper.

[8]For a comparison of these two types of pairs in terms of their internal structure and its interactional consequences, see Schegloff, "Conversational Openings," pp. 1081-83.

Suggested Readings and Study Questions

1. Roy Turner, "Words, Utterances, and Activities," in Douglas, *Everyday Life,* pp. 169-187.

The point of chapter 5 has been quite simple: a convenient place to begin examining how conversations get structured is the unit of conversation called an utterance. All conversation begins with a speaker initiating an utterance, and any ensuing single conversation develops out of the progression, one by one, of these interactional units of speech. If we treat this unit as a basic building block of conversational competence, then we might begin our studies by examining how such units can constitute meaning in any given interchange. We will then be faced with the problem (see next chapter), How do units of interchanges develop into whole occasions and episodes of conversation in a given social context?

We can isolate standard interchanges that in themselves have interdependent structure and meanings. How does Turner show the connection between a given utterance, its neighboring utterances, and the context of a social occasion as defined and recognized by conversationalists? In similar fashion, how does Turner show this connection in "Some Formal Properties of Therapy Talk" in Sudnow, *Studies,* pp. 367-396. What is the significance of Turner's assertion, borrowing from J. L. Austin's terminology, that speech is "performative" of actions? How is talk ordinarily related to action, and what does the idea of performative speech do to modify that ordinary conception of how talk and action are related? Given the significance of a performative, how far does it suggest the primary organizing power, so to speak, of a single exchange of utterances? Can you conceive of analyzing a conversation as a whole, without referring to any of its constituent parts, such as utterances?

2. Schegloff, "Sequencing," pp. 1075-1095.

What are the main structural and sequential features of Summons-Answer interchanges as described and analyzed by Schegloff? In terms of the social situation he selects—telephone calls—how does the problem of conversational availability enter into the analysis? What is a key difference between S-A and Q-A sequences noted in Schegloff's analysis?

3. Make observations of conversational activity in its opening phase. What are some openings you observe, i.e., what is the first interchange of speech? Can you characterize it as a pair of some kind? What specific features of the utterances themselves led you to make one as opposed to another kind of characterization? What features extrinsic to the utterances entered into your descriptive judgments when labeling the opening exchange?

4. After collecting various opening interchanges, look at interchanges that occur anywhere in conversations and also try to characterize these. Do some interchanges occur only at the opening phases of conversations? How is the problem of speaker availability related to any of your interchanges? If three persons speak in turn, who is interchanging his speech with whom? Consider multiconversational situations, and note whether speakers from one conversation make exchanges with those in other co-occurring conversations. Do you find pairs of utterances that are as strongly paired objects as those discussed in chapter 5? Does it make good sense to regard a long string of utterances in a conversation as a series of interchanges in which each utterance is an interchange with the previous one or the next one? Do you think interchange is a concept of limited applicability? Why?

Chapter Six

Elements of Conversational Structure II: The Natural History of Conversational Development*

The last chapter pointed to the smallest unit of a conversation's structure, two utterances or two turns making up one interchange. From the unit of a single interchange we move now to a consideration of the whole course of development of a conversation and its constituent inter-changes.* Presumably at the other end of the analysis, so to speak, we are faced with an empirical fact known as the unit "a conversation," that whole series of concerted speech actions which amounts to one recognizable occasion of talk. We do not mean to suggest, of course, that we know how to measure that amount, so as to be able to say definitively, "The unit called a conversation has N number of interchanges." No such formulation could possibly be made, with the simple exception that a conversation must meet at least the condition that one completed interchange takes place, earlier referred to as a minimal conversational exchange. But beyond that, the number of interchanges in a conversation is entirely a matter of what the participants do to build their conversation into this or that length.

There is one rider to this, however, and it pertains to the nature of the practical activity around which the interactional occasion has been arranged. When such practical activities are prearranged, scheduled, and clocked, then we can see how a conversation that was constructed during that temporally defined occasion can come to a natural close as easily as it was opened within that temporal scheme. Or again, within practical activities, routine events can provide a structurally conducive set of conditions for the recursive opening and shutting down of localized

*Many concepts of conversational development that appear in this chapter are adaptations from Harvey Sacks's conversational analysis; I must express my reliance on his analysis for the skeleton of conceptual machinery which I present the reader.

conversations. For example, conversational interactions in work settings often get built out of mutual work tasks whose duration determines the length of the conversation.

We are faced, then, with the existence of a largely indeterminate stretch of conversation that takes its course from ongoing participation in the occasion. How does it proceed and what is the course of its particular development within the occasion? The issue of conversational development is central to this chapter. How can we study its part-by-part development?

We ended the last chapter with the observation that conversation is twofold in nature: it is speaking to others and listening to others. A proper participation in conversation therefore requires two kinds of attentions. The most obvious analytic attention is to what a speaker says when he takes a turn. The less obvious attention is to what one conversationalist hears. This *problem of hearing is equally central to both conversational interaction and to conversational analysis.*

In fact these two aspects of conversational participation are intimately linked. In general, we can say that a conversation develops because one speaker hears another and shows that he has both heard and understood it. Just as there are rules for speaking competently there must also be rules for hearing competently.

To illustrate what is meant by competent hearing consider the following speech event that took place at a household dinner table:

A. Did you hear what's happening with the mail strike?

B. No, what?

A. No, I'm asking *you.*[1]

We can all read this transcript of a brief exchange within a table conversation as showing how A asks B a question about a current mail strike expecting B to supply some information that A does not possess. But instead B assumes A possesses that information. From the first utterance alone, we could not detect the kind of question that had been asked, namely an inquiry to obtain knowledge from an interlocutor. Instead we might attribute that knowledge to speaker A and assume alternatively that A wants to inform B about it. In other words, the intent of the first speaker is ambiguous. It is ambiguous to B because he hears it the way it was *not* meant to be heard. He asks A precisely what A does not know and would indeed like to know. A shows B how he has mis-heard the remark by correcting B's answer *to show him that he was asked to report about the matter and not coaxed into asking the questioner about it.*

What do we mean by coaxed? Suppose you knew something that you knew *X* would also appreciate knowing. You could start right out to tell *X* what you knew, but another regular way of doing it would be to set the stage, you might say, for telling *X*. You get *X* to ask you about it after giving him an initial topical clue instead of telling him right off. For instance, there is a news bulletin about the astronauts being in danger. You ask the first person you encounter, "Did you hear what's happening with the astronauts?" If he answers, "No, what?" then you know he has heard your remark as the kind of question you fashioned it to be. If instead he replies, "Where have you been, haven't you heard they're in real trouble?" then you would take the next turn to correct his assumption that you did not know and were inquiring of him to find out. You would tell him that, in fact, *you were inquiring to find out if he also knew what you knew.*

In our analysis of this three-utterance piece, we have been taking one crucial thing for granted, that *B* recognizes he is being asked a question, regardless of the special ambiguity built into it. *B* has presumably used some rule for hearing when another asks him a question. The hearing process gets complicated, however, because of the particular construction of *A*'s question. Had *A* asked instead, "Do you know whether there's going to be a mail strike?" or "Do you know that the astronauts are in real trouble?", the ambiguity would not be built into it. It is the ambiguity presented to the hearer in this case that provides for one of the two methodical ways that particular questions could be heard.

This analysis suggests *a general principle* about conversational development. Hearing is not a subjectively idiosyncratic process that might lead one to say, "People hear anything they want to hear." There does seem to be a very definite determinativeness to hearing what another says, which depends very much on what one says in the first place. *Elements for competent hearing, then, are built into the utterances that one offers for others to hear and when one speaks responsively to another he shows that he has understood some possible version of meaning for his utterance.*[2] In our example we find that insofar as *B* listens to *A* asking him a question, *B* shows competence as a hearer. But he knows he misheard *A*'s question when *A* speaks for a second time and shows what he intended the question to be. It may be the case (we can only guess about it) that the opening phrase of *A*'s question, "Did you hear" is regularly used as a marker to indicate that the speaker is informed about the subject he raises.

Question-answer pairs are very basic elements of conversational struc-

ture, and can be found everywhere in conversations. But *another element, even more basic, is the pronoun.* One might say that pronouns
are the cement of conversational structure; they hold it together in very
powerful and necessary ways. They are responsible for keeping a conversation going. What does it mean to say that persons are able to keep a
conversation going by using pronouns?

In order to keep a conversation going interactants must be able to keep
track of their speech relative to given speakers. That is, they must have
methods for referring to things and persons, and to agree about what it
is they are referring to. Speakers must be able to keep track of these
ongoing references while talking. *We shall call this basic phenomenon
in conversational development the problem of making adequate references or, after Sacks, the problem of referential adequacy.*[3] If interactants did not have the means to decide what their utterances referred to,
including references to other utterances, they could not keep a conversation going.

Pronouns are essential elements in the construction of referentially
adequate talk. This use of the pronoun is basic to linguistic as well as to
interactional competence. For instance, a soliloquy, a monologue, or a
written story must provide referentially adequate speech or language
from one line to the next. Pronouns play a big role in achieving this result:
"John used to come to the lake every week with his friends. They were
always with him." The pronouns of sentence two refer back to the
antecedent nouns John and friends in sentence one. That is the way you
would read the sequence of the two sentences as a referentially adequate
and normally acceptable reading.

In conversational interaction the pronouns do this referential work too,
but in more complicated ways which are tied to other elements of the
ongoing interactional activity. We will try to show the way pronouns tie
utterances together to give them referential adequacy and referential
continuity. We would expect to find these phenomena—the pronominals
—at work in any transcript of a conversation.

We would like to show how a conversation proceeds according to the
speaking-hearing relation. *One way to conceptualize the speaking-hearing relation is to observe the use of pronouns as a transformational
operation.* By that we mean very simply that when a speaker chooses
a pronoun it can be heard as a direct transformation of a previous
speaker's pronoun. The following are some examples of how a hearer
shows understanding and referential adequacy when he makes trans-
formative operations with pronouns.

Interchanges	**Transformations**
A. Speaker 1: How are you? Speaker 2: I am fine.	"I" is a transform of "you." Hearer hears "you" as referring to himself.
B. Speaker 1: Are you finished eating? Speaker 2: No, we're not.	"We" is a transform of "you." Hearer hears "you" as himself + somebody else or others.
C. Speaker 1: She's very smart. Speaker 2: Do you like her?	"Her" is a transform of "she." Hearer hears "she" as referring to someone other than self and keeps the third person reference.
D. Speaker 1: We know what you did this morning. Speaker 2: You do?	"You" is a transform of "we." Hearer hears "we" as speaker + somebody else or others.

A little study of these examples—and you may multiply them on your own if you wish—will show that pronouns are interactionally relevant because they specify who is being referred to or talked about, who is being included in the pronominal reference, and to whom the utterance is directed in conversation. Two principles have been pointed out by Sacks to study these sorts of conversational operations of pronouns: *the principle of directiveness and the principle of inclusion.*[4] They are important principles for conversationalists to use competently because they permit them to show how they hear and understand each other's conversational contributions. The two principles are cement in the sense that they tie together strings of utterances in an orderly referential way. The pronouns are methodically selected to do a particular job of showing interactants how present or absent parties are included in the reference or how the utterance that contains the pronoun reference is directed to present parties.

The use of pronouns becomes particularly crucial in multi-party as opposed to two-party conversation, where speakers have to select from among several others the one or ones that their utterance is intended for or applies to. For example, an adult walking into a household room might say, "You forgot to close the front door"; although several persons might be present, all could hear it as directed to and including just one of them. On the other hand, "We'd better be going now" would also be methodically heard as directed to some parties and including some of them, but not all.

These may seem like very obvious facts, but it should be kept in mind that pronouns do more than provide persons with referential adequacy, however basic that may be. They also provide speakers with instruments to get others to hear their conversation in interactionally consequential ways. It is not just that they know what they are talking about, with respect to topics and persons, but that they also know how to keep that talk going, so as to be able to control the direction and continuity of a conversational episode. Pronouns are selected to tie together strings of utterances, and *pronominal tying procedures*[5] internally regulate conversational structure. A hearer exercises his competence at conversational control through the use of pronominal tying procedures. To repeat our point here, then, it is not just linguistic competence that is displayed when interactants use pronouns to make referentially adequate speech, but also interactional competence which enables the effective building of a conversation over its course.

So far we have made the point that a conversation develops by means of rules for both speaking and hearing. This essential fact is built into the basic unit of an interchange. We started out the discussion by examining first a question-answer interchange and then pronouns to illustrate the problem of hearing. It goes without saying that this problem is so general for conversational development that any elements of conversational structure would illustrate the problem. Let us look a bit further into the procedures which interactants use to tie their utterances together so as to constitute a conversational episode.

At several points in our discussions we mentioned the presence of topics in talk. The notion of topic is very readily grasped by the student of interaction and by everyday persons. It is one of the first ideas about conversation that comes to mind as a constitutive element of talk. It is something that conversationalists apparently orient to and can give reports about when describing their conversation to others. For example, you inform another of meeting a mutual friend and he says, "What did you talk about?" or "What did he have to say?" etc. Your answer would presumably try to account for the topical content of the conversation, e.g., "Oh, we talked about skiing, he's been going skiing a lot this winter," etc. On the other hand you might report that your friend was on the run and just said hello, then rushed off. Presumably, this would mean no topical talk took place. Common-sensically we would not treat a greeting as topical, since for conversationalists it appears that to talk topically one must have "something to talk about."[6]

Now, suppose you were given a transcript of some talk, and you found that one of the first things that you attended to in it was topicality. You would presumably have some means of detecting this or that utterance as being related to this or that other utterance in terms of topic. One of the first things you might do, and this seems to be common for beginners, is try to specify the topics, list them out, and then provide a summary of the topics covered. When sociologists do what they call "content analysis" of written documents or some talk, they do precisely this kind of analysis. It is aimed at answering one basic question: what do these particular persons in the society talk about? With such a list in his possession, the sociologist can then proceed to relate what is said to characteristics about who said it such as race, class, profession, personality, mental disorder, attitude on politics, religion, etc. That is, the topical contents become indicators of social conditions and processes.

We propose that this procedure is analytically inadequate because it fails to take account of conversational events and processes as realities in their own right. *For us, topic is but another element of conversational structure around which participants organize their concerted interactions.* Accordingly we are led to ask: *What does a topic do in a conversation,* rather than what are the topics? As part of the study of the mechanics, if you will, of talk, we ask *How do interactants use topicality to achieve a conversational episode and its practical purposes?*[7]

The use of topical talk in conversation involves the methodical control of topics in variously coordinated ways. In conversational development the element of topicality provides a conversation with formal structuring and internal control. Controlling power refers to providing conversational coherence and continuity, maintaining speaker alignments, regulating sequencing, and doing categorizations. By means of topicality, for example, speakers are able to establish social relationships with conversationalists or sustain existing relationships, on each new occasion of conversation.

Consider the idea of *raising a topic* and, conversely, *closing down a topic.*

Suppose you are in a public place and surrounded by strangers, let us say in an airplane. Taking into account the proximate elements of interaction (refer back to chapter 3), if you are seated adjacent to another person and you share that occasion of traveling by plane, you will commonly find that you may open an interactional engagement, a focused one,[8] by entering into a state of talk. You may introduce yourself, including in it some identification of yourself in terms of your occupation. For example:

A. My name is John Wilson and I'm a high school teacher, on my way to a teacher's conference in Toronto.

B. Bill Richardson's the name and I'm a sales representative with Collier-Macmillan. Guess you've heard of us.

A. You're not going to the teacher's conference, are you?

B. No, not this year, but I went last year to the one/*

A. In Winnipeg, yeah, I wasn't able to go but heard all about it.

In this invented scene we can see at a glance that a topic has been raised by the forumulaic way that *A* has introduced himself to *B:* name and occupation, which is returned in the identification *B* makes of himself. The occupation component in these introductions by two strangers has served as an initial topic raiser to build some conversational interaction. Suppose they continue for some stretch of talk to build on this topic, viz. regarding their jobs, last year's teacher's conference in Winnipeg, the upcoming one, the relation between teachers and publishers, school kids and reading habits, etc.—all of which are plausible topics using our common-sense knowledge of the culture.

At some point, however, the talk ceases for some period of time, and there is a lull or silence, and it seems that this topicality has exhausted itself on both sides by unstated mutual agreement. It is a natural juncture in their conversation and, if one of them should want to start up talk again after this juncture, he could continue with the same topic. But if he chose another one altogether he would be showing that the first topic has been formally closed down. However, he might raise a second topic by making some bridge to the first one. For example:

A. You know when I was a kid we didn't have all these paperbacks they have around now. It sure makes a difference for education.

B. Yeah, I know, I can't even keep up with half of them. Sometimes I think there are too many.

Now, in this fictitious scene I have constructed a topical utterance that shows speaker *A* starting up again by referring to the topically previous "stage" of the conversation. But I have built into it the possibility for a new topic, a biographical one pertaining to *A*'s childhood. This could be "picked up" by *B* and carried on for conversational development. But instead I have made him select the previous topic pertaining to the overpublication of paperbacks and the occupational relevance of that remark for him. Suppose, however, that *A* wishes to push his childhood biography topic, for whatever reasons. Then he would have to tie his next utterance back to his topical opener and do what we might think of as asserting a topic, i.e., trying to get it established. For *B* it might be a case of preserving a topic that he may want to reopen, or perhaps, he is a person who does not talk about his childhood easily and sees the new topic as one he would not easily or happily contribute to. To avoid this,

*Symbol we use to show interruptions.

he may try to preserve the previous topic simply to block *A*'s topical opener.

Here is another example of how conversationalists react to topics. A group of people are having a conversation, say, at a party or in the lunch room of an office or factory. They are talking topically about what they were doing when Kennedy was assassinated, where they were when they heard the news, who told them first about it, what the persons did, etc. One of the members of this conversational gathering was in a mental hospital at the time. He does not want to divulge this part of his past for various reasons. He cannot contribute to the conversational development of this topic without falling obviously silent or speaking in a way that might noticeably leave out where he was at the time of the event. To avoid this outcome, he might seek to close down the topic by *topically shifting* to another one. (Of course, he might also suddenly leave the scene.)

Now, we see another example, similar in principle, but different in details. A group of men and one woman are talking and the men have raised the topic of work. The woman is a housewife. She might remain silent but, to contribute interactionally, she might have to devise her speech to develop the topicality, either by fitting her remarks in with her husband's, or by trying to reorient the conversation to how husband's jobs have consequences for family life or married life, etc.—which would amount to a preservation of the topic with a new aspect added on to it. She might on the other hand seek to shift the topic entirely. I am not suggesting, of course, that a housewife could not contribute to occupational talk among men, but it is not uncommon to find that, in the course of a conversation where occupational topicality prevails, those present who are without an occupation find themselves excluded unwittingly, tactlessly, or even intentionally.

The last point suggests some interesting properties of topical talk as they relate to categorization activity. The regulation of topics on the floor involves the participants' consideration of who their fellow interactants are, categorically speaking. That is, there appears to be an orientation toward building a conversation for some particular set of people, where *both* preserving the conversation and preserving certain membership categories of the particular collection of present people are attended to and regulated by topicality, to some extent at least. Topics can exclude speakers.

We have presented a set of concepts for analyzing topicality as a regulative feature of conversational development: *raising topics, closing down topics, preserving topics, shifting topics, asserting topics, topical exclusions, and topical categorizations.*

When we look at the way conversations develop we can detect places in it where persons are talking topically. This involves recognizing topical sequences within a continuous stretch of talk. Take, for example, household talk among mothers doing child-rearing activities and household responsibilities. Two mothers are having a chat over coffee in the kitchen. Their children are present playing around the house, coming and going as the mothers continue to talk. Now, the mothers may be topically developing their talk, but as the children come and go, asking them questions, making requests for things, making various diversions, etc., the mothers attend to their children's interactions and orient to them in the course of their own topical talk. A structure of attentions is required, one for the topicality and another for the kids. The attentions are competing ones, and mothers must be able to develop their own topical conversation in spite of continuing reorientations to their children's interactions. They might often regard the latter as interruptions and negatively sanction the children simply to preserve their own conversation. This calls for *topical continuity and coherence techniques.* For example, how do you sustain a topic that was last referred to several minutes ago, while you "hold on" to the last utterance of that topical talk indefinitely? Some common *reorientation markers* used when preserving a topic are "Now, where were we?" or "What was I saying?" etc. Participants must presumably be able to remember what topics are on the floor and to tie their utterances to the previous ones orienting to those topics. Topical tying procedures are employed for this purpose.

We are not suggesting that in the case of two mothers, topical talk *with* their children would never occur, but that there might indeed be forms of "adult topicality," relevant for them and not for the children, and likewise, "children's topicality," relevant for their interaction with children. As with our example of the men talking about their occupations in the presence of a housewife, in this case the social membership categories of the participants are elements of topicality, namely, mothers, parents, adults and children.

Let us leave the element of topicality and take up another aspect of conversational development that involves the basic rules we stated earlier in chapter 3: *One person speaks at a time* and *speaker-change reoccurs.* How do participants control the turn-taking process when they talk? How do they monitor the speech going on around them so as to fit their own to it in decidedly methodical ways? How does one *begin* to speak? The internal regulation of the distribution of speech in a conversational group must be provided by those who mutually build talk together, and to do this, speakers must be competent to hear all the fine details of the talk around them, one of which is to hear when a speaker completes his utterance.

Two issues should be distinguished here to avoid further confusion. The first pertains to who decides to take a turn, or how it is decided among conversationalists who is to take a turn, the focus of this issue being: *Who is to speak next? We may call this, after Sacks, the speaker-sequencing problem.*[9] On the other hand, there is the issue of how one takes a first turn, i.e., initiates a conversation or joins it.

Let us first consider a conversational encounter, rather than conversational gatherings. Suppose you meet someone you know on the street, coming your way. How is the first speaker selected? Obviously the one who speaks up first as the approach is being made, becomes the first speaker, and from there on out it takes the order of ABABAB, etc., as a general distribution rule. But was there some precedence rule at work that you and your partner used to decide that you and not he would be the first speaker, or is precedence governed by other considerations? If you both made eye contact as your approach was made and both readied yourselves in much the same way for a face-to-face engagement, then it might be that you spoke first without orienting to any particular method for being the first speaker. You simply make yourself the first. Contrastively, if it is someone who does not know you and could not be expected to recognize you and, therefore, make an approach to you, then there would be no issue of who speaks first, because you make yourself the first speaker by deciding to stop him in order to ask for directions, for example. It would never occur to him to be a first speaker.

Now consider another situation, a fairly common one. You see someone and he cannot see you and, because eye contact is not available, you cannot expect this friend to make an approach to you; perhaps he is across the street or walking in a different direction from you. What method can you use to make a contact?[10] You can do something to get his attention, obviously, yell or call out his name, wave your hands, whistle, etc. What you are doing is making yourself the first speaker to effectuate an otherwise improbable interaction. This is not unlike the previous example, save that you have a reciprocal social relationship with an interactional history to it.

In both the previous and the present situation you are in effect required to *initiate* the interaction *by summoning or getting the other's atten-*

tion. You control the outcome of the encounter. In such cases you make yourself the first speaker by being a summoner of a prospective interact-ant. *And in all such cases the distribution rule is simple: the summoner speaks first. In Schegloff's paper on sequencing rules in telephone conversations, he states the rule: the answerer speaks first.*[11] We can see how this applies to the social situation of telephoning because the interaction is entirely achieved by disembodied voices, so to speak, with a total absence of all the normal features of interactional presence. The answerer must be the first speaker because he picks up the phone when the caller rings him, the caller waiting at the other end of the line for his party to pick up and announce his completion of the connection. The caller is the summoner, his electronic signal a proxy for the vocal sum-mons he would use in normal face-to-face interaction. Although he takes the first action, that is, initiates the interaction electronically, it is not a speaking action and therefore he is unable to be the first speaker, as with initiators on the street.

In this discussion we are pointing to the sequential organization of conversational interaction. We began by noting the distinction between an order-of-speakers problem and one that does not appear to be an ordering problem except as the *first speaker* is decided. And in two-party talk once the first speaker is decided, the ordering rule follows quite naturally the ABABAB distribution. But we were suggesting that, where multi-party conversational gatherings are concerned, persons must de-cide when to take a turn to talk next, and that in our culture there does not appear to be a clear-cut rule for doing so, one that would decide the precedence of speakers. What would such an enforced rule amount to? Well, suppose all parties agree to or have a way of enforcing the ordering of each speaker according to some rule of precedence—if four persons are talking, A talks first, then B, then C, and then D, and then to A again, B again, C again, and so on. But we would find that the speakers were locking themselves into an arrangement in which they followed a strict rule of who-could-talk-after-whom or before-whom, and no exceptions might be made. The result would be a round of speech, much the same as a four-part musical round: ABCDABCD, etc.

We can see that such a distribution rule for speech is not common practice, if ever used at all in our culture, and yet conversationalists take turns and sequence their talk. This means that precedence rules are not built into a conversation in our culture by prior agreements or conven-tions not strictly pertaining to conversation as such. But precedence rules originate outside of a conversation in the form of external constraints, as

Albert maintains is true for the Barundi of Africa.[12] Albert states that caste ranking determines the Barundi relative super- or sub-ordinate social positions. Albert is maintaining, therefore, that conversational interaction enforces the social stratification system by means of precedence rules for speakers who, when observed talking, display the caste ranking: the first speaker is from the highest caste, the second from the next highest, etc., and then around again and again in the same way until the occasion is over. But in our culture we can find no such rule at work. Does that mean we do not have rules of precedence?

It might be the case that other things determine who speaks next, without respect to a principle for ordering one speaker vis-à-vis another speaker. Precedence may involve simple things: for example, a person who is asked a question takes precedence over others in speaking next in order to answer the question. The enforcement of that right or obligation of a next speaker to take his turn might be seen in the orientation conversationalists display when demanding the answer or prohibiting others from answering in place of the one asked the question, and so forth. In a game, for example, players share and enforce an orientation to proper turn taking, and should a player wish to go out of turn, he is immediately stopped from doing so or attempting it. Analogously, *interactants can monitor the development of a conversation for the appropriateness of a next speaker,* and such appropriateness is decided by the events of the conversation itself and becomes a matter for internal conversational control. *What this might mean is that it is not a question of* **which** *particular person speaks next, but a question of how one who has been talked to in a particular way gets to talk next.* In other words, it is a matter for interactants to decide depending on the developing course of their conversation.

Since we have raised the question-answer phenomenon again, let us briefly look at the sequential organization of these pairs in conversational development. It should give us some idea of how the two basic rules of conversation are used, i.e., one person talks at a time and speaker-change reoccurs.

Questions get answers and a questioner gets an answerer as a next speaker in a conversation. Sacks notes that the first simple rule of *Q-A* pairs, a proper question gets a proper answer, has the following sequential implication: a questioner gets another chance to speak after the answerer speaks because he has reserved himself a right to speak again. In this way we find that a second interchange is developed out of the first. A sequential pattern of Q-A interchanges can develop into a chain structure of QAQAQA, etc. Sacks refers to this as the *chaining rule*.[13] For example, the following is an instance of the operation of the chaining rule in an interchange:

A. Do you have a car?

B. No.

A. Why not?

Recalling what we said earlier about topicality, we find that questions can be skillful ways of raising topics because of their power to develop a conversational sequence that is initiated by the questioner who might be aiming to get some topic on the floor. An initial questioner is thus able to exercise considerable interactional control over conversational development because of the chaining rule.

However, as you might quickly suspect, Q-A chains need not develop in strict accordance to a chaining rule that goes QAQAQA, etc. Several other alternative possibilities are available for interactants when Q-A pairs are used. For instance, suppose you find that you have answered a question, but that your answer was itself a question:

A. Did you ever buy Fujicolor film? (Q)

B. Why do you ask? (Q)

A. Well, I'm not sure about buying it. (A) Have you ever used it? (Q)

B. Yes. (A)

A. Was it okay, nice colors? (Q)

B. About the same as any other, I'd say. (A)

What is the chaining structure here? It goes Q, then A, but this A is also a Q. *B*'s answer is in some sense a non-answer, but it is positioned in the place reserved for the answer, and it is responsive to the initial question. This is an instance of a general phenomenon whereby one puts off answering directly a question addressed to him. This is something you can do, it seems, for some kinds of questions, when you might want to find out what the questioner is "up to." After all, you are being obligated or coerced by the first rule of Q-A pairs, and accordingly you may want to regain control under its constraining interactional effect. An answer of this sort occupies the structural position of the normal direct answer, and thus allows the answerer to put off that direct answer for a later turn. Furthermore, it now makes a questioner of the answerer and alters the normal QAQ chaining pattern. It, in fact, *reverses it*. The initial questioner is now being asked to give an answer, turning the local control of the conversation over to the one originally under the control of the first questioner.

What this fragment of conversation amounts to is a delay in the completion of a speech act. The direct answer to the first utterance comes in the second and not the first interchange. Were this chain to develop further so that the answerer continued to ask questions back and reverse the pairing procedure, he could be accused or at least suspected of strategically evasive action. The conversational structure of speech occasions known as "interrogations" might be worth inspecting with this problem in mind.

How is a question heard as a question? This is a problem in itself and not necessarily one that involves the sequential organization of Q-A pairs. That is, to get a second item in the pair there must be an act of recognition by the hearer that what was put to him by a speaker consisted of a completed question. Linguists who have studied this matter conclude that not all questions are identifiable by the intonational contour that one often attributes to a question.[14] Whatever way it is that questions are constructed to come out sounding like questions, similarly to the construction of summonses they are methodically generated by conversational participants.

Some psychologists, known as psycholinguists, have argued for the functional equivalence between utterances that do not on the surface appear to be questions but that nevertheless get treated as questions. For example, "I suppose you are going home for lunch again today," is functionally equivalent to the question, "Are you going home for lunch again today?" This may be the case, but it is analytically less useful to treat this utterance as a functional equivalent of a question than to treat it *as some other kind of interchange altogether,* namely one that seeks to find out what another is doing by inviting them to correct your assumption if you are in fact wrong or confirming it if you are in fact correct. *Sacks has called such interchanges correction invitation devices.*[15] That is, they are interaction strategies that invite another to correct you if you have reason to believe that what you are saying is probably not true, but cannot come right out to inquire about what the truth of the matter might be. For example, you want to find out personal information about someone you meet for the first time and you say, "What part of Vancouver did you say you lived in?" when, in fact, you had reason to believe they lived elsewhere.

This example might not seem very personal, but situations can arise where asking about place of residence may be considered too forward or suspicious because of attributable ulterior motives. Similarly, a young man sees a young woman at his office and during the first conversation they have he says, "What did you say your husband does?" where he has not been told anything at all about a husband and he really wants to know whether the woman is married and whether a possible social relationship can be developed beyond the office setting. A straightforward answer might be, "I'm not married," but one that recognizes the correction invitation device as a ploy to take advantage of the woman would be, "I didn't say." This would successfully abort the outcome of the immediate interchange.

There is another issue in Q-A pairs that pertains to who can properly supply the answer. Here the notion of a *proper next speaker* is relevant. If I ask you a question, can another present party answer it? This takes us back to the principle of directiveness we spoke of earlier. How is the direction of a question established? Suppose you need a red pencil and you are in a room with others who work at desks, and you say outloud to no one in particular, "Anybody have a red pencil I can borrow for a minute?" We recognize that as a requestive speech act, but it addresses a body of persons and calls for a volunteer. This is not as obligatory as a specifically directed request. It leaves the next action open to self-selection. What is different about a requestive action?

The above request does appear to be a question too but an answer alone might bring, "*I* do." We can see that just that answer would not be an appropriate next action, even if it is an appropriate answer to the question. Unless the answerer followed it with the offer of the pencil he would not be fulfilling the request. Jokes are constructed around this recognizable distinction between an answer to a question and a proper response to a request. Someone asks you, "Do you have the time?" and, instead of giving it, you answer, "yes."

Our discussion of directiveness presupposes that a questioner formulates his question to get a particular party to answer. We raised the issue of how the answerer is selected and started out by showing that the selection can be determined by the questioner who directs the question to another person. We showed a contrasting case in which no direction was applied to a question that took the form of a request. We introduced requests not to confuse the issue, but because we wanted to illustrate the fact that questions can come in various conventional forms. For instance, you want your husband to come home from his office in time for dinner, and you call him and say, "Are you going to come home soon?" and he answers, "Yes, right away." Now that is a question that gets a proper answer. But it also may be heard as a request for him to come home soon.

In the case of directing a question to a participant who ought to answer, there arise situations in which he does not get the turn to answer because someone else answers in his place. This is what we mean by the issue of a proper next speaker or a rightful answerer. To illustrate this phenomenon, a family is seated around the dinner table and the mother asks one of the children a question. Instead of that child answering, his brother answers. This can be done in various ways. The brother's answer can be ratified by any or all the members of the conversation, or rejected by them. The one whose turn has been taken away can attempt to regain his turn by cutting into his brother's answer before he completes it. Perhaps an adult negatively sanctions the boy by interrupting and retrieving the other child's turn. This brings us to the last features of conversational development to be taken up in this chapter.

When the flow of conversation is broken by various sorts of events as the result of a modification of the basic rule "one person speaks at a time," the term "interruption" is readily applied to these events. But what is an interruption? Is it simply an acoustic phenomenon? Or is it just an obvious case of one speaker carelessly talking when others are talking, a thoughtless interactional intrusion? Let us try to take up some of these considerations and briefly outline some of the ways interruptive events take place and show how they are produced and treated by conversationalists as interruptions rather than as other kinds of events that might look like interruptions but which are not.

First of all, we must be able to distinguish between the intrusion of some behavior upon another from the intrusion of some speech behavior on another speech behavior. We will not be talking about the former, i.e., when someone enters a room and intrudes upon another's solitary activity, such as entering someone's office and saying, "Excuse me, am I interrupting?" Instead we will focus on *the idea of an interruption within a conversational episode,* which means that whatever the formal features of the interruption in question that constitute it as being an interruption, it will be reckoned with respect to the orientations of conversationalists who must take account of that event in carrying on with their talk.

Offhand we might begin with a notion that interruptions are defects in a conversation, petty nuisances for a conversation, proscribed events to be disposed of when they occur, and so forth. It is true that when interactants confront certain interruptions they sometimes treat them as situational defects or undesirables. But that should not color our inspection of them as real features of conversational interaction, because we also want to see that they are not always treated as defects, but as normal features of ongoing talk. The internal regulation of taking turns and *recog-*

nizing when an utterance is completed in order to be able to take the next turn are intimately involved in the idea of an interruption.

Suppose you are talking in a group and you have taken your turn by answering a question, for example. You construct your utterance as an answer and as you do so, the initial questioner starts up again before you complete it. It might go: (You are *B*.)

A. Why do you think the Americans are in Vietnam, to protect the free world or just to shoot up South East Asia?

B. No, no, not just to shoot up obviously, but /

A. And you know as well as I do that they have been called there by the government of South Vietnam, so how could /

B. But they are doing that anyway, aren't they? I mean civilians too, you know.

Is / (the interruption) placed after *B*'s utterance because *A* is interrupting *B* who has been denied the completion of this answer and, therefore, the completion of his turn? This would seem to be a sound notation in keeping with the orientations that participants themselves might have in continuing the conversation as they do. For we see that in the next interchange *A*'s remark gets interrupted by *B*'s next remark. Or is that really another interruption? This question is not asked idly, mind you, but provocatively. We will argue that *it is not another interruption,* and accordingly we would have to remove the symbol / that follows *A*'s second utterance.

The reason is as follows: When *B* speaks the second time, he is completing the utterance he was fashioning in his first turn which was taken away from him before he could adequately do so. Hence, *B* is treating *A*'s second utterance as an interruption and from his point of view *A* is not entitled to take that turn. *B*'s second utterance is an attempt to regain his turn and an opportunity to complete it. He is not willing to relinquish the floor, so to speak, and by speaking again he is not interrupting *A* at all, since *A*'s utterance need not be legitimately acknowledged by *B*. (We might go so far as to say the interrupter is being shown that he is one, in fact.) It seems to be true that, when one has usurped another's turn at talking, he knows that he has taken a turn illegitimately and when the interrupted person holds on to the floor, the interrupter gives way by allowing the interrupted person to complete his utterance, as in the above invented piece of data.

Such an acknowledgment suggests that there might be a rule of precedence at work where interruptions are involved. A speaker may be regarded as having a right to speak in turn and if he speaks out of turn he may be committing an illegitimate action in a conversation. Depending upon circumstances, e.g., the setting and its practical purposes, interruptive infractions can be sanctioned. The courtroom is one such setting. In games, for example, referees and umpires are required to monitor the actions of players for violations of turn-taking rights of precedence. *In conversational interaction a simple precedence rule for the proper continuation of a conversation may be: If a person talking in turn has not come to its completion, then any next speaker who starts up during that turn before that completion is reached is an interrupter, and the one he interrupts takes precedence by regaining his turn without waiting for the interrupter to finish.*

What are the implications of this rule of precedence? It means that interruptive events are not described as simply acoustical instances of overlapping speech. Every time you see a place on a transcript or hear a place in a conversation (or a tape of it) where the rule, "one speaker at a time," seems to be violated, you cannot describe it as an interruption without further investigating how the overlap was organized by the speakers as an intended violation of the precedence rule. This is so because it may very well be that speakers are not overlapping by violation of the rule, but because there is more than one conversation taking place at a time in a gathering. When we say overlapping, we mean that one begins to talk while another already talks. Obviously, two conversations going at once is nothing more than acoustic overlapping, such as a tape recorder might pick up, but not confusing or interruptive to speakers themselves. But when overlapping occurs within a single conversation, it can only be a violation of the "one speaker at a time" rule.

We point to overlapping because often interruptions consist of that phenomenon. However, they need not, and this is the next consideration we examine. To conclude this point, we note that conversations are normally filled with such violations of the rule and participants have at their disposal numerous methods for handling them adequately to insure the continuance of the talk. This does not in any way contradict the existence of the rule, but rather confirms its existence as a stable resource of conversation.

There are places in conversational interaction where speakers pause momentarily. Sometimes these places have in them such expressions as umm, uh, ah, and so on, all of which actually show that a pause is being taken. In these places we often find interruptive phenomena. The use of such expressions seems to be structurally conducive to producing an interruption, because a hearer can take the opportunity to fit his speech into the talk at that point. These *pause junctures,* as we might call them, are monitored by participants for systematic use in constructing another turn for themselves. That is, by virtue of pause junctures, speakers can get another turn and do so in a rather legitimate way. This question of legitimacy comes up with regard to rights of precedence at taking turns and *the problem of hearing when a turn and an utterance are complete.*

It appears very safe to say that there is a linguistic property involved in the problem of hearing utterance completions, namely, the unit known as a sentence. This is a syntactical or grammatical unit of speech and it is a resource for deciding when one has completed a turn, since we find that it is often at pause junctures coming after complete syntactic sentence units that interruptions are made.

For instance, compare the two following cases:

1. A.   I thought he was uh /
   B.   Where did you say he was going?
2. A.   I thought he was uh walking pretty fast for him (pause).
   B.   Where did you say he was going?

In 1, we see the interruption because of A's syntactically incomplete utterance, the "uh" being a pause juncture that gives B a chance to take a turn, but in violation of the previously described precedence rule. In 2, we see the same pause juncture within the utterance and then after its syntactical completion we see another momentary pause that gives B the opportunity to start up in a legitimate fashion. Conversationalists apparently have methods for detecting when a short pause after such a sentence unit offers a slot for their taking a turn in a way that does not violate the precedence rule.

Often the loss of a turn, as in 1 above, does not get contested by the loser, since he recognizes he has provided a pause juncture which his interlocuter might use to jump in. We are not suggesting that speakers must be vigilant or stand on guard against such interruptions, but that these methods are equally available to interactants for coordinating their talk, and as such get regularly used without necessarily becoming the basis for cut-throat competitive conversation, although that too is a fact of certain occasions of conversation, such as political argument. To clarify the point, interrupting by means of monitoring pause junctures may be more permissible than interrupting by overlapping which is done without any pausing phenomenon. In fact, pause junctures are devices that reduce overlapping. They permit a speaker to interrupt without strictly violating the "one person at a time" rule, despite an incomplete turn, since the speaker has at least momentarily ceased to speak. Participants apparently orient to the pacing of others and when a speaker might be regarded as "running down" within his turn, it may be treated as a forfeit of that turn.

On this last point an interesting problem emerges. Pauses are objectively measurable as time intervals between the spoken parts of a person's utterance. One could stop-watch them if he had a mind to do so. However, the conception of a pause in terms of an acoustic interval misses the point of conversational organization altogether. What is at issue is the fact that people do things with their pauses, and *it is crucial to discover that a pause is precisely in the possession of a speaker, that is, a pause can belong to a speaker and to his turn.* In example 1 above, we recognize without any difficulty that the pause belonged to speaker *A*.

Presumably conversationalists recognize the possessive property of a pause and that is what clues them in to taking their next turn in the way they eventually do. There is certain to be some range of elapsed time that can normally occur for a person's pause before forfeiting his turn, but it is most certainly not the case that a specific time interval always in all cases determines the willingness of others to honor the speaker's turn. It may in fact be the case that persons known to us are monitored for their own conversational preferences of pacing and pausing, or that relative membership categories of speakers decide the length of permissible pauses, e.g., a sign of deference in relationships might be displayed by such willingness to let a speaker take very long unbroken turns, etc.

Likewise, the case can be made that silence is not a mere acoustic event of speechlessness. But it can be a meaningful silence insofar as it can be controlled by conversationalists to do various things. Anyone who has witnessed an expert public speaker or a first-rate comedian will readily recognize that silences can be manipulated to achieve desired effects upon listeners. Novelists long ago characterized the silence engendered by a conversation as heavy, pregnant, or uncomfortable. As with pauses, we find that silences can belong to speakers, or to next speakers. As a test of the truth of this fact, try delaying your answer to someone's question next time you are asked one, and see how long you can prolong the silence between the question and your answer. Without doubt that silence would be seen by all present as yours and no one else's.

The last feature of conversational development we will trace out in this chapter pertains to the way in which hearers specifically incorporate previous utterances into their own. By doing so, a next speaker can show

how he understands the previous one. Earlier we showed how pronoun transformations occur in simple interchanges. There we saw that some parts of the previous utterance get built into the next speaker's utterance rather neatly. When we discussed question-answer pairs, we did not take the trouble to point out that whether one answers a question with a simple yes or no involves *a principle of utterance contraction* that we might refer to as *the principle of ellipsis. Very basic to speech, as a rule of speech economy, this principle involves carrying forward parts of a previous utterance which are not repeated vocally but which, nevertheless, become understood as unspoken parts of the utterance.* So, if *A* says, "Did you see John yesterday?" and *B* answers, "Yes," it is understood that yes can be extended elliptically to "Yes, I saw John yesterday." In this way *B*'s utterance is tied to *A*'s and contracts it into a shortened version of a possible answer. This borrowing property is peculiar to elliptical constructions. When young schoolchildren are reciting lessons aloud in the classroom, they are sometimes directed by the teacher to override the principle of ellipsis in order to "say the whole thing" and get practice at making good sentences and showing comprehension of their answer.

Consider now a different phenomenon that involves extension and completion rather than contraction. In cases where speakers want to show that they hear what the previous speaker says just as he intends it to be heard, they will construct their next utterance to fit together with it as a completion. For example, you say, "I was thinking of going" and I say next, "to the store to buy some beer." It is no surprise and gives no cause for surprise that I can do that. Yet, if you think about that kind of phenomenon, a very commonplace one, you will recognize the principle of intersubjectivity: two persons of different mind and body can speak as one. Sacks reports the following phenomenon[17] occurring among some teenage boys in a group therapy session. A newcomer to the occasion is introduced to the boys and one starts to tell about the topicality of their session:

A. We were in an automobile discussion

B. —discussing the psychological motives for

C. —drag racing on the street.

This example very powerfully displays how a group can speak as an entity itself, since together three persons are constructing a sentence for a fourth. Sacks derives the following rule to account for this: If a speaker wishes to extend a previous speaker's utterance, look for a place in his utterance where he uses a predicate noun, participalize it, and continue speaking syntactically consistent with it. What this does is to create a dependent clause that attaches to the first speaker's utterance what is now an independent clause in an extended sentence. For example,

A.: "We were having dinner

B.: "—dining on roast beef."

There are probably numerous ways that such extensions and completions can be constructed by conversationalists. The following is taken from an *Esquire* magazine interview with the Black writer, James Baldwin:

Q.: What you are calling for, then, is a radical change in thinking by government and industry.

Baldwin: Yes.

Q.: And given the inertia plus . . .

Baldwin: Fear.

Q.: . . . fear and whatever else there may be, any such changes seem . . .

Baldwin: . . . seem improbable.[18]

The dovetailing of this speech shows tying procedures at work. The interview situation may be a special sort of occasion; the position of the interviewer as eliciter of information and opinions may build into the talk closely knit tying based on the offering of leading questions by the interviewer and the willingness to accept them by the recipient.

Another issue for the hearership of extensions and completions pertains to the modification or rejection of an extended or completed utterance. Naturally, there is not always a suitable match between the previous utterance and the extension offered for it. The first speaker can take the opportunity to reject or otherwise modify the extension of his own remark, and thus shows misunderstandings in a very unambiguous way. It always seems to be true that an extender is supplying a *candidate extension,* and in some cases he shows that he was not thinking along the same lines as his interlocutor by selecting an unacceptable candidate.

In the above interchange sequence, Baldwin offers "fear" as his candidate extension and the interviewer ratifies this selection by starting up his next utterance with "fear." Presumably, an interviewer wishes to extract opinions in this way, what you might call a fill-in method, leaving a blank slot for the interviewee to fill in as he sees fit. The use of the word "plus" serves this purpose well; it is an extensional aid.

Had the interviewer not been willing to go along with this extension because he did not have it in mind when he constructed his utterance, he might have rejected "fear" by saying in his next turn, ". . . or uncertainty and whatever else there may be like fear as you say . . ."

In this chapter we have outlined some elements of conversational development that need investigation if it is to be understood. These elements are involved in the basic operations of commonplace discourse. They are interactionally accomplished by conversationalists who orient to their use in building talk together in a myriad of human group situations. The study of these elements will reveal the nature of interactional rules for the internal regulation of conversational events. We have not considered any of these elements in relation to practical activities within which conversations might occur and out of which they might be developed. That is, we have not taken into account the development of a conversation within a practical occasion of a concrete sort, not merely substantively speaking but formally within a substantive context. The next chapter will briefly raise some issues in this regard. We will find it necessary to make formal descriptions for natural histories of practical activities, within which interactants organize and develop conversation as a crucial aspect of the activity.

Notes

¹Data from author's observational notes, hand recorded.

²The problem of hearing, as opposed to the problem of speaking, has generally been neglected in linguistic research in preference to analyses of speech production. It is obvious that to speak one must be competent to hear other's speak, if we are talking about speech interaction or speech conduct. Since hearing is only indirectly observable, it might be regarded as too inaccessible for examination. However, a little thought shows that if we are to be competent conversationalists we must have *ways of hearing* our fellow interlocutors. Realizing that hearing is an interpretive process that assigns meaning to others utterances, we must suppose that members can use procedures for hearing utterances, so that they can properly consider, address, understand, extend, contract, reject, etc., those utterances. That is, participants can make inferences quite readily about how to hear utterances and those inferences provide them a stable basis for speaking in response to these utterances. Thus, given you say "hello" I hear it as a greeting and fashion my return greeting. From a psycholinguist's point of view, see the interesting paper by J. P. Thorne, "On Hearing Sentences," in J. Lyons and R. J. Wales, eds., *Psycholinguistics Papers* (Edinburgh: Edinburgh University Press, 1966) pp. 3-25. Sacks has given considerable attention to the problem of hearing in connection with forms of understanding of syntax, of action, and of topic. In his lecture that deals with these forms of understanding (University of California, Santa Barbara, Sociology Department, February 29, 1968, transcribed, unpublished manuscript), Sacks demonstrates that understanding is achieved by fashioning what one says according to the way an utterance is heard for its relevance to (1) the action at hand, (2) the syntactic elements it contains, and (3) the topicality involved. One shows how he has heard another in each of these three different orientations to relevance.

³I have discussed this problem in some detail in "The Everyday World of the Child." See Douglas, *Everyday Life,* pp. 188-217. See Sacks, "The Search for Help," in

Sudnow, *Studies,* pp. 31-74, for the source of my own discussion about children's referential speech.

[4]From Sacks, "UCLA Lecture," 7, Fall quarter, 1966, pp. 8-11.

[5]Ibid., Sack's discussion on pronouns and procedures for using them in conversation first illuminated this problem and led to my analysis of children's talk presented in "The Organization of Talk and Socialization Practices in Family Household Interaction" (unpublished doctoral dissertation, Dept. of Sociology, University of California, Berkeley, 1969), pp. 124-148.

[6]A thorough analysis of topicality in conversations can be found in Albert Adato, "On the Sociology of Topics in Ordinary Conversation," unpublished manuscript.

[7]Sacks has analyzed features of topicality at length in the series, "Five UCLA Lectures," Spring 1968.

[8]On focused, as contrasted to unfocused, engagements see Goffman, *Public Places,* pp. 33-79; 83-148.

[9]Sacks, "UCLA Lectures," 1-4, Spring quarter 1967.

[10]For the most recent lengthy analysis on the regulation of public encounters and the structuring of routine contacts in public places, see Goffman's latest work, *Relations in Public, Microstudies of the Public Order* (New York: Basic Books, 1971), especially the chapters dealing with "supportive interchanges" and "remedial interchanges," pp. 62-187. For specific treatments of eye-contact behavior see Sudnow, "Temporal Parameters of Glancing in Social Interaction," in Sudnow, *Studies,* pp. 259-279. For nice descriptions of these visual interactive arrangements, as they occur in a hospital setting, see Sudnow's *Passing On: The Social Organization of Dying* (Englewood Cliffs, New Jersey: Prentice-Hall, Inc., 1967), especially p. 123, fn.

[11]Schegloff, "Sequencing."

[12]Ethel Albert, "Rhetoric, Logic, and Poetics in Barundi: Culture Patterning of Speech Behavior," *American Anthropologist* 66, No. 6, Part 2 (1964). Sacks called my attention to this interesting paper in his discussions of the speaker-ordering problem, noting that a formulation of the Barundi ordering (for four speakers ABCDABCD, etc.) would be an anomaly in our own culture for normal four-party conversation.

[13]Sacks, "UCLA Lecture," 2, February 24, 1966, p. 15.

[14]Linguists have studied the properties of utterances that are recognizably labeled questions to elucidate classes of questions and question characteristics that reveal not a single, but a multiplicity of question forms, phonologically, syntactically, and semantically. See Dwight Bolinger, *Aspects of Language* (New York: Harcourt, Brace, 1968).

[15]Sacks, "UCLA Lectures," 1966.

[16]I discuss the principle of ellipsis in "Some Conversational Problems for Interactional Analysis" in Sudnow, *Studies.*

[17]Sacks, "UCLA Lectures," 9, Fall quarter, 1966 and 4, Spring quarter, April 12, 1967.

[18]*Esquire,* July 1968, p.50.

Suggested Readings and Study Questions

1. Goffman, *Relations in Public,* chapter 4, "Remedial Interchanges," pp. 138-182.

What are some of the special features noted by Goffman in his analysis of the structure of remedial interchange that constitute development and sequential steps in conversations? How would you relate these structural features to those elements of conversational development we have outlined in chapter 6? Note that Goffman shows interpretive procedures operating in specific linkages of utterances made by interactants. How does Goffman treat the natural unit of a turn at talking in his analysis of remedial sequences or cycles? What is a two-move couplet and how is it connected to standard interrogration-type interactions? What role does Goffman ascribe to question-answer interchanges and to conversational junctures in the context of remedial interactions? What is the relevance of an "anticipated sequence" for a participant's selection and interpretation of a given turn or move in a conversation? Can you provide other instances for the categories of "set-ups" and "cut-offs"? What points are made with respect to opening and closing phases of the sequences?

2. Roy Turner, "Some Formal Properties of Therapy Talk," in Sudnow, *Studies,* pp. 367-396.

What are some features of development in the sequences of therapy talk examined by Turner? How does he analyze topic as a key feature and as related to both the categorization process and to "small talk" in that social occasion? How is accountability a feature of patients' talk in terms of the development of a single occasion of therapy and its recognized purposes of treatment?

3. To study the basic points presented in chapter 6 you will have to rely on your own observations and make up exercises to study them, because there is very little available published material that provides a model for studying conversational development. As an additional aid you should consult Michael Moerman, "Analysis of Lue Conversation: Providing Accounts, Finding Breaches, and Taking Sides," in Sudnow, *Studies,* pp. 170-228. and Gail Jefferson, "Side Sequences" in the same volume, pp. 294-338. Note that it is possible to characterize conversations as accounts or arguments, as containing digressions, etc. Can you see any connection between the issue of taking sides in conversation and the kinds of exchanges Goffman describes as "supportive" and remedial"? Can you collect a specimen conversation of "taking sides" or of an argument? Study its structure carefully and try to analyze how it has developed into an argument, a disagreement, or however you might choose to characterize it. Does the problem of hearing, as we outlined

it, enter into the interpretations of participants about the argumentative nature of their discourse; and can you specify how it does from one utterance to the next? What is the structural relevance of "side sequences," as Jefferson calls them, to the ongoing topical development of a conversation?

4. Other investigators of social life have incorporated conversations into their analysis of social organization in an explicit way, but do not study conversational development per se. Consult Aaron Cicourel, "Conversational Depictions of Social Organization," chapter 4 in his study, *The Social Organization of Juvenile Justice* (New York: John Wiley, 1968), pp. 111-169. How does Cicourel use conversations to show the organization of juvenile justice in situated encounters between juveniles and legal authorities? What are some features of the interrogations that juveniles undergo? As a type of conversation, how does an interrogation develop by means of strategies employed by the police? Consult also Sudnow, *Passing On,* for conversational material used to depict the routine practices of hospital staff. How is "bad news" transmitted in conversational exchanges between staff and relatives of the patient? Can you see a developmental structure in these fairly short communications?

5. The following are exercises to gain understanding of those features of conversational development outlined in chapter 6:

a. Select any two utterances from an observed conversation (you may be one of the participants) and show how the speakers display their hearing for each other, i.e., show that they have understood the sense in which the utterances where intentionally communicated. Can you find cases where the original intentions are misheard or misunderstood? How do the conversationalists show that mistake? What conversational consequences ensue from the mistake?

b. Observe a conversation for the use of pronouns. Can you see the procedures used to detect the intended meaning of a pronoun, in terms of whom it is directed to and whom it includes from among the conversational group?

c. Observe a conversation for topicality. How does a topic get raised, how is it developed? Does the development have anything to do with the membership categories of the participants? Show the sequential connection between topics and phases of conversation, i.e., locate the place topic-shifts occur and topic-digressions arise. How does the topic get closed down?

d. Note in a conversation you observe how speakers take turns. Do you discover some pattern to the ordering of speakers, one that recurs throughout the conversation? Can you formulate the ordering as a principle or method for the sequencing of speech for that group of speakers? Can you discover precedence rules and describe how they work?

e. Observe question-answer exchanges in a conversation. How do they contribute to the conversational development? Can you show how questions and answers are chained? Are there types of questions, both interpretively and structurally, that set up conditions for answering, i.e., the method and content of an answer are responsive to the question?

f. Locate some interruption points in a conversation. Observe how the interruption comes to be seen as an interruption because of the manner in which it is related to the utterance already on the floor. How do various interruptions occur and what interactional consequences can you observe? Can the development of a conversation be normally accommodating to interruptions, or can you locate instances where interruptions terminate conversations?

g. Collect some instances of utterance extensions and completions. What method does a speaker use when he extends or completes another's utterances? Can you construct a rule that would enable you to generate further instances of that class of extension or completion?

6. Does it make any sense to conceive of a conversation's development without conceiving of its special parts contributing to that development? Compare a structural analysis of parts to common-sense analysis such as "The conversation moved along very slowly, not much was really said." What structural and sequential analysis might be done to demonstrate this observation about the tempo of a conversation and its relation to topicality? (This is a purely speculative question.)

7. What is silence in a conversation? How is it part of a developing sequence of conversational actions? How is silence interpreted by conversationalists as a positive phenomenon, rather than as merely the absence of speech in physical terms? That is, can you observe what silence does in a particular conversation?

Chapter Seven

What is a Social Activity?
Some Descriptive Parameters

Thus far in our efforts at making natural histories of everyday social events, we have concentrated on elements of conversational interaction. Throughout our discussion, we have implied some understanding of the nature of social activity that includes other structural elements as well. What in fact is an activity; or better, how can we come to analytic terms with the idea of an activity? This is no simple task, and the best we can do in an introduction to the problem is offer some simple suggestions on how we might get started. In some ultimate sense, we want to develop a coherent theory of human activity in terms of the practical procedures available to everyday interactants whose main task in social life is to make daily activities an accomplished fact.

We may begin by noting that an activity refers to some course of humanly organized behavior, irrespective of its particular shape or content. Activities are constructed by individuals taking joint lines of action, i.e., action oriented to others, as opposed to individual lines of action that take no person interactionally into account. Solitary behavior, such as reading a book in the private confines of a room, is to be regarded as an individual line of action, and as such may be designated as individual activity. We are concerned only with collective activity, i.e., activity including others—this is, what we mean by social activity. This does not mean that an individual in a room by himself is no longer a social being with respect to his own behavior and thoughts, but only that social activity is precisely that behavior called forth from individuals when confronted by the presence of others. The arena of social interaction involves behavior in groups (two or more persons).

Participants in group behavior do things together. They share a mutual orientation to doing things together, and they take account of mutual interests and purposes. Since activities are manifested in the outward actions of group members, as opposed to their inner thoughts which are unavailable except through behavior, the locus of human activities is their practicality. We shall use the concept of social activity to refer to the concerted practical actions of cultural members.

Sociology has focused heavily on uncovering those hidden aspects of human behavior called attitudes, beliefs, values, etc., without fully realizing their basis in everyday practical activities, or at least without seeking to describe that basis. In Sudnow's study of the social organization of dying in hospital settings, he underscores this important point:

This study thus seeks to explore the sociological structure of certain categories pertaining to death. Its foremost concern is not with such an interest as "attitudes towards death," but with the activities of "seeing death," "announcing death," "suspecting death," and the like, where in each case the ways in which these activities occur can be seen to furnish us the basis for a description of what death is as a sociological phenomenon.[1]

And in a similar argument, Sudnow underscores the perspective guiding his study, one that this text also subscribes to:

That perspective says that the categories of hospital life, e.g., "life," "illness," "patient," "dying," "death," or whatever, are to be seen as *constituted by the practices of hospital personnel* as they engage in their daily routinized interactions within an organizational milieu. This perspective implies a special concern with the form a definition should take, that concern involving a search for the *procedural basis* of events. By this I mean that a search is made, via the ethnographic description of hospital social structure and activities, for those practices which give "death related categories" their concrete organizational foundations. Rather than entering the hospital to investigate "death" and "dying" as I conceived them, I sought to develop "definitions" of such phenomena based on actions involved in their recognition, treatment, and consequences.[2]

Natural histories of everyday events must seek to produce formal descriptions of members' procedures for doing social activities, i.e., by including descriptive enquiries into the procedural basis underlying the routine practices of socially organized events.

To begin, consider the problem a normal member of society faces when he encounters the everyday appearances of things in the social world. This will help to indicate how a scientific description of social activities can best be conceptualized. Recall the so-called scientific description offered by classroom observers that was cited in chapter 2. We criticized it for its failure to describe the classroom activities in terms of the methods used by participants in the activity, *as recognized by them.* That is, we argued that the descriptions offered did not allow us to recover the original properties of the classroom events, and in fact failed to show how those events were shaped and structured by the behaviors of the members in the environment. To use Abraham Kaplan's terms,[3] the analysis of an activity ought always to be a reconstructed logic of the logics used by the activity's members. Therefore, if our aim is to achieve a valid scientific description, we must reconstruct the logic of social participants in such a way as to preserve the form of their logics-in-use, rather than violate the integrity of that original form. In other words, we must strive in our analysis to discover how participants see activities and do them. How is recognition and performance accomplished?

The first consideration might be called the problem of recognition. How do we recognize the appearances of an activity? The idea of an unrecognized activity seems absurd. This is not a question of making judgments that are true or false as much as it is a question of making judgments that are possible interpretations of what we see. A witness of any human interaction whatsoever can be pressed into making some interpretation of the events before his eyes. He can describe them, perhaps name them, by using interpretive procedures[4] to make inferences about the appearance of events. In chapters 3 and 4 some of the study questions were directed at your everyday ability to use interpretive procedures to make sense of photographs and unheard but seen conversational interactions. You probably found that your inferences brought into play interpretations about the context of the events, for example, the nature of the occasion, situation, and setting. Taken together with the categorizations you provided for the persons shown or seen, you were using some implicit knowledge about the parameters of social activities. That is, you were able to decide about the meaning of an event in a photograph on the basis of relating the categories of figures to the other observed elements in terms of occasion, situation, and setting.

Looking at the problem of recognition from a different angle we now can inquire into the interpretive basis for making inferences about naturally occurring sequences of actions, as opposed to the still scenes of a photograph. It might be the case that you inferred something about sequence from a still photo, e.g., "They look like they are just sitting down to enjoy that meal," or "I would say they are preparing for a holiday," or still, "That's the end of the race, it's over and number 5 won." In each of these descriptions the activity is recognized or detected, and then characterized in relevant descriptive terms. However, you must temporally project those actions either forwards or backwards, i.e., into the future or past, as possible extensions of what is seen in the frozen image. When it comes to naturally occurring sequences of actions of the sort that surround us in everyday life, how do we engage in recognizing the structure of their appearances?

We have at our disposal a common-sense system of descriptive parameters that we employ to "read out" or decipher that structure. The task of producing natural histories of social activities would therefore seem to consist of discovering first how members routinely use these parameters when doing social activities, so as to be able to see the methodical basis for their own definitions, formulations, and treatments of those activities in their localized social environments. You will recall that in chapter 3 we spelled out these parameters using an invented sequence of actions in Gide's novel. In that discussion we tried to exhibit the invariant features of interactional events that Gide relied on to invest his scenes with socially meaningful actors and courses of action, motivations and strategies. Those same elements found in naturally occurring sequences of action are open to our inspection if we seek out their location in actual social activities.

Let us review that list of invariant features of interactional events in order to see whether each feature can be treated for the construction of descriptive parameters of a social activity:

1. Main activities within which mutual involvements are built up into situations and occasions.
2. Local settings.
3. A cultural apparatus of membership category devices for making selections of identifications of social participants.
4. Temporal orientations.
5. Conversational structuring and sequencing rules.
6. Spatial orientations.
7. Nonverbal communicative behaviors.

What our method calls for, then, is an initial *search* for these invariant features. When we have located these features in observed phenomena in naturally occurring sequences of actions, we can ask of the data how to construct descriptive parameters of the social activities within which that data of invariant features has been observed and located. Our final analytic product should result in a finely detailed account of how members' common-sense descriptive parameters operate. We must stress that this is merely a preliminary list of invariant features and not a logically arranged system or theory of such features.

One is tempted to reorganize this list so as to give all the items on it a subordinate status to the second one, local settings. Given that one normally does descriptive investigations of a concrete setting or locale, e.g., an industrial establishment, a family household, a public place, a professional office, a military establishment, a school, a hospital, etc., it might seem that one could discover the parameters of a setting in terms of the other invariant features we note. That is, for each localized setting the socially organized, routine practices could be formally described in terms of the nature of its main activities that frame involvements in situations and occasions, its organization of membership categories (and the rights, responsibilities, and duties of members occupying given categories), the temporal orientations of participants to activities in the setting, the conversational work as specifically related to the setting, the members' spatial orientations relevant for the ecology of the setting, and the nonverbal communicative practices of interactants.

To do so, however, would be to assert a theoretical orthodoxy, namely that settings are causally determinative of the specific configurations of these invariant features. That is, for every setting the descriptive parameters of its social activities would be different. To view settings in this way would be to alter their status as invariant features of social activities in their own right. Rather than treating them as mere physical establishments that house people in unique ways, it should also be recognized that setting is itself a feature of social activity that enters into members' constituted practices and definitions about what that setting is. Our tendency is to treat a setting as a primary social organizing device, instead of regarding it as but one more feature of constituted social activities.

For example, the university is a behavioral setting: it consists of locales, buildings, classrooms, offices, living quarters, etc., all of which comprise its physical layout and architectural structures. But what does setting mean in this case? One normally categorizes this setting in terms of its purposes, objectives, personnel—in a word, its traditionally recognized features as an institution. It is accordingly regarded as a place where educational activity occurs, where students go to learn from teachers about various bodies of information organized into schools, faculties, disciplines, courses, etc.

Conventional sociological descriptions and ethnographies take for granted the application of a traditional label to a setting like the university, despite the fact that a setting is constituted by the practices of its mem-

bers. Our concept of social organization, in the sense that Bittner describes that concept,[5] must be responsive to members' conceptions of
a setting and to their practices that constitute the meaningful activity of
that setting. *Traditional institutional analyses of work settings, educational settings, family settings, etc., have failed to exhibit the invariant
features of interactional events, simply because they have not been
concerned with the everyday practices that constitute a normal environment, but with describing the institution as a normative idealization.*

In the case of the university as a type of setting, we would not want
to construct natural histories of university activities on the basis of a
normative idealization (an abstract ideal version) that we might have
about the so-called formal structure of the university bureaucracy, e.g.,
beginning with a model of administrative hierarchy, channels of communication up and down the hierarchy, constitutional provisions of rights,
authority, and power in decision-making, etc. Natural histories could not
be built on formal models of social organization, for the simple reason
that they require data on the interactional organization of everyday routine practices. The naturally occurring sequences of actions that make up
routine practices and constitute units of social activity must be first detected and characterized as practical achievements within that setting.

What does this mean in terms of observing behavior? You would need
to study the everyday activities occurring among university members as
an order of communicative competence, to construct formal interactional descriptions of those activities in order to discover how participants routinely bring them off. For example, take the student-teacher
relationship. What activities do occupants of these membership categories organize together? What types of social situations and occasions do
they mutually become involved in? What types of interactional exchanges do they make when they encounter each other? Once you
began to construct natural histories of such interactional events and
concerted activities, you would be in a position to examine questions
about the procedural basis of some important university activities on
which the nature of the student-teacher relationship is itself based, e.g.,
patterns of deference behavior and techniques of using and displaying
authority.

In the previous chapters of the text you have seen how you can search
for conversational structuring and sequencing rules within main activities
and within the structure of mutual involvements for situated and occa-
sioned behaviors. You have also been exposed to the issue of selecting

identifications in interactional circumstances via a machinery of member-ship categorization devices that cultures make available for their members. In the remainder of this chapter we examine the invariant feature of temporal orientations.

One important requirement for making natural histories of everyday events is to describe the temporal characteristics of social activities. If activities are natural units of interaction, can we discover the temporal structure of those units? To look for them we must assume that temporal structures are observable because they provide activities with boundaries that mark one off from the other. *Activities are temporally bounded events.* That is, they have detectable beginnings and endings. The manner is which participants methodically construct beginnings and endings for their activities is a very logical place to begin a formal description of activities if for no other reason than because a natural history is fundamentally oriented to the way in which events unfold or develop across time. Participants' orientations to time are aspects of interactional competence that enter into the recognition and treatment of activities as temporally organized and temporally bounded events.

How do members of activities orient to time? Can we isolate *temporal units* of activity that are organized by means of members' temporal orientations? Can we detect temporal practices as constitutive features of activities and environments?

Kenneth Pike has analyzed the traditional activity of the Sunday service in church.[6] He points out that members of the activity orient to it as a temporally organized occasion and participate in constructing the sequential form of the service. He notes that the activity is bounded by members' preparatory behavior: a prelude of events not part of the main activity of the church service but rather forming a pre-occasion of sociability. Likewise participants orient to closure of the main occasion and reassemble afterwards in some further post-occasion activity. Pike says:

> That the church goers consider the church service to be a unit is seen, then, in the following kinds of stray remarks heard preceding, following, or during the service: *Hurry, we'll be late to church. Has church begun yet? No, you're still on time. Shh. Church has started. We will open our service by . . . Stop whispering, tell me after church is over. In closing . . .*

> Even a young child sometimes recognizes these units. My young son (three years old) . . . has detected the ending of a church service with amazing skill; he will have been quiet, with not a

word aloud throughout an hour's service, and then, less than a half a second following the final prayer (so close that I can hear no pause whatever between the preacher's voice and his—and before the staid members of the congregation have "shifted gears" for the next behavior pattern) he will have started to speak aloud in delighted tones about something irrelevant to the service.[7]

All the remarks Pike excerpted from the talk of members in the church activity are temporal references. They show how members orient to timing, phasing, pacing, etc., of coordinated activities of the service, pre-service and post-service activities included. The latter are temporal conditions that intimately connect to the main activity for which the members have intentionally assembled.

Presumably you can collect temporal references of this sort for any observed activity, e.g., in work places, households, public areas, etc. Temporal practices involve orientations to classes of timed behavior sequences or periods of social activity, e.g., a social occasion. By "timed," we do not mean to restrict this to a clock formulation, but to cover the whole range of temporal phenomena concerned with keeping track of ongoing activities: how long they take (duration), when they periodically recur (periodicity), what starting times are appropriate or inappropriate (initiation), completion dates and deadlines (terminality), the relation of work routines to job time, overtime, and time off, the units of daytime and nighttime, calendrical time units of days, weeks, months, and years, and so forth. There is also a large class of temporal units of reference used in everyday discourse that account for present, past, and future time orientations, such as now, later, in a little while, soon, some-day, a long time ago—all those conversational references to the "when" of interactional events.

In organizational settings where an elaborate coordination of daily work routines happens around the clock, such as hospitals, prisons, military establishments, etc., temporal orientations are fully built into the flow of activities by scheduling structures[8] that markedly constrain how activity units occur within the flow. Sudnow points out how hospital staff members orient to events of dying and death by using quantitative procedures for keeping track of typical death-relevant occurrences, i.e., counting deaths. In like manner he notes:

> The day is the relevant unit of temporal specification, and counting "deaths in general" is merely part of counting a host of daily, recurrent happenings . . .

Any given death, however, is always a potential candidate for later retrospective comment when, for some reason, an instant death suggests a principle of categorization and provides for the relevance of searching over "past ones."[9]

In the event a patient dies in the hospital, the ensuing "bad news" requires special methods of transmission to relatives of the deceased. Sudnow describes the temporal structure of this situation:

Should staff members wish, for whatever reasons, to avoid telling the waiting relative some news in such circumstances, their main strategy is to avoid contact with him. The more such occasions are structured as episodes, with clear beginnings and ends, the more difficult it is for the announcer to appear before relatives without news. Surgeons, for example, carefully arrange their rounds in the hospital so that once they go into surgery, they will emerge from behind the scrutinized doors only when they carry the news being awaited. Once the surgeon has been behind the doors for some time, he must stay back there until ready for his final emergence. Only in the first few minutes or so does the surgeon have a degree of freedom such that should he reappear within that time, the assumption is that things "haven't yet begun."[10]

Sudnow reports further on the temporal structuring of the surgeon's activities:

Physicians use the ecology and perceived expected lengths of procedure in a variety of ways. In the surgical setting, surgeons were observed to finish the critical parts of an operation, turn the sewing-up tasks over to residents and interns, and then take an extended break before having to greet relatives. In one instance, a surgeon was observed to remove his cap, mask, and cloth shoecovers as he adjourned from the operating room proper to the doctor's lounge and then, after chatting for a half hour with his colleagues, put his cap and mask back on, with the mask hanging around his neck in that position which suggests it was just taken off. He then left the area and talked with the family.[11]

In any setting, whenever persons come into each other's presence for intentional communication, we can observe them orienting to the temporal feature of interaction. They must be able to open a face-to-face engagement, carry it through some stages of development, and finally bring it to a close. The temporal organization of interactional events, from units as small as brief exchanges to drawn out conversations, centers around event units that might be referred to as openings and closings.

These events demarcate the limits of an episode of interaction or activity and give to them their most recognizable bounded characteristics.

Let us consider the temporal boundaries of *openings* and *closings.*

Earlier we suggested that participants have ways of showing each other that they are starting some interaction and some activity. There is a ratification of copresence, as we might think of the process whereby two or more persons recognize and treat each other as accessibly communicable. How do interactants communicate that they are preparing to take part in an encounter and an activity? That is, we are suggesting that they do not suppose that once they confront others, they merely have to open their mouths or show their faces to get an interaction going or to establish their participation in an activity. Rather *they must orient to the fact that they are about to begin.* In some cases it might indeed be the simple need to get another's attention by opening one's mouth, to shout or call. That is always an act of preparation, it seems, for what is to follow, viz., the reason for the interaction to take place.

This suggests another issue for our interests, namely, interactants cannot always expect and may, in fact, fail to get an interaction going. For whatever reasons, an interaction may be aborted and an initiatory action may be rejected. For example, I am sitting in my office and someone comes by, sticks his head through the open doorway and says, "Are you busy?" If I answer, "Yes," that is a rejection rather than an invitation to the visitor. If I say, "No, come in and have a seat," that provides an opportunity for further sustained interaction. If a child approaches a parent in the household while the latter is talking to another adult, he can be told, "Please, don't interrupt us; wait until he finishes what he is saying to me." This aborts the child's opening with his father. Or if you are at a party and you want to find out if someone will dance with you, "Can I have this dance" might get back, "I think I'll sit this one out if it's okay with you."

Knowing that rejections or uncompleted interactions are possible, particularly in certain circumstances, one can build into his opening some method that promotes its success and likewise minimizes its failure to get interaction going. Children regularly use "You know what?" to open an interaction with an adult, because it works well as an initiatory utterance. It has the property of being an open question that allows the child to speak again and get an interaction going.

The connection between openings and settings comes to mind quite readily. The same utterance can be used in quite different ways depending on the setting. The opening, "Do you have a light?" meaning a light for a cigarette, can be asked by one man of another in an office, and it means he is out of matches, normally. Two co-workers in an office do not need to rely on this as a method for achieving sociability, but might just as well light their own cigarettes and begin an interaction. "Do you have a light?" asked by a solitary woman of a solitary man in a bar or beer parlor could be a method of making a contact, since the civil inattention persons accord each other in public places usually promotes reluctance to have sociability with strangers. One needs usually to find or construct a "ticket," as Sacks has called it, to make an appropriate opening in a public place. In this example it may be a prostitute setting up a potential customer, or just a woman who cannot afford to pay for a heavy drinking habit, or perhaps just a lonely woman desiring some male companionship.

We are not suggesting that there is some simple repertoire of opening utterances that can be used interchangeably in various settings, but only that there is some interpretive basis for an opening given its concrete setting. It may be linked to routine activities that participants are very accustomed to performing in that particular setting. On the other hand, one can use openings quite independently from settings, insofar as the particular opening may not be as much regulated by the particular setting as it is by ritualized interchanges that are available for very general use in constructing social situations.

Take the speech act known as "greeting," for example. One can have greeting exchanges in a multitude of social arrangements. It stands perhaps as the most basic kind of opening for the simple reason that it is normally an opening and nothing else. That is, it is a *boundary marker* for conversational interaction. It occurs at the start and could not be appropriately done after interaction has got under way (with the same set of participants). It can be done again, however, within a single occasion, when one participant has disappeared for a while and his reappearance calls for some reorientation to his membership in the activity, e.g., "Oh hello, where have you been?" It is not as though a first hello were never performed, but that after some period of nonpresence it is a way of showing the missed person that he was in fact missed. He is seemingly *restarting* his participation. It can also for that matter be a mild negative sanction to show one that he ought to have been present or ought to have informed others of his temporary disappearance.

Just as greetings are boundary markers that come at points in interactional sequences that are decidedly the beginning for some participant, so are summonses. Unlike greetings, which call for a return greeting either with spoken words or with some recognizable nonspoken substitute, summonses place a different obligation on the other party. They call for his initial acknowledgment of the presence of the summoner. This is a necessary first step in the development of the interaction. It must be cleared, so to speak, before the next interchange takes place. Summoning is a property of the start of a sequence, or as Schegloff describes it, a summons has the property of "nonterminability."[12] That is, the Summons-Answer (S-A) interchange could not occur appropriately as a closing to a conversation. In the obligatory structure that is generated by the summoning procedure, the caller makes himself available for further interaction and the answerer makes himself available in return.

Schegloff studied S-A interchanges in telephone calls. In this case the conditions are quite clearly describable. The opening structure of the call is based on a simple asymmetry between the caller and answerer. The answerer cannot normally know he is going to be called by a given person; that is, he cannot be certain that a particular party will be at the other end of the line when he picks up the phone. He may have some idea, say by prearrangement, but even then he cannot be certain it is the party he expects. The answerer speaks first. This is an invariant feature of telephone interaction. The answerer might pick up the telephone and say, "Hello," then making voice identification with the other party, he might say, "Oh, hello." The second hello is a greeting, the first just an answer to the summons. It is as though one cannot start to interact sensibly until some basis for recognition of the other party is first made. From the point of recognition onward, the interaction gets calibrated with a second hello.

The speech acts of greeting and summoning both involve a basic property of interactional development. They involve the initial presentation of oneself and the initial constructing of an encounter. They are speech events that mark off the boundary of interactions. One can seek to discover whether members of different settings use the method of opening with greetings and summonses to organize the interactional events that these openings start off.

Are greetings normally used to get interactions going in routine office work? Do persons make greeting exchanges whenever they encounter each other over the course of the work day? Is there a first of the day greeting and then, in progressive order, a series of greeting alternatives, e.g., a nod, a smile, a raising of the eyebrows, a wave of the hand, etc.? Are participants constrained from making greetings under various circumstances? Can greetings be exchanged in rounds or otherwise among a group of interactants coming together; by means of precedence rules for who greets whom first and who can greet whom at all? For example, greetings can occur in combination with other speech acts, such as introductions. How do such combinatory acts work? Do customers normally greet or get greeted by sales persons? Or does one in this type of setting get right down to business, so to speak? If so, are greetings very optional openings in sales establishments? And when a customer gets a greeting is that intended to be a way of showing friendliness and courtesy? Or identifying a regular customer? Given that the interaction in such settings is based on a service offered by the representative of an establishment, what is the tie between the practical purposes of the activity and the construction of a typical opening, e.g., "Can I help you"?

These are all questions to keep in mind when studying the phenomenon of interactional openings. To use the example of meetings again, persons arriving at the place of the meeting can engage each other in pre-meeting activities. They can resume their relationships with greeting openings or summon each other across the meeting room. But the opening of the official activity of the meeting is not accomplished by this pre-meeting activity. There are usually boundary markers that signal to participants the beginning of the official business of a meeting. Someone who presides over the meeting may have the right to be the official opener. He may be specially entitled to organize the boundary marker, and this entitlement may be recognized in the fact that others will continue to engage in pre-meeting sociability until the word is given to start by the one presiding over the party. Things such as "Well, let's get under way, it's getting late," or "Shall we start?" etc., can be employed as boundary markers for an activity. This is an occasion in which persons assemble themselves together for a practical purpose and together they constitute a viable group, willing to coordinate their interaction as a group towards some commonly accepted set of practices.

One can go to a place for some common activity with others and yet not have the appropriate conditions for that activity to be achieved. For example, assemblies can be made and readiness be shown by participants, but if some party required for the occasion does not show up then the meeting never officially comes off, despite the assembly and all the talk persons may do. The occasion is transformed from one kind of activity to another. The opening never occurs, just numerous interactional openings between individuals, where the sum of all their interactions does not constitute a regular meeting.

What can we say about closings? Unlike opening zones of interaction, they must be fashioned out of what has preceded them. *Closings are also different in that they can be redundant.* The repetition of greetings is rare, and perhaps with the few exceptional cases in which the resumption of social relationships calls for prolonged greeting sequences (such as at airports or other transportation centers), there is never a redundant greeting exchange. Once it is done the interaction proceeds along its course. But as everyone well knows, there is a repetition possible when good-byes are performed. This may be the result of social inertia, as one might call it, having to do with coordinating the closing of an occasion and the breaking off of interaction among face-to-face interlocutors. The nature of the occasion and its setting are once again relevant for the study of this phenomenon, because we find closings at a dinner party to be quite differently paced from those at a work setting, say, which often are quite circumspect. Let us consider some of these problems.

When we say that the closing of an interaction or an activity is contingent upon those events that came before it, what do we have in mind? Does that mean that you choose particular closing utterances depending on what was said or done previously? *Or does it mean that the utterances, whatever they might be, are selected and deliberately placed to effectuate a closing juncture?* One interest we have in studying bounded activities is to examine the sequential process of interactional development in a social occasion. Having interactionally developed into a conversation within an activity, a series of interactional events can be closed off, and with that closure comes the end of its development. In the course of developing an interaction participants can, in fact, prepare for the closure, or to put this another way, they can watch its development for places to stop its further development. This is so, irrespective of the length or depth of the interaction already developed. Members can shut down conversation or an activity almost immediately after its opening, for various practical reasons. Or on the other hand, they can elaborate an interaction into marathon proportions.

Whatever the case may be, *participants have methodical ways of orienting to a closure at any point along the course of an occasion's development.* Here again the relevance of the constraints of the occasion and the setting may enter into the method participants use to select a particular place to make a closing juncture. Notice we say "make," because there is no independent system of enforcements that rules when an activity is to be closed down, except in special cases that dictate a strict time schedule for the completion of an event, as in certain athletic games. Normally in interactional circumstances, one must work out the method for terminating an interaction with others that is acceptable to them. *Closings are negotiable.* For example, a closing appears to be taking place in a conversation, but then the interaction is reopened or reinstated; this necessitates preparing for and doing another closing interchange to bring it to an end, however brief or swift it may be.

In the paper by Schegloff and Sacks, called "Opening Up Closings,"[13] the authors point to the fact that conventional "terminal exchanges" can be used to close off interactions (the terminal exchange is another paired object in which the first item of the pair, such as "good-bye" elicits the second item, another "good-bye"). However, they also point out that one cannot simply drop in an utterance from a terminal pair of utterances and expect that a closing has been accomplished. Rather, they argue that a closing is a unit event in itself, a section in a conversation, and as such it must be a section that is properly initiated to effectuate a closing. There are pre-closings that form what we have been referring to as boundary markers. For example, "well," with its own special intonational patterns, or "so" followed by a pause.

There are also markers that can reinstate the conversation after some closing has been prepared for and even actually completed. One common one is "by the way." This is a kind of *conversational extender.* By using it, one can attach onto an already completed conversational unit some more conversation, and it is conceivable that a whole new conversation section can be generated by this device. It becomes quite clear in studying these structural aspects of terminal phases of a conversation that closing interactions are coordinated phenomena, wherein interactants control mutual activities by looking out for each other's initiation of a closing section. It is always negotiable in the sense that one seeing the closing section being initiated by another, he may be quite reluctant to close off, for whatever reasons, and this may lead him to reject the preparations being offered by the other party. He rejects the section and continues to talk on the topic. This amounts to an unwillingness to release the other party from the conversation and forces a continued development.

Certain activities may close in which *all* participants uniformly orient to the closure of the activity unit at the same time, e.g., a normal work day, the end of a movie. The participants mutually make preparations for the termination of these activities. They enter into closing sections of activity units. At the office, persons prepare their desks, their personal appearance, their supervisors, co-workers, etc., for the opening of terminating rituals. Sales persons will often show the customers that they are entering this closing section of the work day activity and expect the customer to cooperate in releasing the obligations of the sales clerks from further attention. You might look at a store at the work day's end and see a juncture occurring: cash registers are being closed off and counted up, cashiers are leaving their posts, salesmen are reallocating their involvements and looking at their watches, etc.

Now you might think that they are doing this in complete oblivion to you, as though your presence were not being taken into account. But there is always the problem, providing there is at least one customer left, of showing him he is now entering a zone of terminal time, so to speak, particularly if he is unable to make up his mind about a purchase. Doors are conspicuously locked and remaining persons are let out by a staff member who unlocks it each time anew, until the attrition of customers is completed. The clerk waiting on remaining customers may shift her treatment of them to a more uninvolved mode of interaction, hurrying them, showing signs of patience or impatience, or even going so far as to close off the interaction with, "I'm sorry, Sir, it's closing time." Activities in settings like this one always involve the dispersal of the participants, who both break off the routine sequence of the work day and also go through closing rituals with the others around them. But such ritualized terminal exchanges are made between staff members, not between staff and customers. The proper leave-taking ceremonies assure persons who stand in stable social relationships on a daily basis that they are part of the same order of activity, the ceremonial "good evening" preserving these membership ties.

The movie theatre illustration is different from the work setting, because it involves an occasion in which participants are all participating members of an audience. Their own interaction among themselves is governed by their mutual involvement in the presentation of the film they watch. (In special places that are used for nonwatching activity other interactions may, of course, take place, e.g., "necking" in the balcony or "cruising" around rest rooms or talking at the candy counter, etc.) There is no preparation for a closing section of this film-going activity, but the closing is a part of the film itself, a section of the end of the movie that signals the audience that it is indeed coming to the end. This is available to the audience in various standardized formulas for ending films, just as it is available to the audience of musical performances, when a singer or an instrumentalist deliberately paces his performance near the end in such a way as to tell his audience he is about to finish. This preparation for the ending is conventionally achieved by retarding the tempo of the music in the last bars. An audience must orient to the boundaries of such performances in order to know when to participate properly by applauding. On this score, an audience sometimes improperly claps at the end of a movement of an unfamiliar symphony instead of at its finish.

This chapter has focused on the nature of social activities and on some of their descriptive parameters, particularly temporal orientations. One way of making natural history investigations of the bounded features of activities—features that give to an activity, whatever it is, the semblance of a completed unit event or episode—is to consider the structural zones of activities and interactions known as openings and closings. We have briefly noted some of the structural aspects of opening and closing interactions and their relevance for the development of social activities in concrete settings, situations, and occasions.

We have not discussed, however, the aspects of opening or closing that involve nonverbal communicative elements of interaction. They must also be brought into the investigation, naturally. The use of eye contact and the organization of the face and the body in interactional circumstances offers further evidence of the methods members of the culture have for entering into social intercourse with others, making junctures in social activities, and terminating copresence. Some simple examples of these nonspoken elements at work are: the regulation of the eyes in doing greetings and introductions; the regulation of body contact on the bus; the regulation of bodily spacing at work desks and work areas; the reorganization of the face when showing attention, surprise, detachment, anger, impatience, etc. These may all enter into the construction of activities, as for example, when you are approached by someone and you do not make eye contact with them to avoid their glance and possible contact, or when you put on a face of annoyance or impatience because someone is late for an appointment, the facial behavior performing a negative sanction at the opening of the interaction.

Notes

[1] David Sudnow, *Passing On: The Social Organization of Dying* (Englewood Cliffs, N.J.: Prentice-Hall, 1970). Reprinted by permission of the publisher.

[2] Ibid., p. 8.

[3] Abraham Kaplan, *The Conduct of Inquiry* (San Francisco: Chandler Press, 1964), pp. 3-11.

[4] I use this term "interpretive procedures" in the sense attributed to it by Aaron Cicourel in "The Acquisition of Social Structure. . . . " The basic premise of a phenomenologically oriented sociology would seem to be the role of subjective interpretation in

human actions, and the ethnomethodological extension of this premise is to the study of the procedural basis of interpretive behavior.

5 Bittner, "Concept of Organization."

6 Kenneth Pike, *Language in Relation to a Unified Theory of the Structure of Human Behavior* (Glendale, California: The Summer Institute of Linguistics, 1954).

7 Ibid., p. 33.

8 On scheduling behavior see Julius Roth, *Timetables: Structuring the Passage of Time in Hospital Treatment and Other Careers* (Indianapolis: Bobbs-Merrill, 1963). Also see the analysis of time as related to space and situated behavior in Boughey, "Time, Space, Occasion."

9 Sudnow, *Passing On,* pp. 40-41.

10 Ibid., p. 119.

11 Ibid., pp. 121-22.

12 Schegloff, "Sequencing," p. 1081.

13 Unpublished manuscript, delivered at the Annual Meeting of the American Sociological Association, San Francisco, 1969.

Suggested Readings and Study Questions

1. Sudnow, *Passing On.*

What has been emphasized in chapter 7 is the concept of a social activity in relation to its interactional and communicational components. Sudnow's study describes how death-related practices in two hospital settings are routinely organized by staff members' management of dying or dead patients. How is his description or ethnography constructed around units of activity in the settings? What specific features of these activities are characterized interactionally? How does Sudnow show conversational interchanges in the context of activity units and interactional sequences? What concepts are employed by Sudnow to analyze how death-related practices are recognized and treated by hospital members, and how are these concepts related to the definitions employed by hospital members themselves in doing their activities? What are some of the spatial and temporal boundaries organized by hospital members in the course of their work routines?

2. Goffman, *Presentation of Self; Public Places; Relations in Public.*

Find discussions in these works that pertain to the issue of the boundaries of social activities, i.e. where Goffman makes general statements about bounded behavior. What specific concepts does he originate to analyze boundaries? Consider region behavior, for example. How are physical boundaries or territories interconnected with ones marked off by temporal units in the performance of a social activity?

3. Don Zimmerman, "The Practicalities of Rule Use," in Douglas, *Everyday Life,* pp. 221-238.
How does Zimmerman describe activities in a county public assistance setting in terms of task structures? What temporal features does he specify as normal features of the activities?

4. Locate in standard bibliographies any sociological reports or anthropological ethnographies that describe cultural activities and determine what components of the particular activities are included in the descriptions. Are definitions of activities derived from observations of interactional sequences, and are the latter spelled out? Does the author make reference to conversational phenomena or does he leave out interactional references altogether, when offering abstractions about how activities are socially organized?

5. Collect specimen openings and closings in overall activities. What structural features can you isolate that seem invariant features for opening and closing phases in the natural history of the type of activity you observe? How do openings differ from closings?

6. Collect specimen openings and closings to interactional events that occur within given activity units, i.e., within a complete occasion of activity. How do these form constituent temporal and structural components of the activity? Are they recognizable "micro-units" in themselves, and what is their relation to the larger units that are recognized as activities? Do the larger units supply contextual meaning and interpretive bases for the enactment of the smaller ones? For example, in a retail store, observe the interchanges between a clerk or sales person and a customer, and compare their natural boundaries to those of the temporal unit, "a single workday."

7. Select any natural setting accessible to you and scrutinize it for sequencing behaviors, i.e., for the methodical way members sequentially organize their mutual activities. How do you detect sequential units? Do you perceive junctures, phases, episodes, repeated segments of behavior, or behaviors that appear out of phase, incompleted, etc.? Are your inferences based upon observations of the interpretive process of partici-

pants or are they based judgments of your own that do not consult the participants' interpretations (by "consult" is meant any checking of behavioral data in participants' performances, conversational or otherwise, that provide the grounds for some interpretation)?

8. Describe an observed activity in terms of allocations of involvement without any reference to temporal features. What problems do you run up against? Can you distinguish between main and side activities?

Interpreting a Social Scene. Analyze the methods you use to assign meaning to the activity shown, i.e., figuring out the who-what-when-where of the scene. (photo by Marian Penner Bancroft.)

Sequenced Actions. All action occurs in temporal sequence. Can you tell if the above is the original sequence in time or if the photos have been put out of order. How do you decide? (photos by Marian Penner Bancroft.)

Chapter Eight

Substantive Applications

Now, that your readings have included a study of a particular aspect in the social organization of hospital practices, *you have entered upon the domain of "substantive sociological analysis," which means simply that sociological analysis is always directed toward elucidating some forms of organized behavior in the culture.* But, you might ask, where does one look to study such forms? Surely, everything that passes for social activity must be fair game for us. How can you decide, as a matter of principle, what is a substantive study? If you were to make an investigation of greeting activity, would that be less substantive than studying the institution known as the family? It would certainly encompass less interactional data than the study of family interaction patterns, but would that make it any less substantive in result?

In sociology it has become customary to examine institutions (e.g., familial, religious, economic, etc.) as major substantive areas of inquiry. Sociology has reserved certain categories of subject matter for substantive areas of knowledge in the discipline. A conventional text, such as Leonard Broom and Philip Selznick's *Sociology,* [1] surveys the discipline's knowledge of these categories; for example, the family, religion, education, minorities, crime and delinquency, and so forth. There is, of course, no reason on earth why these timeworn substantive labels must remain the definitive subject areas of the discipline. They correspond to common-sense conceptions of social life, some of them traditionally being regarded as social institutions, and the others referring to socially differentiated characteristics of society and to the problems societies have of socially controlling their members by a system of legal rules.

The point of view we are presenting in this text calls for an inquiry into the interactional foundations for everyday life activities. One of the basic facts we are confronted with is that participants of the culture organize their activities and interactions in complex ways that cannot be nominally subsumed under the conventional categories of social life without taking a completely orthodox position. That is, we cannot assume that everything that transpires in the arena of interaction in a work setting, or in a family household, or in a church service meeting, is understood by participants as being relevantly occupational, familial, or religious. *To make this assumption is to commit the error of deciding which principles of relevance interactants use to accomplish activities without consulting their own criteria for relevant behavior in constructing those activities.*

On the other hand, we have stated that settings and relevant behaviors are intimately tied together, but the notion of a setting requires an examination of a set of concrete instances of behavior regularly occurring within that setting. Settings are locatable; they occupy space and time. They are not simply convenient abstractions that label institutional areas of life. Obviously, we can study many church settings or work places all over the culture, and in some sense we could subsume our study under the heading of "religion" or "occupation," but having each concrete interactional study in hand, we would not find it to be very analytically useful to do so.

If we did try to analytically make more of these labels, we would likely be providing each one with an abstract theory about the workings of the institution it allegedly represents. This can be done quite easily and without recourse to observing how concrete settings work, how their specific day-to-day practices are socially organized by their participants. *That is, one can easily bypass interactional questions and go right on to ask questions that are seemingly quite relevant for the substantive study of an area of social life.* For example, one might have an implicit knowledge of family interaction and family arrangements in our culture and formulate problems about the functional elements of family life in regulating the needs of a society as a whole, e.g., mothers raise children and provide emotional models and support, supply succor and warmth for new generations of the society, while fathers are instrumentally providing the economic support and filling the occupational roles of the society, etc., etc.

One such study is a well-known work by Talcott Parsons and Robert Bales called *Family, Socialization and Interaction Processes.* [2] But nowhere in this volume do the authors describe interactional events. Instead, they fill out a theory—"a Grand Theory"—of family interaction based on presumably relevant and valid abstractions about the social behavior of family members, none of which are derived from the study of interactional events in that setting but rather from an initial substantive theory about family as an institution.

The position we recommend is one that renders the traditional meaning of substantive sociology problematic, for the simple reason that *any finding about how human interactions work can be regarded as a substantive finding.* This is true despite the fact that our emphasis is always on natural histories of activities and on the formal characteristics of interaction. In other words, the timeworn distinction between form and content may be actually a fallacious one. *Whenever we study the form human interactions take, we must also of necessity be studying the shape of some particular concrete contents of human behavior.* It may, in fact, turn out to be the case that whenever we start to look for content, we turn up with form, and vice-versa.

For example, we have made a formal distinction between opening and closing an interaction and that distinction seems quite sound and indisputable. But can we separate the content of an opening, say a greeting or a summons, from the form it is given by interactants to achieve these events? What would that separation look like? Would it make any sense, or be of any use to us, to single out standard or key words and phrases and variants of them, all of which taken together would comprise a list of the "contents" of, say, greetings, e.g., hi, hello, howarya, howdy, etc.? It does not seem so.

What this amounts to is a view that says, whatever interactional events take place and develop, their specific contents are chiefly organized around considerations of form, so much so that where there is no form, there is no recognizable content for interactants. That this is so can be demonstrated by a simple exercise.[3] Take any conversation that you find or collect and systematically disorder its individual utterances, such that you put the second utterance fifth, the third one twelfth, the first last, and so on. Now, try to figure out the contents of that interaction and see what you come up with as compared to what you decide about it in its original form. If it were simply a matter of inspecting words and sentences without consideration for their sequential relationships from one speaker to the next, the content of a conversation ought to be understandable in terms of its original meaning to the interlocutors who produce it. But you will find it is not. *You must assign some meaning to a conversation on the basis of the order in which the utterances presumably occur—that is precisely what we mean by a formal phenomenon.*

We have raised this issue about form *vs.* content because it is some-times believed that a study of formal characteristics must somehow be able to stand on its own and not deal with substance, whereas substantive sociology can avoid formalizations. But we argue the contrary in this text. It is through formal investigations* that we will come to discover what content is all about, and vice-versa. The two ought not to be separated.

With this position, can we go about making substantive applications of the point of view we are offering? It should be made absolutely clear, it must be stressed, that we are going to use the idea of substantive socio-logical analysis in its traditional meaning in order to show what kind of substantive applications we might make to various sociological excur-sions already laid out by the conventional substantive labels. What we will in fact be doing is treating these as common-sense labels, consonant with the naturalistic idea of looking at some area of social life that seems to have some coherence of its own, at least on the surface. We cannot take up all the areas in an introductory text as brief as this one, but we will concentrate on limited discussions in four well-established substan-tive areas of interest in sociology:

1. Childhood Socialization
2. Work and Occupations
3. Deviance
4. Social Stratification

Whatever the traditional issues have been in these subdisciplines of the field, we want to reconsider them strictly in terms of the point of view of this text. Our discussions are more suggestive than definitive and we cannot engage in too much critical reviewing of the literature on the traditional approaches to these subdisciplines. Our concern here is not to review, but to reformulate materials into new directions for inquiry.

1. Childhood Socialization[4]

Learning To Be a Member of Adult Society

The traditional interest in studying childhood has been directed toward the fact that children are regarded as raw material for cultural learning. Over and above their physical and biological growth, they have been looked at as entrants to society who must learn how to adapt to their

---

*By "formal investigations" is meant formal descriptive analysis of the natural history type, not formal as intended by modern formal theorists in sociology, e.g., axiomatic theorists, who use empirical data to test their formal theories, not generate them.

social environment. The obvious fact that any newborn child can be transplanted from one culture to another and develop into a normal member of the adopted culture proves that man is a thoroughly adaptable cultural animal, and that what he becomes in the eyes of other humans is not so much a person of flesh and bone as a member of one cultural context over another. We might call this conventional interest in cultural learning *the social induction problem*. It is not restricted to children, but to inductees in any social environment who must learn to adapt themselves to its particular ways, e.g., immigrants, university students, workers, soldiers, etc. But the socialization problem, as traditionally conceived, is given its most general and central importance in the case of children.

Accordingly, the traditional focus has been on the process by which a child becomes an adult of his culture. What this interest has led to on a large scale of inquiry has been a preoccupation with questions of child development. In some instances the focus has been on mental or cognitive development, in others it has been on the developments of social habits related to class, race, and family background, and in still others, the focus has been on personality development.

• The framework for this developmental process has always been *a normative one,* based on an implicit understanding of an adult view of social life, his norms or rules for properly going about that life. The notion of normal development is well established in the biological disciplines dealing with human physical growth and maturation, as in genetics, for example. The notion of normal development has also found its way into sociological inquiries of social life. The model of a normal, typically competent adult is implicitly understood—more accurately, it is required by the traditional perspective on child study. Development has been necessarily treated as a historical process and a biographical one. For example, one can make a longitudinal study, as it is called, of individuals over a long period of lifetime.

Sociologists have used a set of concepts to aid their inquiry into children's social behavior. They include values, norms, goals, and agents, for example. Presumably, the socialization process involves the child's acquiring the values and norms and the various social goals of his society, i.e., of the adult members of this society, at least those with whom he comes into regular contact. These persons, those with whom he significantly interacts and has relations, have sometimes been referred to as the agents of socialization. These become models for his own behavior, it is argued.

The traditional view has promoted inquiries that seek to learn the reasons for a child's acquisition of a set of values or a pattern of behavior. The process is said to take place by a conditioning of learned responses to the social environment. So, if a child has a given class background, this presumably influences or socially conditions his behavior to the extent that he acts in one learned way while he is growing and when he finally grows up, as opposed to another learned way. When he acts in an appropriate way to the satisfaction of other adult members of his community, he is treated by them as properly socialized. The problem is complicated by the existence of multiple groups, all of which lay some claim and have some influential hold over a child. Thus, it is not just parents and family members, but also peers, other children, and teachers, for example, that mold the child.

All of this interest in the development of particular behaviors, values, styles of life, etc., is aimed at answering the basic question, How does a child become an adult? Alternatively, investigators have asked, How does an infant become a child? That usually means looking at infantile development and the acquisition of motor skills, intelligence, etc. Studying children has also meant examining the lives that children lead in schools, for example. The educational process, as well as the family household environment, has presumably contributed to the social conditioning of a child into a member of society. But the immediate concrete activities involved in the process are normally disregarded in favor of a preference for studying long-term effects of this or that social influence on the child's life.

Now, these seem like important and reasonable questions to raise where children are concerned. Recently, some sociologists have returned to asking the question, "How is society possible?", originally phrased by the classic sociologist George Simmel,[5] as one way of looking at the sociological relevance of childhood. That is, it is only possible because society continually provides mechanisms for its own cultural reproduction, so to speak. It does this by systematically orienting its new entrants, its children, to what needs to be done for them to function effectively in society. The adaptations of the individual and society are interdependent processes.

The Adult Ideological Viewpoint in Studies of Childhood
However, these traditional interests have neglected some very basic matters. *They have neglected what we are calling the interactional foundation to human group life.* The traditional perspectives have over-

emphasized the task of describing the child's developmental process of growing into an adult at the expense of a direct consideration of what the events of everyday life look like in childhood. *Thus, instead of seeking to discover the interactional processes at work when children and adults say and do things together, sociologists have sought to support their theories about how children become adults and how societies are functionally possible.*

The intellectual and analytic position of sociologists is essentially ideo-logical in the sense that they have used an adult notion of what children are and what they ought to be that is like that of the laymen in the culture. That is, adults in our culture have theories of socialization, namely com-mon-sense theories about how children ought to learn and behave in a range of appropriate circumstances. They have notions about what the end product of a child should look like, a person of this or that sort, of this or that moral background, etc. For example, the acquisition of rules of etiquette, proper moral conduct, and social awareness with increasing age are all features of adult socialization theories about child rearing. Likewise, the sociologist has incorporated his status as an-adult-in-society into his thinking about childhood. He asks the very same sorts of ques-tions that adults in the society might ask or conceive of as worthwhile problems for study. For this reason, we are asserting the claim that his adult viewpoint is ideologically carried over and contained in the formu-lation of his research problems.

Consider the following definition made by Alex Inkeles which is typi-cally found in the literature of the field of socialization. It clearly shows the orientation that we have been ascribing to the traditional formulation of the concept of socialization. Inkeles says, that child socialization is

the process whereby a person acquires the attitudes, values, ways of thinking, need dispositions, and other personal, yet social, attributes which will characterize him in the next stage of his development. The social scientist is not alone in his sensitivity to the implications of current childhood experience for the subsequent organization of the personality and the public behavior of a social member. In their interaction with the child, parents and other socialization agents generally have in mind some conception of what the child is "supposed to become" and of the role which any particular child rearing practice may play in achieving or hindering the desired outcome. In other words, *both the practice and the study of child socialization are inherently "forward looking."*[6]

The basis of study is therefore the ideological conception adult members of the society have in orienting to children, rather than an interest in the interactional events of childhood. In a footnote to this passage, Inkeles makes a telling remark for our discussion:

> To say this is not to deny that very often what is done to the child is influenced by no more long-term a desire than to get Johnny to be quiet for the next five minutes or to sleep for the next six hours.[7]

These interactional events, prosaic or mundane as they are, are conceived of as short-term phenomena by Inkeles. They are not incorporated into the broad time sweep of the traditional analytic focus on personal and social development, the alleged outcome of socialization, and therefore play no part in the analysis of childhood.

To break free from the hold of this common-sense perspective on our conception of a research problem and to better understand that perspective as an adult ideological position, one needs to study how children are interactants, while in contact with adults who hold that position and also while constructing a daily social world of their own—this despite the fact that children are not entitled to control their own lives without the essential supervision of adults who organize households, schools, playgrounds, etc., for their activities.

Studying Children's Cultures

The fact nevertheless remains, that children have cultures of their own.[8] Children's cultures are evidenced in the long history of children's games and play forms that have been transmitted from one generation of children to the next, for centuries, without the help of adults. Children's cultural activities have a viable organization of their own and it is this organized world that is not very visible to adults. The nature of the child's organized world is hardly understood as yet. This is mainly because adult theories of how children ought to be socialized into the society of adult activities have been an impediment to the direct study of children's daily activities. The recent volume by Iona and Peter Opie, *Children's Games in Street and Playground,*[9] together with their earlier book, *The Lore and Language of School Children,*[10] demonstrate the wealth of material that can be gathered on children's cultural activities (the Opies have spent 20-odd years collecting material for these books).

Accordingly, the study of childhood forms of social experience needs to uncover what children do together, how they mutually build social occasions and activities in each other's presence. The noted Swiss psychologist Jean Piaget has attempted to show the way in which children

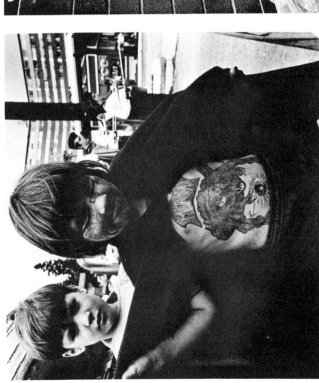

Children's Culture. Compare these two photos. In the photo at left, the presentation of self relates to children's own cultural activities, i.e., those activities not commonly practiced by adults.. In the photo at right, the child's presentation of self is clearly related to adult social organization. Adult appearances are resources for children's play activities. This child has won a prize in a contest sponsored by adults, which is not play. (photos by Marian Penner Bancroft.)

Children's Culture. Here again is an activity in children's lives organized by adults, the visible effect of adult ideology about children. Compare these two pictures for their different communication contexts in relation to children's self-organized cultural activity. (top photo by Marian Penner Bancroft; bottom photo by Rudiger Krause.)

develop morality and how they share a moral code for group conduct. He looked at the rules of some children's games to study the problem of the child's acquisition of moral judgment in *The Moral Judgment of the Child*.[11] His book is instructive on the manner in which an adult scientist goes about asking a child questions about the rules of a game in order to elicit moral rules from the child. But, unfortunately, Piaget leaves aside any consideration of the interactional elements in his observations of children's games and fails to study the relevance of his own question-answer sessions with them for understanding the nature of adult-child interaction. He also fails to see the relevance of children's cultural activities for his own interpretations of their games. Instead, adopting a classic psychological stance, he studies the children's answers to his questions as indicators of stages of intellectual and social development. This he does according to a theoretical framework he imports into his observations, a framework that is antecedent to them and that is clearly an adult ideological position on children in society.

Consequently Piaget never shows, nor is interested in showing, how children mutually build social occasions, such as this or that game activity. The formal properties of children's interactional events are never considered. Given that Piaget is aiming to say something valid about the child's systems of morality in daily life, as evidenced by their games, he cannot possibly succeed unless he addresses issues presupposed in interactional analysis of childhood activities. That is, he would need to study the methods children use to organize their particular games and how these game situations constitute more than just playing by the rules of the game. The unclarified presuppositions about interaction in Piaget's work are the same as those we noted in the traditional ethnographer's reports of everyday activities shown in chapter 4. The interactional foundations to social knowledge and common-sense understanding, and to the pragmatic behavior of everyday life, have been bypassed by Piaget, who uses common-sense resources without turning them into topics of inquiry.

Redefining the Concept of Socialization

How are we going to deal with the concept of socialization, then? Ought we to throw it out altogether? No. The concept should be removed from our set of analytic tools for making interactional studies of children, and retained only as a common-sense construct about the world of child rearing: *Socialization is a lay concept, or lay theory, about the appropriate methods for raising children to become adult members of the society.* As such, it only makes reference to one-half of the phenomenon, so to speak. The other half pertains to children themselves. As Sacks has provocatively suggested,[12] children may have their own theories about socialization that enter into their daily judgments and actions about the appropriateness of other children's actions. We adults tend to view a ten-year-old, who sanctions a five-year-old for spilling his ice cream, as imitating an adult, from whom the older child is presumed to have picked up the corrective orientation. But, it may be that a child's conception of a good or bad child is not an imitation at all, but one that is constructed out of the systematic interactional habits and constraints that children enforce upon each other. It may be that children also have conceptions, enforced judgments, about what a good adult is, just as adults have their own conceptions that are enforced about what a good child is, as Sacks has pointed out.[13]

One of the consequences of using an ideological perspective in the study of childhood is that it typically produces a view of children's behavior as inadequate or in some way defective. The child is treated as a defective member of the society, with a very imperfect sociability. This is strictly an adult viewpoint—among children themselves we cannot assume without an investigation that they view themselves as imperfect social participants.

A word of caution is necessary here to avoid misunderstanding the point of our discussion. We are not advocating that adults have no right to treat children as imperfect (although some psychologists have argued that treating them this way makes life between parent and child ungratifying and harmful) or that adult viewpoints on children are defective and to be abolished. We are only saying that to study childhood one would need to get out from under the burden of pursuing research from within that ideological containment, simply because it is the result of an enforced judgmental system among those who have to manage children and not one we can use to better understand children's activities, as such.

For example, a mother sees two boys in the living room at home. She chides them for making a mess or for roughing around indoors instead of outdoors. To her they are dirt-makers or trouble-makers or noise-makers, or whatever else might appropriately label their behavior. But to the boys, they are building model airplanes, or wrestling, or the like. The definition they give to their own activity is not contained within the practical definitions the mother gives to them. She must attend to their actions in a way that corresponds to her duties and responsibilities as mother and housekeeper. The relevance of viewing their activity is determined by her own household activities rather than by the children's activities. In fact, it seems to be the case that for adults, anything children do between, say, the ages of one and ten, can be characterized as play. Now, surely that is not what children always recognize and treat as their own constitutive definition of what they do, if we are going to be objective about it. That is, two children might be having a conversation on the grass while two onlooking mothers can speak of them as "playing nicely together."

The point we have been making so far is that a course correction is needed to steer socialization research into an area of problem formulation and conceptual thinking that is not encompassed by our adult formulations—ideological ones primarily—about what children are like and how they ought to behave. We need instead to ask questions about how children go about organizing their own activities and daily contacts with adults and other children. This raises the next point in connection with the claim that children's culture has a viable group structure of its own.

The first problem is to examine interactional events in children's cultural activities, such as talking, play, and games. The second problem pertains to the distinction between children's and adult's cultures. *In effect, what this supposition points to is the side-by-side existence of two cultures. We borrow a classic notion from anthropology that is used when the anthropologist will speak of one culture as in proximity to another: culture contact.*

Adult-Child Interaction as Culture Contact: Some Specific Issues

Now with this notion in mind, the question of children's activities becomes more interesting, because it entails the possibility of seeing the two cultures as coexisting in the daily world and requiring some means to effectuate social contacts essentially cultural in nature. That is, when children are confronted with the presence of adults, circumstances arise in which adults intervene or interrupt their activity or, conversely, children themselves attempt entry into adult interactional scenes. Observation of adult-child interactions shows that there are orientations to making contacts that owe much to the cultural distinctions between the groups. For example, if you were to try to enter a game being played among a group of children, you would need a method that takes into account the fact that you are an adult and they are children—you would have to take into account, in other words, the difference in cultural membership categories that are omnirelevant for the society. *By omnirelevance we simply mean that whenever adults come into contact with children, despite the type of setting, they orient their behavior to the cultural distinction between the two categories.*

So, for example, a child so categorized can be seen in a department store and an adult can treat him as a child rather than as a customer, whether or not he is in an ecological area especially organized for children's consumer activity, i.e., the toy department. A child can sit idly on a street corner or a curb, watching things go by, and as adults, we can recognize that as peculiarly childlike behavior. Adults do not normally conduct themselves like that in public. Viewing idle adults on the streets involves the recognition of a whole other set of social organizational properties; adults normally go about their business in public, save certain categories reserved for those whose business is hanging about in public. To summarize the point, seeing human beings as "children" is not just recognizing biological or physical properties, although to be sure they have those distinctively. It is the cultural recognition of children's practices.

One issue worth exploring is the nature of adult-child contacts, not within the conventional mode which ascribes the adult ideological position to the treatment of children who come into contact with adult figures, but as contacts between two distinct groupings of cultural participants. What methods are found within each cultural set of participants for striking up interactions with each other? This pertains to the way in which actions get initiated, or opened. Do children use particular methods for making such openings, ones that are noticeably distinct from those used by adults who initiate interactions with children? This is a very general issue in social life that deals with the nature of adult-child encounters and approaches in various social settings.

It appears to be a fact of childhood that a child is in a special position vis-à-vis adults as a conversationalist or interactant. He has not the same access to adults as they have to him. His rights seem to be definitely restricted in the matter of initiating interactions with them. He must first get the attention of adults around him to get the opportunity to enter into a state of talk or start a conversation with them.

A regularly used form of interactional control by children in our culture is the "You know what?" opening. What this does is get the adult hearer into a state of readiness as a prospective interactant by using the simple first sequencing rule of Q-A pairs,[14] namely, that the question obligates the hearer to answer. But more strategically considered, this is a question that is entirely open, being an unspecified one leaving little else open to the hearer than a straightforward "What?" This guarantees the child another turn at talking and prepares the stage for conversational development. Thus, it may be the case that a child, because of his very special status as a conversationalist with adults, is constrained to establish initial attempts at obtaining the adult's attention to effectuate a face-to-face engagement.

This consideration of children's openings with adults can be extended to include such things as *announcements of presence and arrival on the scene,* using greetings—e.g., "Hello! Anybody home?" as when a child returns home from school—or using a summons to signal presence to others—as when a child precedes his greeting announcement with a summons for his mother, "Mom! I'm home." Greetings can also be ceremonially focused on others, as when a child enters the house or a room and, seeing his mother, opens with "Hi, Mom."

The development of these opening interchanges can be studied for their sequential properties, as for example, when they do not get returned or when they are noticeably absent from the initial phase of an encounter. There are cases where the interactive process is cut short before it can start because greetings are avoided. When children do this, they can be sanctioned for it by adults who take it as their business to socialize a child to make suitable or appropriate openings. For example, a mother will notice the absence of a greeting in the opening position of an encounter between the child and another adult and point it out with a corrective "Say hello to her." In this instance, we find that parents can enjoin their children to perform classes of speech acts for ceremonially entering into a conversation, or at least for properly establishing the child's presence. This often involves the presence of adult visitors to the household. Visitors and visiting occasions call for these forms of appropriate interactional openings. In the above case of a mother correcting for an omitted hello, we find that one standard parental method for teaching sequencing of openings is the use of what we might call the "say formula," simply an instruction to a child to say what the parent says or expects the child to know how to say, e.g., "What do you say?"

Other aspects of adult-child interactions that can be studied in detail are those features of conversational development we spelled out in chapters 5 and 6. Take the issue of initiating conversation, for example. Once an initiation has been made, either by the child or through the efforts of adults (as when parents seek to get their children to be sociable with household guests or adult strangers in public places), we can see that a state of talk has been undertaken and an opportunity for conversing exists. How does a child participate in a conversation with adults? If he is on his own the development takes place without the overseeing of his parents, who often make the procedural basis of parenthood quite visible, namely, if it is your own child you can methodically prod him to speak up, and your practical task may be to get him to be sociable. For example, one kind of parental entitlement includes the right to make requests of one's own child to attend to others (children included) as sociable objects, e.g., "Why don't you ask her what her name is?" or "Tell Mary what you did at school yesterday?" etc.

If the child is alone, however, how does he enter into interaction? How does he topically construct his conversation, for example? Often a child will call upon an adult strictly for help with some task. Sometimes this involves the adult physically moving from one place to another and with that the adult's removal from his own situated activity, e.g., "Can you come here and help me with this? I can't do it." Now this raises another interesting issue for childhood study.

It is often believed and asserted that children are very dependent on their adults. And adults come to view this as an ideological condition: children are helpless and demanding. However, a little thought should reveal that it is the adult who may be constructing appropriate solutions for initiating the child's interaction with adults. That is, the adult provides the necessary structural conditions for a child's right to call on him for help. Believing that a child is helpless, the adult creates the situated conditions of helplessness for a child, who learns to rely on those conditions for making interactional contact. This is true despite the fact that a particular child might in some objective sense be physically able to complete a task, but regardless of that fact, he can rightfully call on an adult who is under some obligation to respond to calls for help. In childhood activity all kinds of interactions are constructed on just this general basis. *The issue is not, then, that children are helpless, but how they present themselves as helpless persons in order to construct routine interactional events with adults.*

Adults' views of childhood are productive of a childhood state of helplessness, insofar as they provide continual opportunities for interaction on that basis. In this respect, adults are as dependent on their children as their children are on them. In fact, a child who shows independence at too early an age is not always accepted as a model of good development, from an adult standpoint. It can be viewed as restricting the adult's opportunities to continue to interact on the basis of the child's ascribed dependency, and, therefore, diminishes the authoritative and controlling aspects of parenthood. It seems quite clear that this ascribed dependency is used to justify authoritative behavior toward children's activity.

This point is in harmony with the cultural distinctions we are stressing as a point of departure for analysis. The child who shows competent behavior in some form or other can always be commended or singled out, his behavior can be reviewed, reported about to others, awarded or rewarded, etc. This entitlement of adults to monitor the activities of children for their competence and age-appropriateness is asymmetrical. The child is not normally in a position to do likewise, with the exception of those occasions in which adults enter upon the domains of children's culture and children bring to their attention the adult's incompetence within that domain. But it seems to be the case that an adult can always query the child's competence, can always look over whatever the child does, in those terms. The adult is also entitled to make correctives that the adult feels will promote and/or sanction normal forms of behavior, positively or negatively.

With respect to conversational development, for example, adults can correct a child's failure to abide by the two simple rules pertaining to turn-taking, i.e., one person speaks at a time and speaker change reoccurs. If a child talks when others are talking, it is open to an adult to call a child on it, thus treating it as an interruption, e.g., "Stop interrupting us now, you just wait until Nancy finishes telling me about this." *A child may not have used one method for getting a turn that adults normally use, namely, attending to a topic on the floor to construct his turn.* A child who is regarded as interrupting may indeed be deliberately or unwittingly introducing another topic altogether. Let us consider this further.

First of all, on the issue of topical talk, are there topics that are central to each of the cultures and, therefore, noticeably distinct? *Are there, in other words, different rules of topical relevance for the members of each of the two cultures?* Anthropologists have often noted cultural preoccupations with some facet of nature or social life, the result of which is a relative importance placed on those aspects of nature or social life in talk and language. For example, the Arabic cultures traditionally make considerable use of camels for many purposes and a linguist can show that the terms in the native language for camels are very numerous, being formed to show the camel's numerous purposes or characteristics. Likewise, the Nuer of Africa have a cattle-raising economy and venerate them as religious or ritualistic figures, and presumably much talk is made about cattle. The Eskimos place great importance on the phenomena of snow and ice, and so on. *The point here is that a culture may provide some key topics for conversation because of the relation of the topic to the main activities of the culture.* To give one simple example at home, the topic of toys may be a very key one to children, and their conversational interactions may be built around that topic.

Remembering that our concern is mainly with what a topic does for a conversation and for an interaction, we must be able to study the phenomenon of topic as part of the organization of talk and social activity. What, then, can children do with topics to build interactions with adults? Can adults construct conversational occasions that take children's topicality, if such should exist, into account? The birthday party would seem to be a case in point where these questions can be investigated.

At the dinner table, how does a child get topically included in the talk? Does it require some special "cross-cultural procedures," as we might call them, whereby the adult offers up child-relevant topics to bring the child into the conversation, e.g., "What happened at school today?" If a topic is on the floor among adults, how does the child construct his own contributions? *Where children are concerned, and this is most interesting, interruptions may in fact be defined as talking off-topic.* That is, were an adult to talk before another adult finished his utterance, but talk to the topic, that might pass as an acceptable interruption; or were a child to do it, that too might be acceptable. But given the case of a mis-topical piece of talk by a child then this might be a negatively sanctionable interruption.

Another issue can be raised in connection with children's use of topics to achieve conversational participation with adults. It pertains to children initiating contacts with adults in groups. Because of the requirement it places upon interactants of the respective cultures to show that they are able to attend to each other as the situation calls for it, this issue highlights the cultural distinction. Adults particularly must attend to their children's demands upon their attentions. *A structure of differential attentions exists between children and adults.* This is very readily observed when two mothers, for example, are having coffee at the kitchen table and their respective children periodically enter their presence, call on them for help, ask questions, get into trouble, etc., all of which calls for the restructuring of interactional attentions, or allocations of involvement on the part of the mothers. This interactional "demand condition"[15] on adult activity calls conversational techniques into play that must be designed to circumvent the destruction of a conversation. That is, the two mothers must have methods for getting around these periodic conversational stoppages in order for them to be able to continue to talk on a topic.

Looking at transcripts of situations such as these, one sees very quickly that the conversation proceeds on the course of a chosen topic despite the children's intermittent contacts: here the topic is broken off to answer a child's question or to leave the room to see a child; there the topic picks up again. *Presumably, one feature of any conversation is that participants keep track of the progress of a topic, a feature we have referred to as topical tying and continuity.* This is done to preserve the conversation, and where children's interventions are concerned, there may also be the feature of protecting a conversation.

Still another issue can be developed out of this problem of divided attentions between cultural participants. This is the issue of how one adult talks to his, as opposed to another's, child. Looking at transcripts where two or more parents and their respective children are present, one can readily identify by inspection who is the parent of whom. This is a striking fact, because if it is true—and you can quickly confirm this with a transcript of your own—then there must be some structural feature at work that we can isolate to empirically account for this difference in speech patterning. *Apparently, a mother can formulate her utterances for another mother's child.* A correlative issue pertains to whether the other mother is absent or present, as when a child visits another child. If the mother of the other child is present, there seem to be some operative rules for speaking and hearing that are contingent on her presence, i.e., speech gets formulated for another mother as well as for the child. This is one way that motherhood can be accomplished as a mutually enforced and sanctionable system of understandings about child rearing.

Typically, the speaker will include politeness markers in her utterances to the other mother's child when she is present, rather than criticisms of his behavior, because, so it seems, to criticize another mother's child in her presence is also to criticize her as a mother in some respect. Parents are treated as accountable for their own children's actions and development. They can be called on that, when it is noticeably lacking. But more regularly, such criticism is politely avoided; parents are normally accorded special rights to govern the lives of their own children. Teachers traditionally have averred to this common-sense principle about the relation between parents and their children: a child is a reflection of his parents. But social occasions in which teachers critically evaluate a child's school performance to his parents are legitimate forms of communication between adults, unlike the case of one mother telling another mother, for example, "You know, you have a very destructive and selfish child," which can be heard as a complaint and not just as an evaluation.

These issues are all subject to study in depth and all of them pertain to adult-child interactions and likewise to interactions within their separate cultures. We must also consider the interactions of children in other cultural environments: streets, playgrounds and parks, household areas, schools and schoolgrounds, public places, etc. Naturally, adult-child interactions are not restricted to the family household. The school has a lot of interaction going on between children on their own, and between teachers and school officials and those children who are there every day. One project of study would be to inspect the methods teachers and children use to construct daily schoolroom activities together. The lesson-plan schedule, however much it enters into the organization of activity, is, of course, not the full basis for how interaction proceeds in the classroom, but more likely a blueprint for temporally organizing the class activity.

Issues we have raised elsewhere can be adapted to the school setting, with the main difference being the special category of the adult as "teacher"; one who is involved in social arrangements that have the practical job of educating children, viz., the teaching profession, its own organization of educational activities in the school plant, the ideological and philosophical bases for teaching methods, the specialized methods themselves, etc. It would seem that the problem of classroom management is central to running it, irrespective of the educational persuasions, approaches, etc., teachers may use. How does the teacher get the concerted activity of the day achieved? What are the commonplace routines that occur in the bounded activities of the typical class day? How do children go about participating in the activity, e.g., how do they initiate interactions in the classroom; how do they orient to taking turns at talking, to the raising of topics relevant for the classroom environment; how are they sanctioned for violations of basic conversational rules; and how does an activity or a set of interchanges temporally develop in the episodic work of the class? What do children learn about the ways of referring to others and other cultural activities when they talk in the class or participate in a lesson? These are but a few questions worth pursuing.[16]

Children's Cultural Activities: Play and Games

Finally, coming back to the theme of children's culture, we need to study how children organize their own activities exclusive of adults' direct or indirect participation. Forms of play and games are best known products of children's culture, though by no means the only ones. A basic problem in the analysis of childhood behaviors would be the investigation of the formal properties of games. This would require a study of the structural features of games in and of themselves. That is, we would examine the established rules of particular games and observe how players follow them. Obviously, one could locate a rule book for a given game and then list out the rules relevant for proper playing. But the study of games, their rules and possible strategies, must include data from the arena of game interaction. *One has to consider games as social occasions and "gaming" to be but another group activity requiring concerted methods for successful performance.*

Children's performances of games are essentially occasions for sociability in children's cultures. While it may be a popular lay conception that game activity is divorced from the realities of everyday life, one consequence of children's games may be that children initially find out how social order works through game participation. Sacks suggests that, if so, it may be that the principle of interchangeability of personnel over a stable set of social categories—a principle operative in games—is a lesson in social organization.[17]

Some of the important questions at first glance turn on issues of game interaction and organization. How do children get a game going? How do they "map" players into game categories, given that games with names normally have a stable set of game categories into which persons must be mapped for the game to start? The activity boundaries of games are a pertinent issue relative to the study of game openings. What criteria do children use to select participants; are other categorical characteristics relevant for the initial selections of players from a pool as possible players? Are there basic categorical features that qualify some participants and disqualify others, e.g., age, sex, size, equipment ownership, etc.? How are the rules of games interactionally organized so as to preserve the occasion of a game, to permit the play of one completed game? Just as there are interactional rules for closings, are there completion rules for children's games? How do conversation and action develop over the course of a single play of a game?

One regular type of game consists of pretended activities that are obviously intended as a version of adult activity, such as house, doctor, police, etc. Take playing house, for example. We might think of this as a simulation of adult activity among members of children's culture. It is important not to treat these simulations as defective or imperfect versions of adult counterparts, as though they were to be checked out for their scientific accuracy to adult forms of social life, and upon finding that they perhaps do not match them, deciding that children are obviously unsocialized. Rather, the occasions in which children do pretend activities, such as "house," can be inspected for their methods of constructing typical family household arrangements. Interestingly enough, this is one setting children are bona fide members of, unlike "doctor," for example. There is an internal regulation of the interaction that governs the way it structurally and temporally develops as a social activity.

Take the following actual transcript as an example of household simulation. Three girls and three boys, ages three to seven, are playing house on a front porch:

Playing House Transcript

Participants: Sheila, seven yrs.; Laurie, six yrs.; Michael, three yrs.; Roy, six yrs.; MaryJane, five yrs.; Eddie, three yrs.

1.   S Daughter, you stay in to do your work.
2.   L. I *am!*
3.   S. These are little *babies.*
4.   L. I *am!*
5.   S. These are little children. They'll go outside and play. Remember, I don't want you havin' any fights.
6.   M. All right!
7.   S. You goin' outside? You better not go outside. You're too small. Everybody stay close to the house. Now pretty soon it's breakfast time. (long silence)
8.   R. Mother! Mother! Mother! Those guys are (playin' with the thing . . .) you cut the grass with.
9.   S. Oh, daughter, will you take care of your baby!
10. M. *I* will!
11.   L. Now you helpin' my baby? You be good now.
12. M.J. I cut my finger!
13.   S. You shouldn't play with that thing (. . .) Let the big boys cut it. O.K. You stay close to him. Pretty soon I'm gonna call you for breakfast.
14.   E. I'm the daddy.
15.   S. I'm gonna call you all for your breakfast.
16.   L. No you're not. You're the little boy.
17. M.J. And I'm the daddy! Pretend there'll be two daddies, O.K.?
18. L.   No.
      (some inaudible voices of the boys)
19. M.   I'm the father.

20. M.J. And I'm the father too!

21.   R. I'm the fatha too!

22.   M. I'm the father too.

23.   R. I'm the fatha too.

24.   S. Everybody can't be the father. I told Eddie he could be the father.

25.   L. *One* person has to be the father. And that's Mikie.

26. M.J. Cause I, I want to be the father.

27.   S. You gonna be a g . . . lady, young lady, and he gonna be a young man.

28. M.J. Well, I'm gonna be a man too!

29.   M. I wanta to be a man too.

30.   S. You're not no man. You're a girl.

31. M.J. I *wanta* be a man if I *want* ta!!

32.   R. You're not.

33. M.J. Yes!

34.   R. You're not no boy.

35. M.J. Well (I'm not teasin' . . .) I wanta be a daddy, I want to!

36.   S. MaryJane, girls don't be a father. Laurie, do girls be fathers?

37.   L. No! Boys!

38. M.J. Well, I want to be the father if I want to, Laurie!

39.   S. O.K. ....

Looking at this transcript, we can see how the children go about initially mapping each other into viable game categories of the family household set. More generally, if we return to a feature discussed in an earlier chapter, we find that there is an identification selection problem that confronts all the interactants. In this case the children, who know each other's names, select identifications for each other in order to construct the simulated environment of a recognizable family arrangement. They use the consistency rule for categorization we spoke of earlier.

Who does the selecting? All, or just some of the children? We can see from a glance at the transcript that the oldest girl, Sheila, is a self-appointed selector for the others. In some way, this process is like that of choosing players for categories of a ball game, where Sheila has chosen herself as leader and it gets legitimated by the others who cooperate with her selections. Sheila has selected the category of "mother" for herself, but not explicitly. Notice that the whole sequence is very rich in categorizations. This itself is a clue to the nature of the activity. By their speech, the participants come to control the domain of their interaction under the relevance of the type of setting simulated and its set of categories and relevant events.

The most striking feature in this sequence of activity is the structural division of the episode into two distinct parts. This is very instructive for an understanding of the interaction as a progression of coordinated definitions of the situation. How interactants mutually define a social situation is, of course, a basic component of its perceived organization—a fact long ago pointed out by the noted sociologist, W. I. Thomas.[18]

The episode is altered by the children at a point when (utterance 16) a dispute arises about the proper methods of playing at a pretended environment. During the first half of the sequence, the children are engaged in a smooth set of interactions, going through the activity by activating some implicit rules about household organization, i.e., who the relevant categories of persons are, what they can be called or addressed as, what domain of appropriate actions is attached to those positions, etc. After utterance 16, "No, you're not, you're the little boy," the children perform an analysis of appropriateness rules applicable to the simulation: How can players be properly mapped? Who is entitled to be an incumbent of a particular position in the set of categories? Is there a proper or adequate incumbent of a particular category? Is category interchangeability among the players unconstrained?

When the issue of interchangeability arises, the children's activity and conversational interaction shift into an argument over the proper incumbency notion. The principle being argued over appears to be whether or not simultaneous occupancy of the category "father" in the set, can properly exist. Noting that "father" is not normally a duplicated category for this set in real life—that is, there is normally only one father to each family—the five-year old girl, M.J., wants to pretend that two daddies are in the activity (utterance 17). Other categories, such as kids, little children, babies, sisters, brothers, all are duplicatable. M.J.'s request for a duplication of a nonduplicatable category in the structural arrangement of a family is treated as a violation of the proper method for playing house. Consequently, M.J. is sanctioned by the others. She is also denied the right to enter into that position because of a disqualifying characteristic, namely, her sex. We find two sets of utterances occurring that constitute rules of play.

24. Everybody can't be the father. I told Eddie, he could be the father.
25. *One* person has to be the father. And that's Mikie.
36. MaryJane, girls don't be a father. Laurie, do girls be fathers?

37. No! Boys!

Although we can see in this transcript a "reflection" of normal real families in the culture, in which the category "father" is singular, *we emphasize that in their activity the children attend primarily to organizing their own behavior as interactional and cultural activity in its own right.* The children interactionally control the ongoing development of the interaction by reference to a system of internally regulated rules for membership in the activity. Clearly the breach made by M.J. reconstitutes the activity and her proposal calls for explicit consideration of the way to make their version of a cultural grouping acceptable. By acceptability is meant the containment of a set of categories by use of the consistency rule. We simply do not find the children mixing up the categories for different MCDs, just as we do not find M.J. proposing to be the "first baseman" or the "nurse."

Throughout this segment players construct their actions with an orientation to their incumbency in categories. That is, they mutually recognize what actions go with what categories. Mothers do certain rightful and dutiful actions because they are indeed mothers. Given you are a mother, you can be called on for help, direct the actions of others, give orders and commands, etc. The transcript demonstrates this tie between categories and rightful domains of action, or what Sacks has called "category bound actions."[19] The children go through sequences of typical family activities and routines that the categories methodically generate.

These are only some of the many issues one can explore in the study of childhood within the interactional frame of reference being proposed. Aside from the playhouse sequence, we have not touched upon the way children develop conversations among their own cultural peers. We would like to construct natural histories of interactional events and activities that are found in children's culture. Such adult speech acts as greetings, introductions or name exchanges, invitations, rejections, insults, might have counterparts in children's activities. These would provide opportunities for students to pursue long-term projects.

2. Work and Occupations

This section will be quite brief. It is intended to make some simple suggestions for the student who wishes to consider what might be done in this area of the discipline.

Traditional Problems

Traditional problems in this subject area have focused on labor and industry, divisions among management and workers, organization of work tasks in factory and office settings, trends in professionalization and specialization of labor, related economic problems of employment-unemployment, recruitment patterns to various sectors of the labor market, and so on. Very early sociological investigations of occupational life were closely tied to policy-making decisions in the management of labor forces in given occupational settings, with particular emphasis on work conditions and productivity. Efficiency experts were called upon to make studies of work schedules and rate of production, so-called time and motion studies being one example of this interest.

Our concern is merely to suggest that there is almost no data at all that present how work routines of the most mundane sort are accomplished as interactional phenomena. Instead, the classic works in this field have focused on more abstract issues in the functional aspects of work organizations. For example, Chester Barnard's *The Functions of the Executive*[20] has taken up the problem of work incentives as systematic agents in the nature and output of production and work morale, e.g., such things as statuses on the job, fixed lines of authority, channels of communication and chains of command.

Questions about lines of authority and communication have developed out of Barnard's work, such as those analyzed in B. B. Gardner and D. G. Moore's *Human Relations in Industry*.[21] Here the authors inquire about the ranking of positions into lines of authority from the top to the bottom of an organization, what they recognize as its hierarchical characteristics. They seek to explain the principles of human relationships which center around subordinate and superordinate social positions and the resultant differential rights and obligations that enter into work activity. They explore the idea of control and discipline by work superiors and make observations about the constraints apparently working on persons lower in rank when dealing with those higher, or what has been referred to as "distortion up the line." Here they suggest that workers will mask their behavior by trying to cover up their activities in order to present an image of "what the boss wants." In this hierarchical system no one passes bad information up the line to the boss. The problem of conveying "bad news" is one that requires special handling by a person down the line. Defenses are developed by persons at various levels in the hierarchy of authority in order to protect themselves from criticisms, and so on.

Another classic in this field is Melville Dalton's, *Men Who Manage*.[22]

Here, interest-group formation and leadership characteristics are examined in work organizations, centering on the problem of the relation between management and labor. Interest groups are expected products of the division of labor in a stratified set of work arrangements. Staff and management are differentially oriented by their competitive claims on specialized duties and responsibilities. Dalton points out that staff is relatively weak compared to the line, which is in part due to the vested authority of the top officials of the line. Staff-line conflicts are taken to be key organizational phenomena for the working relationships of occupational co-workers. Staff organization is made up of specialists with research and advisory functions in the work plant, while the line refers to foremen and their superiors who are responsible for production and who actually direct the work routines.

Dalton points to the sources of friction between staff and line in terms of their social background differences, for example, that are brought with them to the work place in combination with their different social positions in the plant. Categorizations such as "college punks," "slide rules," "chair warmers" are applied by line members to staffers. Dalton used conversational observations to document these different styles of presentation of self and action that entered into everyday interactions between line and staff members. He quotes a line officer, "They (staffers) don't go into the cafeteria to eat and relax while they talk over their problems. They go in there to look around to see how somebody is dressed or to talk over the hot party they had last night. . . ."

An Interactional Approach
Now, for our purposes we would need to see these kinds of interactions in their original sequences. Only in that way could we detect the formal properties of communicative acts among coparticipants in a work setting. These studies have almost invariably been concerned with the social importance of seeking solutions to the reduction of conflictual relations in industry. Yet, they point to the interactional basis for that conflict in routine communication among the participants. In our examples throughout the text we have made reference to work settings. The world of work is perhaps the most pervasive aspect of everyday life activity. In some sense it is synonymous with adult life. But knowledge is lacking on the most fundamental details of how members routinely construct organized events in work settings.

Although questions of conflict, work satisfaction, power and authority, and organizational policy have all played an important part in sociologi-

Men at Work. How do work tasks structure communicative behavior for workers? Is there always room for relating outside occupational categories in work situations? (photo by Marian Penner Bancroft.)

cal studies of work settings, we propose beginning our studies on a much simpler basis. The main task might consist simply of gathering ethnographic data of routine concerted activities in work settings. Here is a short list of questions: How are routines performed by participants and what do they take to be their main involvements in practical work tasks? What is the arrangement of the typical work day? What are the temporal junctures in that day and how is temporal structuring accomplished? How is responsibility delegated and enacted by those in positions with duties and obligations towards others? What are the actual day-to-day spatial constraints on interaction in the setting? What special entitlements, privileges, and qualifications do persons have that define spheres of rightful behavior for them but not for others? What typical conceptions of the work establishment do participants share and how do they relate to it ideologically? Do they use a special vocabulary of terms and motives especially meaningful to describe their activities? What temporal conceptions of an employee's career are related to interactional histories at the work place? How do job categorization practices and work routines shape sociability on the job? Are there job topics and special techniques for building conversations with other personnel or in customer contacts? Can deference patterns be located? And so forth.

Student projects in the past have taken up such researchable topics as interactional control in buying-selling situations in car lots, department stores, and other retail shops. Standardized procedures for opening and closing interactions between salesmen, clerks, cashiers and customers were studied. In the car lots the students investigated the way in which the salesman first decides the eligibility and seriousness of a potential customer, the way in which a sales encounter is opened, how the customer is qualified and controlled with respect to the salesman's inferences about the type of person and purchase involved and, finally, how a sale is accomplished and closed or how it is left unmade. In department stores, students attended to the richness of the ecological features of the environments, the distribution of activities in regions staffed by locally placed personnel. They studied how customers are approached and, if in fact they are not approached at all, how they initiate contacts with visible representatives of the store. The nature of help offered and the method of showing a customer around or suggesting how to make an appropriate purchase are part of the sales person's routine activities that are open to study. When persons present themselves to a sales person, do categorizations take place and become the basis for opening the customer-clerk talk? What kinds of interactions routinely take place between staff members? What special unit events are found in the department store setting, e.g., complaints? What is the structure of accountability of personnel to each other? How do customers locate objects in the store if interactional inquiries must be made for that purpose? Do customers talk to strangers? Under what conditions? What happens in back as opposed to front regions?

To put problems into terms spelled out by Goffman, regarding public places where everyday persons come into contact with sales persons: How do they regulate their mutual conduct when doing their main business? What is the nature of the face work that transpires among them? How do establishments provide mechanisms of interaction through physically arranging the environment for types of traffic flow and types of encounters? How is social embarrassment handled, or how does it arise? What are the forms of deference and demeanor that come into interactional play when routine encounters are made? Does the work establishment provide places for the private use of any categories of its participants? For example, are there involvement shields built into the work place? Are customer shields of a different interactional nature or purpose from staff shields? What part do non-spoken elements of interaction play in mutually regulating group activity? How do persons orient to the right of way of others when cueing up for services? And so on.

Many work settings, most in fact, do not provide routine contact situations with the public. Instead they are organized into self-contained units of members who assemble routinely every day in some physical plant and go about their work together. This has been the main focus of traditional studies, as, for example, those in industrial sociology. The issues explored by Dalton, Barnard, and others, center on privately situated work activities, where persons are arranged in stable, or fairly stable, social relationships, mostly oriented to cooperative work tasks. So, we can see that the degree of contact that a work place has to maintain with outside persons varies a great deal among establishments.

Within the establishment, there may be differential contacts among participants, with some persons regularly requiring each other's presence or telephone contact, and others requiring virtually no contacts. The grouping of persons into categories, such as those defining work duties or management and supervisory responsibilities, creates a body of preferential communicative rights. That is, some categories of persons can initiate interactions with any others, either directly or through others, whereas other categories of persons are limited in their entitlements to

initiate such contacts. The meaning of supervisory, management, or simple "boss" activity involves a consideration of legitimate forms of direction and control, including the sanctioning of others' behavior. What are
conversational interactions like in a typical business office? How is talk
governed by constraints and purposes of the setting and its personnel? Is
there something called "shop talk" that has describable formal characteristics as conversational interaction? That is, does shop talk do something
for participants on the job (and when it is done off the job, what are its
interactional consequences)? How are forms of deference and types of
power relationships interactionally achieved through talk on the job?

Other issues worth taking up as projects might be the search for employment, i.e., how does one locate a job? What procedures are used by
the one who is looking and by the ones he approaches as a candidate
for a job? This would involve hiring activity in employment offices. Here
work qualifications and credentials would provide an organized basis for
categorization practices in terms of assessments of competence made in
interview activity. Another issue would center on the professions, those
bodies of persons grouped together into an association of professional
workers with common training and standardized occupational requirements. For example, there are the professions of doctors, nurses, lawyers,
teachers, etc. Here, the issue of common or divergent professional orientations in the form of ideological positions[23] would be worth pursuing
insofar as they become sources and resources for interactional events
among members of the profession. For instance, in recent years in the
United States a development that has divided the nursing profession has
been the emphasis on university training and technical skill as opposed
to the more traditional apprenticeship orientations of nursing.[24] The
place of a nurse in an occupational team has become central in modern
hospital organization. How can we observe these features of the profession in interactional circumstances?

Professional agencies that deal with the public, such as social welfare[25]
and county-supported hospitals,[26] are also worth investigating for the
simple problem of how agency policies and ideological positions regulate
the routine interactions between clients and staff, on the one hand, and
between staff and other supervisory staff, on the other hand. For example, what are the typifications that social workers have of their clients,
their social characteristics, and accordingly what moral inferences about
their character do they make in the line of their work? How does a social
worker present himself to his clients? How does he manage his conduct

in accordance with his formulations about his clients' social characteristics—formulations acquired primarily on the job, a set of "demand conditions" for work, to use Bittner's phrase.

We should remember that simply because we have labeled settings as occupational, there may be no reason to expect we will discover some distinctive features of work settings without considering what invariant properties of interaction they might share with all settings. This is a persistent problem for our analysis. We may simply find that in the long run our common sense classifications will break down where many interactional features of human environments are concerned. This once again raises the issue of so-called substantive studies. For example, it may be irrelevant in the last analysis whether the setting is a General Motors automobile plant or a Safeway market insofar as leave-taking rituals among employees go. Yet, we know that there are bound to be many other features of conversational interaction that must remain invariant in these settings, such as question and answer sequences, summoning and greeting, taking turns at talking, etc. The internal regulation of conversational interaction may well be so invariant from one setting to the next, that we must seek other descriptive justifications for studying the practical activities in which these conversations occur, e.g., the structure of activities and organized settings as conversational environments. We may feel that work environments are constituted differently for employees of Safeway as compared with employees of a General Motors plant. But we must always exercise caution in order to avoid being seduced by surface appearances. Often when we study the formal characteristics of social phenomena we discover powerful resemblances lying at a deeper structural level.

3. Deviance

What is Deviant Behavior?
The field of deviant behavior is a very broad one covering many areas of possible study. For instance, there are the subject areas of crime, juvenile delinquency, legal administration and justice, mental illness and psychiatry, nudism, prostitution, forms of sexual deviance, drug addiction, alcoholism, etc. They have always been avidly studied and equally as avidly followed by students and laymen alike, because of the intrinsic attractiveness of the material. In fact, one look at an average daily newspaper in any large metropolitan area will document the fact that editors

believe that citizens are most likely to be interested in reading news items about the kinds of events around which such topics can get constructed. But what exactly are the events?

Considerable attention has been paid to defining the concept of deviance.[27] Some have pointed to the individual as deviant, meaning his actions and his personality. Others have pointed to the process whereby persons become labeled as deviants, a process in which persons assign deviant attributes and status to another's actions. Some have said that deviance is not a property of persons as such, but a property of social relationships among persons. Most have looked at deviant behaviors— whatever form they presumably take—as remediable, in need of correction, either from the point of view of those who commit deviance, or for the benefit of those who are subjected to deviance by others. *But there has been a widespread and unfortunate tendency to bypass the study of those characteristics that produce the appearances of deviant behavior as a perceived departure from normal environmental characteristics.* That is, what is usually bypassed is the attribution process whereby some actions are treated as deviant ones, the issue being, how it is that one can decide in a given concrete case, that some breach of the normal has occurred. *What this involves, naturally, is some set of rules for perceiving normal environments with which to recognize the deviant case.*[28]

The whole process of recognition of deviance by means of normal rules for perceiving the everyday social order that constitutes the mundane world has been presupposed and left entirely unclarified in studies that take for granted the existence of common-sense forms, or lay concepts, of social deviance.[29] For example, it is possible without studying the interactions of young boys who form groups called gangs and commit acts of violence, crime, and destruction, to go straightforwardly into an explanation of their social backgrounds as causes for their actions. *In other words, the stress has traditionally been placed on the etiological basis and remedial aspects of social problems believed to be present, instead of on the interactional and procedural basis of the gang's activities as a topic in its own right.* The latter orientation is exceptional.

For example, Werthman has studied the methods gang members have used to control the evaluations made of them by high school teachers.[30] The situation involved a consideration of the gang's acceptance, or terms of acceptance, of the teachers' authority in the school. Gang members would methodically construct hypotheses about how grades were assigned by particular teachers, i.e., what criteria the teachers used for making grades, and then seek to influence the teacher if the grade was judged to be unfair in order to change it. One simple and more conventional observation of the same phenomena would be: gang members are dissident rule breakers who need to be either rehabilitated or disciplined, because they do not accept authority. But Werthman instead gives us a richly detailed description of the way in which the interactions are structured by gang members around principles they socially organize for their own daily survival in the school. We see how the so-called deviant behavior operates.

To elaborate this point in other areas of interest, consider for a moment the phenomenon called prostitution. There was an interesting nationally televised documentary on forms of deviance, including prostitution, which was oriented to psychiatric issues. Its theme was love and hatred. The interviewer asked a female prostitute why she did her job, wasn't there something that was wrong with it, wasn't there other work she could do, etc.? The interviewer's implication was clear that the absence of normal love in sexual relationships must be mentally unhealthy for the prostitute. The answers given by the woman were illuminating of some of the points in this text. She did not grant that she was mentally disturbed by her "profession." She said that she was doing it strictly as a financial proposition, that her behavior was governed by her own estimation of what her value was on the labor market. She felt it was very low due to her lack of experience and education. She could not make as much at any other job she might land. She did not mind selling men her body, it definitely did not mean anything to her beyond an arrangement for pecuniary purposes, so she maintained.

Now, we will not ask whether she was telling the truth or not. That cannot be proven. But we see no necessary reason to assume she was lying. She clearly made the program's purpose seem foolish, however, for the simple reason that the interviewer was concerned with getting at the emotional or psychological basis of this illicit form of human activity and he could only get indications from her about the sheer practicality of the activity. Were we to adopt the interviewer's line, as is most often done, we would want to show that the activity is indeed mentally and morally degrading in order to remedy, reduce, or otherwise control it. *In the process, we would not be likely to ask questions about the competence and routines of the prostitution.*[31] That is, we would not care about the organized activity of her daily life, except as we could show in some ideological fashion that it was depraved or morally and mentally deficient in some way. By so doing, we would, of course, fail

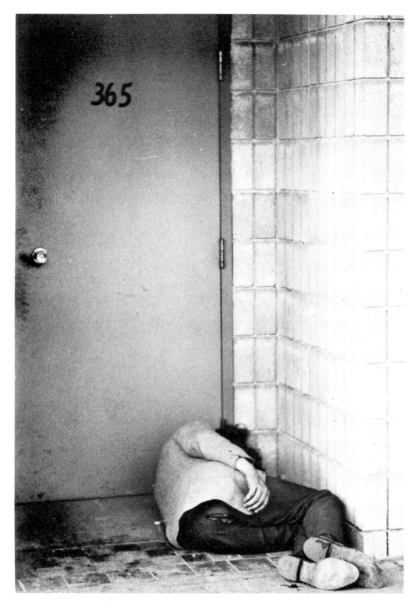

Deviance. What warrants the inference that this is deviant behavior? Street life is culturally organized into normal appearances for different ecological domains in a large city. (photo by William Darrough.)

to see the world of those persons we study in the way they see and make that world a reality. We might not like prostitution and really prefer to develop theories about its harmful effects on human beings, *but the sociologist's first task ought to begin on an evaluative-free basis, otherwise he will not describe the subjective reality of those he seeks to understand and his position will be moralistic rather than scientific.*

Another example pertains to drug use. The subject has become very popular in recent years. It has reached the proportions of a major social problem where middle-class youth is concerned, as opposed to its earlier connections with criminal activity and lower-class life. One finds many studies on the causes for drug addiction,[32] but one would have to look hard for detailed descriptions of drug-taking or drug-dealing activities. For example, an extensive set of observations could be made of known drug-taking or drug-selling hangouts in order to study how users organize their activities around the practical activity of drug transactions. One would have to place himself in a suitable position to gather this data, noticing the mundane aspects of everyday life and transactional routines in the setting.

Deception Practices and Masking Techniques
When transactions are not legitimate ones, such as we find in regular business establishments, the orientation of participants must take illicitness into account. By doing so, how do they accomplish their tasks and regulate their interactions with an eye to preventing detection of what they are really up to? *The deviant aspects of the activity, then, are discoverable by looking to those forms of behavior that build into their activities barriers to their recognition or detection, or what we might call deception practices and masking techniques.* That is one important issue to develop in an analysis of drug-taking deviance.

Of course, we should bear in mind that for the participants these practices and their texture of everyday life are not at all deviant insofar as their routineness goes. *They are in fact the normal conditions for these activities.* But insofar as they operate in ways that would be sanctioned by the legal rules of the society and those who execute them— the police, for example—and insofar as they would be judged by others in the society—citizens and professionals—as immoral, they must be treated as deviant activities by the consequences they would receive were they to be made public. One consequence is legal punishment.

If deception practices are not used, the exposure of illicit actions and the legal consequences that follow upon exposure may be calculated to bring public attention, rather than preserve the conveniences of secret activity. When this attention is sought after, the alleged deviant activity presents itself as a challenge to established legal rules and morals. It is often argued that drug use among the young is a form of social rebellion against established conventions, and from this argument a search for the reasons for the presumed rebellion is made: what are they rebelling against, etc.? Concerted breaches of legal and moral rules of society often take on the character of a social movement, which enters into the political domain of social life.

character of a social movement, which enters into the political domain of social life.

Our point here is simply that instead of treating activities such as drug use among young persons along lines defined by the society as "social problems" and embarking forthwith on a program of remedy or eradication, we must first seek the interactional foundations for the activity in order to understand what it actually amounts to as planful and methodical human group behavior. This is simply an attempt to understand the way in which the phenomenon works for those routinely organizing it into structured or patterned cultural activity. *Once again, we are proposing that to characterize the social world is to do sociology.*[33]

For those of you who would prefer to do social criticism—and there is room for much of this in an obviously imperfect human world—you may be asking how such a proposal for doing sociology includes criticism. It simply does not; at the outset, at least. *This does not mean I am personally unwilling or unable to make social criticism, but only that a science that is indeed a respectable and creative science of social life cannot begin with problems formulated by members of the society for solving their own problems. The problems of science are not the same as the problems of people or of living.* A science of some natural phenomena, whatever they might be, must decide what its problems are for itself. It must supply constraints on the intellectual discipline it is committed to creating and developing.

Does this mean that a scientist is irresponsible or unethical because of this decision to promote the problems of his science rather than solving those of his society? Since the eighteenth century it has been the hope and promise of the institution of science, that the products of scientific inquiry will be applied to the eradication of social evils and the solution of social problems. This may indeed be the end-result of the approach we are proposing here, but that is a question whose answer evades us right now. However much we might want to see it answered affirmatively, the promise of an answer cannot be guaranteed from the start or necessarily used as an initial justification for doing scientific work.

A microbiologist or biochemist may start out with the deep conviction that he wants to eradicate cancer from the world, but he needs the tools and problems of his science on which to build any successful outcome, since conviction alone is not enough. If you take Sudnow's *Passing On* for example, you will certainly find much material that points to the inadequacies and social problems of county-run hospitals, and you could propose changes that would improve human life in them, but that is not where Sudnow started and it need not be pursued to gain what Sudnow's analysis alone has to offer as a naturalistic description of human interactions. *However, this kind of analysis could most certainly be used as a detailed blueprint for locating and correcting bad practices of organizations (i.e. bad from the humanistic point of view). The real question is: how will valid social information be used and who will use it?*

Distinguishing between Characterizing and Evaluating Deviance

Here is another example of what we mean by this distinction between characterizing and evaluating a way of life. Skid road is a well-known way of life in many big cities. One kind of activity common to this area is known as "panhandling." People who do this have traditionally been called bums. They are unemployed, are often heavy drinkers, and sometimes are serious alcoholics. They are often viewed as human wrecks, spoilage, and wasted human resources. One student made a study of the panhandlers' daily activities.[34] He situated himself in skid road and made observations of panhandlers he got to know on the street. He watched them making approaches to people, and made films of their actions and interchanges with others. The result was a highly illuminating set of findings about the nature of a panhandler's "occupation." This term is used advisedly, because a bum is supposed to be unemployed. But the study of the activity showed that they are engaged in a *form of work,* soliciting persons in the street for small change.

Panhandlers use methods for going about this work of selecting "customers" or "marks," as we might think of a person who is asked for spare change. One term used by the panhandler himself is a "hit." The approach pattern varies with the ecological conditions, with the proximate elements of interactions, and with the time of day or amount of success during a given temporal unit devoted to the activity. Panhandlers may work together and man certain locations. They may often pool their take. They are apparently concerned only with reaching a certain threshold of income for a given stretch of time during a day, beyond which they stop the activity and shift to buying things with their money.

When the films were studied very carefully, using slow motion, reverse motion, etc., the exact patterns of interaction organized by the panhandler for making a hit could be analyzed. They were broken down into sequential elements beginning with the question of identification and selection of a suitable mark, the problem of physical access to him and the approach path taken, the opening of a contact by summoning, non-spoken gestures, and the possibility of it producing a return, a "dig," from the mark.

The interchange that develops is built around the panhandler's request, e.g., "Spare a dime, bud?" It can be rejected or ignored entirely, a total rejection or nonrecognition amounting to strict refraining from sociability. Eye contact techniques were crucial to establishing a line of action. When a mark responds with words that indicate he cannot give, e.g., "Sorry, no change," etc., the panhandler invariably thanks the mark, which is a politeness rule acknowledging the mark's willingness to recognize his presence. Panhandlers recognize their own competence or skill at making an approach and will allow a competent member to take the position of solo-panhandler in a group of two or three at a particular location. These are just some of the findings that characterize the activity, stated in the most general terms.

Deviant actions can take many forms within given normal environments: children can be sanctioned by parents for acting inappropriately, adults can be treated as displaying symptoms of mental illnesses, workers can violate strikes and picket lines applying to them, crisis centers can talk to persons who call because they are suicidal, an entrapment procedure can lure a suspected homosexual into a public restroom to to commit a sexually illicit act, students can cheat during examinations, children can steal from a grocery store, and so on. These are all cases of so-called deviance, because of the treatment they would get in their normal environmental contexts.

Does this mean that deviance is only consequential if it is interactional? If persons' acts were to go unrecognized and undetected, would they still be deviant? It seems intuitively incorrect to answer yes to that question, because we know that illicit practices go on all the time, but because they go undetected does not mean they do not exist. There are many events in social life that are "negatively eventful," to use a term of Goffman's. That is, they are not normally noticed until someone breaches the normal procedure for carrying out his actions. For example, we all obey traffic lights and do not notice that there is a system of enforcements operating until we go through a red light. It is not that we are unaware of the rules we use to drive with respect to traffic lights, but we are so accustomed to the normal driving pattern of orienting to the signals, that when that pattern is broken, we find it a negatively eventful occurrence that throws the normal occurrences into sharp relief.

This being the case, it seems perfectly plain that if deviance means anything at all, it must be understood with reference to the concept of normal environment. That means, then, that we need to know how to describe a normal environment first in order to describe the kinds of normative departures that can occur within it. Another way to think about this is that the best way to observe a rule in action is to break it. Much earlier in the text you were asked to read some papers by Garfinkel. Garfinkel's "experiments" demonstrate the existence of a normal environment by principled breaching behavior. To return to a point we have made, if illegitimate activities take place in unseen or undetected ways, the deviance that occurs is a breach of legal rules, for example, but it is also constitutive of a normal environment. The notion we want to take up is that of "normal deviance," a term which is not a contradiction.

Normal Deviance

In two papers, one by Sacks[35] and the other by Sudnow,[36] you will find the notion of normal deviance explored—with respect to police procedures in dealing with suspicious persons, on the one hand, and with respect to lawyers' procedures for dealing with criminally charged persons, on the other. Both topics deal with bodies of professional persons who have methods for handling criminal behaviors relevant to their occupational work.

Consider the suspicious person problem for a moment. How does a policeman detect from among passers-by a probable criminal? Let us consider this with respect to the detection of deviant behaviors again. If a person engaged in illicit activity organizes his interactions and illicit business with an eye to preventing their being seen that way by others, then his organization of action must have built into it some careful methods of deception. He must not be giving off those signs of his behavior that would clue others into seeing it as illicit. Likewise the police, whose job it is to spot such illicitness in otherwise innocent-looking activity, must know that deception practices get built into criminal activities. The masking techniques that persons use to cover up their illegitimate activity must take on the appearances of normal and unsuspicious looking environments, otherwise the masking technique would be useless.

Take the example of a con man. *The con man is a perfect illustration of building deception practices into normal behavioral appearances.* In fact, the con man is only successful if he masters the appearances of the normal environment. He trades on others' competence to make normal interpretations of social life and relies on their taken-for-granted perspectives of everyday activities. Once he has gained the trust of others, he is in the advantageous position of doing them in without their suspicion. Criminal activity can mask itself by putting out a front of normality. You will read the extent to which this can be skillfully accomplished by pickpockets, for example, in David Maurer's book, *Whiz Mob.*[37] Sacks points out the use of "street operatives" who do normal activities as the basis for passing as legitimate persons while they engage in illegal activity, e.g., a postman could easily pass around information for an illegal activity, such as betting, without fear of detection.[38]

Just as those engaged in masking illicit activity have methods for making their actions look normal, so do policemen who must not give away their methods of detecting and combatting crime. It is obvious that if police methods were so well known as to be predictable, this knowledge could be used to undercut the practical purposes of police activity. Thus, police on patrol may randomize their movements, so that criminals cannot plan on their whereabouts at any given time of the day.

Just as police are oriented to a territory of appearances, as Sacks points out,[39] so too are everyday persons who come and go in various territories of a community. We have already mentioned skid road as one such territory where there is presumed to be much deviance, e.g., drug addiction, homosexuality, prostitution, alcoholism, residential instability, unemployment and poverty, panhandling, etc. Early sociological studies of crime and social "disorganization"[40]—as they were called (there is actually considerable organization to any social territory)—focused on ecological areas of large cities. They pointed to the relation between given territories, like skid road, and criminal and deviant behavior.

Persons who live and work in skid road orient to common-sense conceptions of the daily life activities and interactions that transpire there. For example, public agencies, such as the police department, the coroner's office, the fire department, the social welfare department, etc., have typifications about the organization of social life on skid road, and these typifications enter into their occupational routines when they deal with members of skid road. What are these conceptions of normal deviance on skid road? How do they enter into the coroner's procedures for deciding about the cause of death, for example, or the policeman's procedures for making up official reports? The study of these procedures in action would tell us much about how these agencies construct their facts and compile their statistics.

The issue of statistics of deviance can be mentioned briefly here.[41] The main point is that statistics are methodically produced by agencies who have special interests in keeping records of actions and activities relevant to their agencies' practical purposes. Behind every statistic stands an unexplicated set of human interactions that permitted, in various sequentially organized ways, the progressive generation of some statistics. The construction of statistical measures of one or another crime, for example, is itself a social activity, and its objective appearance as a number or percentage figure should not obscure that basic fact of social statistical life. What becomes an event in a policeman's report is based on an actual encounter with a person, and the way in which that encounter is coded can become the basis for future uses of the report in other statistical summaries that compile the facts of such reports. It is, of course, impossible to recover these original generative features of statistics when reading them in national compilations, for example. Cicourel explores this issue in detail on the subject of juvenile delinquency rates in *The Social Organization of Juvenile Justice.*[42]

Returning to skid road, Bittner examines the typification of police who work in that area and what methods they use to keep the peace in that territory.[43] Bittner's report outlines the mundane activities of police in which no charges of criminal behavior nor any arrests are made. The legal code cannot be employed as a guide to making decisions about peace-keeping and Bittner outlines some of the "demand conditions" for peace-keeping activity that do not involve invoking the penal code. One of them pertains to police duties involving persons who are viewed as not fully accountable for their actions, such as minors, mentally ill persons, and those who occupy the status of outcasts, although this last type of person is not explicitly acknowledged as such by police. Such persons usually include ghetto residents, known criminals, vagabonds, etc. These persons, in policemen's eyes, necessitate special handling and procedures in the line of their peace-keeping duties. Bittner traces out the practices of peace-keeping, which include the policeman's organized common-sense perspectives on the locale and its inhabitants, such perspectives becoming the basis for interactional events between police and skid road residents. For example, the policeman develops a rich body of particularized knowledge about the territory. It becomes the source material for ascribing characteristics, standard forms of behavior, typical motives, etc., of skid road activity and interaction.

In a similar manner, the lawyers working in the public defender's office in California, as reported by Sudnow,[44] use a body of recipes and standardized lore for the interpretation of criminal types and criminal actions. Once again, the point is made clear that to understand the workings and procedures of the public defender—his initial interview with the defendant, the preliminary hearing, and finally the actual trial—one cannot rely on the rules of the penal code for an explanation of the social characteristics of this legal activity. Because there is a social code, as well. It determines how the reduction of a guilty plea is made from a greater to a lesser offense, the lesser offense bringing the defendant a lighter sentence in exchange for pleading guilty.

This "deal" by the public defender and the district attorney to reduce the charge for the guilty party is a social as much as a legal form of arrangement. How the reduction is actually made in each case is procedurally accomplished not by reference to legal statutes, but by reference to what Sudnow calls "normal crimes." Crimes or types of criminal offenses are normal for given places and times and types of offenders. The focus of activity is not on particular individuals but on offense types. Those features attributed to offenders and offenses are often without any import for the statutory conception of a crime. There is a community-specific character to the features of offense types and, correlatively, offenses are ecologically specified and attended to as normal for particular locales within which they occur. Thus, while for society's members such criminal types may be regarded as deviant individuals, for those who deal with them on a routine, occupational, and legal-administrative basis, they constitute normal criminal activity.

These studies we have briefly noted all focus on the methodical or procedural basis for routine interactional events in specific settings. Each takes a well-known area of sociological interest—juvenile delinquency (Cicourel describes police-juvenile encounters on the street, in the station house, during interrogations, etc.), skid road life, police activity, criminal procedures and the administration of justice, the workings of the court. Each tries to show how the activities are organized interactional events on the part of the participants. The material is substantively within the field of deviance, but it is also within the areas of occupational routines, social control, urban sociology, criminology, and so forth. *The point is, that it is not as important to be definitive about the substantive placement of a study of an aspect of social life as it is to be clear about how a given set of social arrangements is methodically organized into a daily life world by its normal participants.* In none of these studies do the authors begin with a decision to treat their material for its socially important aspects. They do not call for the improvement of the social activities they describe, whatever they might personally feel or desire about changes in those social arrangements they detail.

More basically, what these studies actually focus on is not an orthodox substantive label to give their work some place in the discipline's intellectual terrain, but on the concept of social organization which is basic to the study of any social phenomena. Here, we might recall the conception of social organization, as Garfinkel defines it:

> ... the term "an organization" is an abbreviation of the full term "an organization of social actions." The term "organization" does not itself designate a palpable phenomenon. It refers instead to a related set of *ideas* that a sociologist invokes to aid him in collecting his thoughts about the ways in which patterns of social actions are related. His statements about social organization describe the *territory* within which the actions occur; the *number* of persons who occupy that territory; the characteristics of these *persons,* like age, sex, biographies, occupation, annual income, and character structure. He tells how these persons are *socially related* to each other, for the talks of husbands and wives, of bridge partners, of cops and robbers. He describes their *activities,* and the ways they achieve social *access* to each other. And like a grand theme either explicitly announced or implicitly assumed, he describes the rules that specify for the actor the use of the area, the number of persons who should be in it, the nature of activity, purpose, and feeling allowed, the approved and disapproved means of entrance and exit from affiliative relationships with the persons there.[45]

This definition is taken from Garfinkel's earliest writings (1956) and must be qualified in his own terms as they are expressed in his papers in *Studies in Ethnomethodology.* What the above definition points to is the nature of the sociologist's abstraction called "organization," and as such it is indeed a set of ideas. But what the definition does not make clear, and this is vital to Garfinkel's own work, is that there are indeed palpable references to the empirical world of social actions which the concept is used to describe, and these palpable references are the methodical procedures that everyday persons employ when they organize their activities into structurally meaningful units of action. In other words, the definition almost appears to be saying that the concept of organization is the sociologist's invention, but in fact, *it is not a concept or a phenomenon that originates with the sociologist, but with the social participants of everyday life who take it that their main task in practical living is to organize their daily lives around other persons, activities, territories, etc.* The job of the sociologist, as we have proposed in this text, is to make formal analytic descriptions of the organizationally constituted events of human activity.

Conclusions

How do the studies we have cited meet with the stipulations we have laid out in making formal interactional descriptions? Are they formal descriptions in the sense that we have proposed? Insofar as they focus on the way participants of the activity and setting organize their interactions by means of methodical or procedural orientations to their practical involvements, the studies are in accord with our discussions. They make considerable use of conversational materials gathered in field work, and show us by illustrations what comments were made and how these comments are analytic resources for their analytic conclusions.

The aim of these studies is to understand aspects and processes of organizational arrangements that cover a very broad range of routine interactions. Their characterizations are made to encompass very large streams and segments of activity that deal with the most crucial practical concerns of the persons involved. In this sense Cicourel's, Sudnow's, and Bittner's papers are attempting to study a whole process, or chain, of actions, motives, routine events, social accomplishments, etc. One could easily break into that chain at any point and ask detailed questions about the interactional formalities of interchanges organized by participants. For example, what does a typical encounter between a policeman and a resident of skid road consist of, such that the particularized knowledge he has, or is at that moment gaining, enters into the construction of the encounter, to bring it off this or that sort of procedural way?

It seems to be true, in closing this discussion of deviant behavior, that the concept of deviance is so intimately linked to normal interactional environments and properties that it is not feasible to separate it into a subdiscipline of its own—save the possibility of studying those organized arrangements whose practical task consists mainly of sanctioning and controlling those who breach the legal and moral rules of the culture.

Keeping in mind the vital point that agencies set up for these purposes are not merely receiving points for those who commit illicit or immoral acts, but are actively involved in the identification and treatment of those who would be defined as deviants in the society, as such, these agencies of social control contribute to the meaning of deviance by supplying criteria for recognizing and judging it, or, in other words, producing socially pre- and proscribed understandings of what deviance actually is. But insofar as *any* departure from conventional procedures are opportunities for the attribution of deviant behavior, this would include all socially situated behaviors, and would require nothing less than a complete understanding of the interactional foundations of the culture in all its workings.

4. Social Stratification

The idea that a society is stratified is a very ancient one. It is a notion based on the common-sense perception of social differences that exist among cultural populations and which serve to align their members into various groupings in cooperative and contrastive ways. The study of social stratification has traditionally been oriented to what we might think of as social differences in income and wealth, class and race. The fundamental distinction between leaderships and their followings, or underlings, has been a source of continual thinking about human hierarchical arrangements and the issues of power and justice inherent in ruling group phenomena. Perhaps the most influential thinker in the classic tradition of these issues of social stratification was Karl Marx.[46] His analysis of class interests, power, and competition has, of course, been the basis for a vast amount of thinking and writing, and for social actions along political lines, as well.

Today, issues of class have become interested not so much in traditional Marxian interpretations as in the functional or disfunctional relations between classes of persons who differentially contribute to the production, distribution, and consumption of goods and services in a society. The study of human rights, civil rights, and equality of opportunity, has focused especially in recent years on lower, or so-called declassed persons, e.g., "the invisible poor," as Dwight MacDonald referred to the one-quarter of the population of the United States that lives in substandard conditions (conditions as defined by economists in the federal government). The history and development of the social position of American Blacks[47] has also become a very major area of interest in studies of stratification, and along with Blacks, other minority groups that are in a similar socially and economically deprived position. Questions of human welfare and a guaranteed national income for deprived persons have been raised by critics and analysts of these problems.

We are glossing over these issues, quite obviously, and only suggesting the highlights of the field called social stratification. To take them up in terms of the approaches and conceptions used by sociologists who analyze these issues would take us far afield from the point of view of this course, for the simple reason that analyses in this area are invariably preoccupied with formulating problems that are considered for their social importance—because of their traditional origin in political and social theory, and because they are invariably directed to studying global, institutional and historical phenomena, rather than interactional events.

For example, one concept is that of social mobility. How do persons born into one class or one set of socioeconomic conditions move into different class positions during their lives? If a class system is presumably very tightly structured, like that of a traditional caste system where movement from one caste to another was virtually impossible, how can mobility be achieved? Then, too, mobility can be downwards as well as upwards. Studies of the characteristics of mobility, such as income, occupation, education, generation, sex, etc., have been made in an attempt to see how the global process works.[48] Race is one characteristic that suggests mobility is always restricted on the basis of racial ancestry, and in some cases, e.g., the American Black, severely so. Recent trends in the political life of Blacks, show a powerful and militant attempt to organize activities designed to overcome this barrier to social acceptability, as measured in terms of social and economic opportunities of equality.

Now, these are well-developed issues within their own frames of reference and we could not add anything new to them in that sociological context. How then can we make some news about the facts of socially stratified human groupings?

Interactional Issues in a Global Substantive Area

The first point we want to take up pertains to the interactional foundations for these alleged facts about social structure. Recalling the conception we have of social organization, how do the members of a society—our own culture—orient to socially stratified behavior and activity? Is the notion of social stratification the conceptual invention of sociologists or political theorists, who define human arrangements with the points of view the members themselves have in mind? To what do the conceptual notions of stratification correspond as empirical occurrences in the everyday world? For instance, do members orient to class identifications and organize their daily life interactions with the guidance of that orientation? Are persons orienting to their own mobility from one type of occupation to another, from one level of income to another, or from one residential area to another? Do such orientations, if they exist, form the basis for daily decisions about planful activities? Can we observe the workings of principles of stratified social organization?

Do persons align themselves with others or do they membership themselves into groupings that are based on the alleged characteristics of social stratification? First of all, are all groupings, whatever their nature, arranged into some stratified positions with respect to other groupings? The idea of stratification is apparently applicable only to groupings that form, as the concept implies, strata. This means that there is an order of relative hierarchical positions for each stratum. For example, the ranking of persons in work organizations into super- and sub-ordinate positions, where all members live by an understood agreement to honor the relative ranking arrangement, comprises a stratified system. A geological analogy is—the strata or layers of mineral material one over the other comprise an arrangement which lends itself to a natural order of super-subordinate relative positioning. The key to the phenomenon is its recognized ordering or ranking principles among social positions and relationships. An illustration was the Barundi caste ranking system that Albert reported about (see chapter 5).

If ranking is the central feature of stratified behavior, then how can it be accounted for, under what circumstances does ranking become a principle of social organization? First off, we must insist on the subjectivity of the principle, that is, on the way it is incorporated into orientations to the actions of others and into mutually constructed activities. This is contrasted to the traditional notion of objective principles of organization which presume the existence of social distinctions without checking to see whether those distinctions, e.g., class, are meaningful orientations for action for those to whom they presumably apply.

That is, a traditional approach to the problem of stratification has been to select certain social characteristics of persons and treat them as indicators of class position. For example, you select a sample of persons in the society and inquire whether they earn X amount of dollars, whether they had X number of years of schooling, where they reside, what kind of a job they have, and so forth. You may also inquire, by asking pointed questions, about the prestige of the occupational positions available in the society, with the aim of getting persons to show a ranked preference of the same. You survey their attitudes, say, on politics, religion, or whatever, and inquire about the kinds of associations they make with others in life, and so on. But, and this is our main point here, the criteria for bunching persons into class positions is already decided by the indicator questions on income, residence, occupation, etc. The sociologist may wish to compare the class position of persons decided in this way, with the way they rank themselves or others into classes or prestigious occupations, when asked to do so. With the objective indicators of class position at hand, you are able to compare it to their own class estimation of themselves to see what the discrepancy is, and perhaps show how their personal opinion or attitudes are out of phase with their "actual" class status in society.

One of the criticisms of this kind of approach is that persons come to be regarded as "cultural dopes,"[49] to use Garfinkel's phrase, since they are looked upon as poor scientists of their own society, because they are not aware of the objective conditions of their socially stratified lives. Similar in one sense to a Marxian type of position, sociologists are intellectuals who prove to be "smarter" than the members of the society and who can tell them what class determinations actually order their everyday lives without their knowing it. Whether or not they assume a Marxist position, sociologists who adopt this stance are claiming that members of society do not perceive the objective conditions determining social-economic life because of an ideological inability to see them.

The previous paragraphs are a considerably oversimplified version of modern sociological survey approaches based on traditional notions of the meaning of the concept "class." Yet, the argument has a kernel of truth in it. *This boils down to one basic issue on which our argument stands or falls: Can we validly construct a concept of social class, using traditional indicators of the sort we noted, without first studying the ordering principles that are interactionally founded in persons' everyday orientations to social rank?* This, of course, requires the supposition of social rank. It also requires some rethinking of the notion of the concept of social action. To recall the idea you came across in reading Blumer earlier in the text, can we validly talk about principles of social organization, interactionally conceived, without respect to what Blumer has termed "acting units" of persons? Do members of our society organize their activity on the basis of abstract concepts of social membership or on the basis of concrete acting units of social membership? For example, do all "blue collar workers" form an acting unit of members? Are all Blacks uniformly tied together into a class of persons who act with a uniform orientation to that group classification, and does the so-called middle class constitute some real grouping of society's members, real in the sense that it has an internal organization to act as a unit of persons?

Conceptualizing "Race" and "Class" in Terms of Categorization Activity

It would appear that these questions cannot be satisfactorily answered without recourse to the empirical facts of membership categorization practices in the culture. When we speak of a member of the culture as orienting to a category of social membership, we mean that from among many such classifications that could be assigned to him, only those from among a coherent family of categories is operative for a particular social occasion or situation. Now he is a father, and now again he is a blue-collar worker. The selections and decisional procedures for these concrete applications constitute organizing principles for his activities at hand; that is, they must always be interactionally mobilized, many of the possible categories of application being inert and simply irrelevant for the occasion. Now, what has this to do with our discussion of class as a concept, and ranking as a social phenomenon?

To study the arena of everyday social interactions by approaching it with a prior theoretical stencil or blueprint for the organization of those interactions, is to approach it by using a theory of how it works in order to show the value of the theory as an explanatory device. *But what is needed is an investigation of the organizing principles of persons' cultural lives, not an investigation of the organizing principles of a theory of their cultural lives.* To use Garfinkel's notion of "theoretical representation,"[50] studies in social class, perhaps more than other studies, are most guilty of committing the fallacy of theoretical representation. This is the error of constructing a theory of social organization without consulting the actor's methods for organizing his own behavior with respect to others.

Where class is concerned, as with any abstract construct, the normal task of a sociologist is to decide which social characteristic applies to persons he lumps together into this or that socioeconomic class. However, the sociologist's lumping of people into various socioeconomic categories of membership tells us very little about the structure and process of everyday life. *Rather, it is the lumping that everyday partici-*

pants do that tells us that.[51] Using common sense, we can entertain the idea that this or that category is applicable to this or that person in society and we can theoretically posit social groupings on the basis of common-sense theorizing. But what we want to discover, so as to come out with news about society's workings, is precisely how members decide for themselves what social categories of membership they are in at any interactional moment in their daily intercourse. How do they honor these assignations they make or that others make of them? That is what social competence involves: the actor's methods for deciding, honoring, and enforcing social characteristics that apply to the participants at hand.

Thus, if we see a man driving a car and the make of the car is a Cadillac, for example, then it is not "that he is driving a car of this make because he is a Black" which ought to be our inference as sociologists. *Given that persons see a Cadillac, they look to that social characteristic of the driver that presents itself to them as a socially relevant fact about driving Cadillacs.* We then have to ask the simple question: *How is it they see a Black and not a man in a black suit or a young man, etc., driving that Cadillac?* Why is that categorization more relevant for a viewer than the others? For us to say, he is driving the car *because* he is a Black is to jump or by-pass the central issue: Why is it you describe him as a Black driver?

It is the common-sense perspective persons use that warrants their saying he is driving the Cadillac *because* he is a Black. *It ought not to be the sociologist's perspective.* What this has led to is a formulation of sociological problems that seeks to check out whether in fact 1) persons have the opinion that more Blacks drive Cadillacs, and 2) whether in actual fact proportionately more Blacks do drive Cadillacs. These problems, however, are actually strange sociological formulations, because they treat common-sense reasoning as bad science and therefore search out its truth or falsehood, that is, as scientifically correct or incorrect judgments. Why should we ever treat common sense as bad science or as in need of being scientifically assessed? To prove that social and racial prejudice exists we do not have to show that social members are bad scientists. *We have to show how prejudice is interactionally achieved in categorizing activity designed for that purpose.*

To consider class, then, would mean to consider what principles of common sense members of our culture use when treating others around them—and themselves vis-à-vis those others—with respect to class categories, as they conceive of those categorical possibilities. Behind the traditional categories of membership that sociologists use to indicate class position stand interactions or actual behaviors that presumably have class relevance. For example, if high education is allegedly a characteristic of higher class position, then presumably the fact of one's higher education must behaviorally or interactionally display and provide stable orientations to class categorizations. Do persons with a college education, for instance, therefore categorically treat higher education as a class-relevant feature in their mutual activity with others? If a man is reported as being of working-class background is that a reference to his education or his income or any such characteristics, or might it refer to the fact that he hangs out in a longshoremen's beer parlor in his spare hours—which is not an indicator in an abstract concept but a palpable natural fact of life that provides persons with the methodical means of saying, so-and-so is working-class because he hangs out in a place where it is known that longshoremen often congregate.

And when members of that labor union get together they all orient to their common membership in that group, despite any topic they might talk about, and it provides a set of social categories that can be invoked at any appropriate point in their interactions. But they may order their beer, exchange greetings, talk about their wives, etc., not unlike others in ordinary conversations. But when a strike vote is called, all union members are co-membershipped into that activity as an acting unit of persons. Whether one would want to call all that behavior lower class or lower-middle class or working class, because they all have about the same education, income, residence locations, etc., does not seem very helpful to understanding these behaviors.

To summarize the previous points, we find that sociologists have traditionally asserted a cluster of social categories as omnirelevant for so-called social class behavior, at the one end, and at the other extreme, they have tried to characterize life styles of social classes. But between these two poles, there exists a whole world of identification techniques and behaviors that must be consulted in the natural activities of members themselves. It may actually turn out that the concept of class has to be either discarded or reserved for political rhetoric, or at the very most, reserved for a common-sense shorthand method of referring to vast collections of persons who are so categorized for the convenience of a theoretical argument, and categorized from without their own interactional patterns of cultural life. The latter would not satisfy the requirements of empirical validity, however.

The basic concepts for the processes of social stratification are empirically very problematic. Such concepts as power, influence, prestige,

Social Class. How is the concept of social class tied to concrete settings and their inhabitants' daily life patterns? (photo by William Darrough.)

control, etc., are only understandable, it would seem, by reference to the realm of interaction. For example, the following set of exchanges, found in an article in the *New York Times Magazine,* are by a Black doctor who reports his experience on a street in the United States:

"What's your name, boy?" the policeman asked . . .

"Dr. Poussaint. I'm a physician . . ."

"What's your first name, boy?"

"Alvin."[52]

A common-sense accounting of the above might be: the scene is the deep South and the custom of policemen is to address Black men with "boy" because of racial discrimination. By choosing to call all Blacks "boy," regardless of any other characteristics they display, one enforces a local policy of racism. This is an interactional event and it displays the properties of social ranking. Now, what kind of interactional ranking is taking place? How is a principle of super-subordination at work here? The policeman monitors the appearance of the man, and he chooses to select one social category in addressing him on the basis of that perceived category—from the MCD "Race." The address term "boy" is a ranking term from among other terms that could be used to rank the addressed person.

One rule for ranking persons might be:[53] Select a category which inappropriately ranks them, from a set of possible ranking terms which might apply to them, because it is lower in rank than what they appear to be. This would be a *downgrading* ranking procedure. For example, if a boy is acting inappropriately you might say, "Stop acting like a baby," where baby is lower in a set of applicable categories than the one by which he normally gets treated. *One can interactionally do subordinations by this procedure.* One can see instances of interaction in which a person shows another that he has been mistreated, by being downgraded, by responding to an overly superior command with, "Okay, boss," where in that activity of working with another, receiving his directions, etc., there is a possible set of ranked categories of membership, "boss" being the top rank.

In the street scene reported by the Black doctor, the policeman was ranking according to race categories, but what made this particularly poignant was his enforcement of that ranking procedure after being offered an alternative category that was contrastively very high with respect to both man-boy, and policeman-doctor ranking pairs. The convention is to accord deference to the holder of titles like "doctor," particularly physicians. To maintain the local convention of downgrading

Blacks by using "boy" when addressing the holder of the title "doctor" is to accomplish a double insult to the recognition of a social identity. It is a way of saying that even normally highly honored characteristics are irrelevant qualifications where incumbents of the perceived racial category, Negro, are concerned.

In this sense, the category Negro is a disqualifying or discrediting characteristic calling for principles of subordination on the part of the policeman, who speaks as a white man in a position of social power.* One could look at this incident and come away with the conclusion that the policeman is doing what he does in order to maintain or perpetuate a system of social injustice; that is, he is enforcing a stratification system where Whites are high and Blacks are low in the hierarchy. But one might also look at the way the interactional events are a system of internal enforcements of their own, not unrelated to a political system of racial injustice, of course, but a system of internally regulated interactions that generate social structural realities on the spot.

That is, by their mutual encounter they construct a presentation of themselves which methodically controls the cultural apparatus that provides each participant with a way of treating the other as this or that kind of social member. For example, the Black did not correct the policeman after his second use of "boy." He gave him his first name, which presumably is for the record as far as the policeman is concerned. He might have attempted a correction with "I would prefer to be addressed as 'doctor,' if you don't mind," for example. But the interactional consequences of this might be increased downgrading on the part of the policeman.

We have to ask what other kinds of ranking procedures take place and involve the use of principles of super-subordination. They would presumably constitute stratified behaviors with recognizable and decomposable interactional structures.

We might look at work settings and how they get activities organized around stratified interactions, as when certain categories of persons are especially entitled or privileged to give order and directions to others, and also have the right to enforce rules of organization for the activity, including sanctioning powers. The existence of authority in human activities is something that needs rethinking, because conventional studies have stressed the reliance on the concept of social status in understanding the meaning of authority. But it is not a status, as such, but the social relation-

*Recognizing this, dark-skinned persons have recategorized themselves from Negro to Black, thus casting off the oppressive category historically imposed upon them and replacing it with one of their own choosing, one that now stands as self-crediting.

ships that persons have, whereby a person in one categorical relation to another can call for certain behaviors from others, and get that reciprocal action legitimately.

One might think offhand that a hospital surgeon has more power and authority than a staff nurse, yet, the basis for his authority over the nurse may be restricted in various ways and may be subject to numerous constraints and obligations to the work schedules and requirements of nurses. Authority and power may take many different interactional forms, so to speak. When a mother puts her foot down to her child, she is exerting authority, but her son may have considerable power over her in getting her to do things for him the way he expects them to be done, e.g., certain eating or dressing routines. It is probably correct to say that naked or brute power is the rare case in human interactions. Again, the power and authority of a political system, say, may be exerted in a multitude of ways in daily interactional circumstances. *To see it working, one needs to undertake a detailed inspection of these interactions and on the basis of this inspection, one may go on to say something more rigorous and useful, more newsworthy about social stratificational systems in the large.*

In actual fact, there would appear to be as many classes involved in the use of power and authority, and in the daily achievement of social rank, as there are stable collections of membership categories. The conventional division into lower, middle, and upper class would seem to be entirely inadequate to account for the interactional facts of everyday life where power, authority, rank, and social differentia are involved.

Notes

[1] Leonard Broom and Philip Selznick, eds., *Sociology: A Text with Adapted Readings* (New York: Harper & Row, 1963).

[2] Talcott Parsons and Robert Bales, *Family, Socialization and Interaction Process* (New York: Free Press, 1955).

[3] I have done this exercise with students, using natural conversations in which the utterances have been written on individual slips of paper and disordered, and then handed to the students who are asked to order them back together; the resulting sequences were put on the board and justified, and finally compared to the original sequence. I got this idea from Harvey Sacks's discussions on disorderability and nondisorderability in conversational sequences.

[4] This section condenses material and ideas I have presented elsewhere plus some new considerations. See Speier, "The Child as Conversationalist: Some Cultural Contact Features of Conversational Interactions Between Adults and Children," presented at the Meetings of the Canadian Anthropological and Sociological Association, St. John's, Newfoundland, 1971. This paper is to appear in Roy Turner, ed., *Socialization: The Acquisition of Membership* (New York: Basic Books, forthcoming).

[5]Kurt H. Wolff, transl. and ed., *The Sociology of George Simmel* (New York: Free Press, 1950).

[6]Alex Inkeles, "Society, Social Structure, and Child Socialization," in John Clausen, ed., *Socialization and Society* (Boston: Little, Brown, 1968), pp. 76-77. Italics added.

[7]Ibid.

[8]It may be disputed that this is indeed a fact, and perhaps it can be regarded as only a supposition that I have adopted to explore the possibility of its existence. Much has been collected by students of children's lore and games over the years to substantiate this claim, however. (See Notes 9 and 10). The thrust of my argument that we treat children's behavior as cultural rather than as an incompleted and poorer version of adult cultural forms of behavior was initiated by my hearing a taped lecture delivered by Harvey Sacks at the "Language, Society, and the Child" lectures and workshops that I participated in the summer of 1968 at the University of California at Berkeley. Some of the ideas in the lecture that I incorporate into this discussion are sufficiently provocative to overhaul the basic orientations thus far used by researchers in socialization and to provide a powerful impetus to strike out in an entirely new direction.

[9]Iona and Peter Opie, *Children's Games in Street and Playground* (London: Oxford University Press, 1969).

[10]Iona and Peter Opie, *The Lore and Language of School Children* (Oxford: Clarendon Press, 1959).

[11]Jean Piaget, *The Moral Judgment of the Child* (New York: Free Press, 1948).

[12]See note 8, this chapter.

[13]Ibid.

[14]See note 6, chapter 5.

[15]I borrow this term from Egon Bittner, "The Police on Skid-Row: A Study of Peace Keeping," *American Sociological Review* 32: 1967, 699-715, and use it to mean the established and routine constraints that confront the work of parents in their daily management of children and that involve their achievement of competent practices in so doing.

[16]The recent explosion of interest in classrooms and alternative learning environments has led to numerous inquiries and studies which are change-oriented. It appears that out of this evaluative and often ideological orientation there is a new appreciation for describing classroom environments, if only to document the rationale behind arguments for change. See for example Charles Silberman, *Crisis in the Classroom* (New York: Random House, 1970) and John Holt, *How Children Learn* (New York: Pitman, 1969). Yet there still are very few interactional analyses and ethnographic descriptions of classroom behaviors that illuminate the kinds of problems discussed in this chapter. See Robert Mackay, *The Acquisition of Membership in First Grade Classrooms*, Unpublished Master's Thesis, Department of Anthropology and Sociology, University of British Columbia, 1967.

[17]Harvey Sacks, "On Some Formal Properties of Children's Games," Unpublished manuscript, August 27, 1965.

[18]Edmund H. Volkart, ed., *Social Behavior and Personality, Contributions of W.I. Thomas to Theory and Social Research* (New York: Social Science Research Council, 1951).

[19]Sacks, "Search for Help."

[20]Chester Barnard, *The Functions of the Executive* (Cambridge, Mass.: Harvard University Press, 1938).

21 B.B. Gardner and D.G. Moore, *Human Relations in Industry* (Chicago: Irwin, 1950).

22 Melville Dalton, *Men Who Manage* (New York, Wiley, 1959).

23 For information on professional theories and ideologies in practice see Anselm Strauss et al., *Psychiatric Ideologies and Institutions* (New York: Free Press, 1964). Also see the earlier volume on the training of medical professionals, Howard S. Becker et al., *Boys in White* (Chicago: University of Chicago Press, 1961).

24 S. Schulman, "Basic Functional Roles in Nursing: Mother Surrogate and Healer," in E. Gartly Jaco, *Patients, Physicians and Illness* (New York: Free Press, 1958).

25 See Don Zimmerman, "The Practicalities of Rule Use," in Douglas, *Everyday Life,* pp. 221-238 for a general treatment of a bureaucratic public assistance organization in terms of reception procedures of applicants for assistance. Zimmerman is concerned chiefly with the practices involved in "the operational meaning and situational relevance of policies and procedures for ongoing, everyday organizational activities" in the setting. His study is suggestive of ways for doing similar analysis into other areas of a public welfare organization.

26 Sudnow, *Passing On.* While there are many studies of hospital organization, e.g., E. Mumford and J.K. Skipper, Jr.'s *Sociology in Hospital Care* (New York: Harper & Row, 1967), there are very few observational reports of routine interactions on the wards. In this regard Goffman's *Asylums* (New York: Doubleday Anchor, 1961) is very useful as a study of the interactional features of hospital institutions, especially the essay on total institutions, those which are normally divided between those who manage and those who are managed, e.g., staff and inmates.

27 See, among the numerous readers and studies available on deviance, Earl Rubington and Martin S. Weinberg, eds., *Deviance, The Interactionist Perspective* (New York: Macmillan, 1968); Howard S. Becker, *Outsiders: Studies in the Sociology of Deviance* (New York: Free Press, 1963); R. Quinney, *The Social Reality of Crime* (Boston: Little, Brown, 1970); Edwin M. Lemert, *Social Pathology* (New York: McGraw-Hill, 1951); Jack P. Gibbs, "Conceptions of Deviant Behavior: The Old and the New," *Pacific Sociological Review* 9 (Spring, 1966): 9-14.

28 Understanding the framework of a normal environment is an analytic prerequisite for postulating and observing deviant practices. This is the central orientation that ethnomethodological researchers have adopted when addressing the topic of deviance. The normal environment is construed to mean the properties of perception at work in members recognizing and treating the objects of the environment for their interactional consequences. In this sense "normal" does not refer to a probabilistic or statistical notion of the expectancies of an event, but to common-sense usages of "normal" in practical discourse and routine interactions among those who experience the environment. See Garfinkel, *Ethnomethodology,* and Aaron Cicourel, *Method and Measurement.* In particular see Cicourel's application of the notion of deviance vis-à-vis the normal environment in *The Social Organization of Juvenile Justice* (New York: John Wiley, 1968).

29 Recall Durkheim's treatment of the topic of suicide, in *Suicide,* pp. 41-46. (See chapter 1 of this text).

30 See Carl Werthman, "Delinquents in Schools: A Test for the Legitimacy of Authority," *Berkeley Journal of Sociology* VIII, 1963, 39-60.

31 On this approach to the subject see James H. Bryan, "Apprenticeships in Prostitution," *Social Problems* 12, No. 3 (Winter 1965): pp. 287-297.

[32] For a general discussion with accompanying references and readings in the area of drug use see William A. Rushing, ed., *Deviant Behavior and Social Process* (Chicago: Rand McNally, 1969), pp. 328-358; I do not know of many participant studies of drug user's settings. I am grateful for the opportunity to have advised Kenneth Stoddart in his study of a local drug setting, a cafe in Vancouver, in which he situated himself as a field worker and observed many drug transactions and their surrounding social events, reported in his unpublished Master's Thesis, Department of Anthropology and Sociology, University of British Columbia. Additional recent studies of drugs are: Allen Geller and Maxwell Boas, *The Drug Beat* (New York: McGraw-Hill Paperbacks, 1971); David "Language, Society, and the Child" lectures and workshops that I participated in York: New American Library, Signet Books, 1968).

[33] We are proposing that this approach is the only fruitful one if the task deemed relevant is doing a scientifically respectable sociology. By respectable we mean nothing snobbish or elitist, only that science must build its theories and applications on a firm descriptive foundation of empirical particulars. There is nothing that prevents a sound descriptive body of knowledge from being used to effectuate social change (as well as it might also be abused to make undesirable changes or to prevent desirable changes).

Some might argue that one does not actually need science to make a moral change in society, and that scientific application to change-oriented policy-making is politically unnecessary. Without taking up the various lines of argument here, in defense of the political relevance of the approach we are offering there is every reason to believe that detailed knowledge of how a social setting is organized can be used by persons or groups committed to programs of change in such a manner that their intelligent appraisal of social conditions promotes their ethical interests in improving these conditions for the members of the setting living in those conditions. Moreover, such finely grained knowledge could allow reformists to precisely locate sources of problems in a setting and provide a rational basis for devising strategies to make effective changes.

Expressions of dissatisfaction and moral outrage, no matter how strongly registered or recognized, can never be a substitute for planful action intended to replace existing conditions. To combat the abusive use of power in human organizations, for example, one must know more than the existence of power and its use by particular individuals. One must know how power is used in a whole variety of interactional circumstances and human relationships; one must be able to articulate the consciousness of power as social activity, i.e., its treatment, recognition, and consequences.

[34] I am grateful to Alan Newsome for sharing his film footage on panhandlers' activity gathered for a class project on Vancouver's skid road. He filmed sequences of sidewalk activity in order to reveal the formal characteristics of an activity that is financially crucial to some members of this locale. His footage uncovers the procedural basis for social contacts between panhandlers and pedestrians. On the social life of skid road alcoholics see Jacqueline Wiseman, *Stations of the Lost: The Treatment of Skid Row Alcoholics* (Englewood Cliffs, N.J.: Prentice-Hall, 1970).

[35] Harvey Sacks, "Methods in Use for the Production of a Social Order: A Method for Warrantably Inferring Moral Character," unpublished manuscript, nd. Also Sacks, "Notes on Police Assessment of Moral Character," in David Sudnow, ed., *Social Interaction,* forthcoming.

[36] Sudnow, "Normal Crimes: Sociological Features of the Penal Code in a Public Defender Office," *Social Problems* 12 (Winter 1965): pp. 255-276.

37David Maurer, *Whiz Mob* (New Haven: College and University Press, 1964).

38Sacks, "Methods in Use."

39Ibid. On the notion of normal appearances and its relation to territorial behavior, see Goffman, *Relations in Public,* pp. 238-333.

40For an analysis of the relation of criminal behavior to the forms of association in group life as a problem in studying the causes of crime see Donald R. Cressey, "Epidemiology and Individual Conduct," in Donald R. Cressey and David A. Ward, eds., *Delinquency, Crime, and Social Process* (New York: Harper and Row, 1969), pp. 557-577. In the same volume see the various papers bearing on this topic, pp. 244-556. Also for a critical approach to the main theoretical orientations expressed in these papers see Quinney, *Social Reality of Crime,* pp. 207-233.

41See John Kitsuse and Aaron Cicourel, "A Note on the Uses of Official Statistics," *Social Problems* 11 (Fall 1963): pp. 131-139.

42Cicourel, *Social Organization,* pp. 22-110.

43Bittner, "Police on Skid-Row."

44Sudnow, "Normal Crimes."

45Garfinkel, "Some Sociological Concepts and Methods for Psychiatrists," *Psychiatric Research Reports* 6 (October 1956): pp. 181-195.

46There have been many books written on Marx from varying political viewpoints. A good introduction is T. B. Bottomore, transl. and ed., *Karl Marx, Selected Writings in Sociology and Social Philosophy* (New York: McGraw-Hill, 1964). Also see C. Wright Mills, *Images of Man* (New York: Braziller, 1960) and H. Stuart Hughes, *Consciousness and Society* (New York: Random House, Vintage Books, 1961), pp. 67-104. For a treatment that deals explicitly with Marx's writings in terms of social class, see Bendix and Lipset, "Karl Marx's Theory of Social Classes" in Reinhard Bendix and Seymour Martin Lipset, eds., *Class, Status, and Power,* 2d ed. (New York: Free Press, 1966).

47There are numerous books on the subject of American Blacks. One type of recent book to appear is the autobiographical account of life in the Black ghetto. See for example Claude Brown, *Manchild in the Promised Land* (New York: Macmillan, 1964). A very good reader that deals with the educational problems and aspects of racial differentiation and discrimination for Blacks, and one that has an excellent bibliography of studies on Blacks, is Meyer Weinberg, *Integrated Education* (Beverly Hills, Calif.: The Glencoe Press, 1968). The material in this volume has been selected from the journal *Integrated Education.* Other books include, Jewel Bellush and Stephen M. David, eds., *Race and Politics in New York City* (New York: Praeger, 1971); Henry Allen Bullock, *A History of Negro Education in the South* (New York: Praeger, 1970); Warren D. TenHouten, "The Black Family: Myth and Reality," in Arlene Skolnick and Jerome Skolnick, eds., *Family in Transition* (Boston: Little, Brown, 1971), pp. 419-431.

48See the various papers in Bendix and Lipset, *Class, Status,* especially, S. M. Lipset and H. L. Zetterberg, "A Theory of Social Mobility," pp. 561-573; William J. Goode, "Family and Mobility," pp. 582-601.

49See H. Garfinkel, *Studies in Ethnomethodology,* p. 68:

By "cultural dope" I refer to the man-in-the-sociologist's-society who produces the stable features of the society by acting in compliance with the preestablished and legitimate alternatives of action that the common culture provides. The "psychological dope" is the man-in-the-psychologist's-society who produces the stable features of the society by choices among alternative courses of action that are compelled on the grounds of psychiatric biography, conditioning history, and the variables of mental functioning. The common feature of these "models of man" is the fact that courses of common sense rationalities of judgment which involve the person's use of common sense knowledge of social structures over the temporal "succession" of here and now situations are treated as epiphenomenal.

[50] This notion is synonymous with that of cultural dope or judgmental dope, as I understand it, i.e., typical actions and actors of the social scene are represented theoretically without recourse to the actor's own methods of socially organizing their "class" behavior.

[51] Cited by Susan Ervin-Tripp, "Sociolinguistics," Language Behavior Research Laboratory, Working Paper #3, University of California, Berkeley, 1967.

[52] Cited in Susan Ervin-Tripp, "Sociolinguistics," Language Behavior Research Laboratory Report, unpublished manuscript, n.d., University of California, Berkeley.

[53] I am grateful to Harvey Sacks for suggesting this idea as a possible method or formula for doing a degradation by means of categorizing others. From a set of possibly ranked relevant categories applicable to an interactant, one can select one that is noticeably lower than normal appearances would warrant or allow for, and thus by so choosing, the degradation is effected, although its total context as an interchange might qualify the intended sense behind it, e.g., humorous, sarcastic, ironic, serious, etc.

Suggested Readings and Study Questions

This chapter has presented conventional materials in substantive socio-logical areas and stressed innovative and alternative issues that one could ask of those same areas. The study questions can be organized to review the conventional readings referred to in each of the four sections (socialization, work and occupations, deviance, and social stratification) and then to outline a plan for a term project that would examine some aspects of each of these four areas in an alternative framework of sociological reasoning suggested in the text. Each term project might follow the following steps:

1. Review the conventional literature cited in one of the areas, plus any additional reading material suggested in the readings or that is very current. Trace out the major issues in *one* such reading that you select from this bibliography, using your own personal criteria to make the final selection, e.g., a study of juvenile delinquency or of a hospital, etc.

2. Using the approach presented in the text, including all the aspects of making formal descriptions of naturalistic activity and face-to-face communications discussed throughout the text, select a problem around

which the same substantive area could be examined, but which is barely or not at all touched upon in the reading you have selected.

3. Critically assess your reading in terms of the suppositions laid out in chapter 2 of the text. How does your formulation of a problem call upon you to investigate these suppositions in the selected reading? That is, what specifically will you have to study to take these suppositions into account?

4. Using your findings and thinking in these three steps, can you plan a simple study that would take you into the field to investigate your problem in the innovative framework you have adopted? In your plan include the following items:

    a. What type of setting will you study?

    b. Which particular instance of that type can you study in your community?

    c. Can you gain access to it, and if so how? What problems arise in introducing yourself into the setting, what role do you cast yourself into, whom do you contact to initiate the visit?

    d. What kinds of observations do you plan to make? What kinds do you actually make? What kind of data do you collect and in what form? Do you use any data recording instruments (e.g., tape recorder, still camera, movie camera, video-tape recorder, pencil and paper, etc.)? What are some units of interaction and activity that you observe? Can you collect naturally occurring sequences of behavior? Do you have "specimens" of communicative behavior, such as conversation sequences or bodily communications?

    e. How do you assemble your data for analysis? Do you make transcripts from tape recordings, edit movie films, make photos from video tapes, arrange written notes into some order?

    f. What are some of the findings in the application of your problem to your data? What are some formal characteristics of the normal environment you have observed? How do these findings of the formal properties of naturalistic interactions and communication patterns give you deeper insight into the common sense realities of the social worlds they encompass and of the everyday methods the members use to accomplish their routine activities together?

    g. Can you see generalities that might extend to interactions of a similar nature in different types of environments?

    h. Can your findings be applied to change-directed questions about the social organization of the setting?

Indexes*

Author

Adato, Al *109*
Albert, Ethel *97, 182*
Amidon, E. *26*
Austin, J. L. *83*

Baldwin, James *107*
Bales, Robert *136*
Barber, Bernard *194*
Barker, Roger G. *11*
Barnard, Chester *160, 164, 191*
Becker, Howard S. *192*
Bellush, Jewel *194*
Bendix, Reinhard *194*
Berger, C. Q. *48*
Bergson, H. *48*
Birdwhistell *49*
Bittner, E. *16, 17, 118, 130, 156, 176, 179*
Blumer, Herbert *28, 183*
Boas, Maxwell *193*
Bolinger, Dwight *109*
Boll, Eleanor *67-68*
Bossard, James *67-68*
Bottomore, T. B. *194*
Boughey, Howard N., Jr. *48, 130*
Broom, Leonard *135*
Brown, Claude *194*
Bryan, James H. *192*
Bullock, Henry Allen *194*

Casagrande, J. *65-66*
Catlin, George E. C. *10, 11*
Chomsky, Noam *22, 26*
Cicourel, Aaron *ix, 26, 27, 70, 111, 129-130, 176, 177, 179, 192, 194*

Clausen, John *191*
Cohn, Norman *10*
Comte, A. *9*
Conklin, Harold *65-66*
Cressey, Donald D. R. *194*

Dalton, Melville *160-161, 164*
David, Stephen M. *194*
Douglas, Jack *26, 28, 47, 70, 83, 108, 131*
Dreitzel, Hans Peter *ix*
Durkheim, Emil *9-10, 14-17, 28-29*

Elliot, Henry *ix*
Ervin-Tripp, Susan *71, 195*

Firth, Raymond *11*
Fischer, J. A. *64-65*

Gardner, B. *160*
Garfinkel, Harold *viii, ix, 26, 28, 47, 70, 174, 178, 183, 184, 192, 194*
Geller, Allen *193*
Gibbs, Jack P. *192*
Gide, Andre *31-34, 36, 39-45*
Goffman, Erving *ix, 27, 35, 47, 53, 72, 82, 109-110, 130, 164, 173, 192, 194*
Goode, William J. *194*
Gumperz, John *ix, 71*

Hall, Edward T. *49, 53*
Harvey, O. J. *26*
Holt, John *26, 192*
Hughes, H. Stuart *194*
Husserl, E. *48*
Hymes, Dell *71*

Inkeles, Alex *141*

Jaco, E. Gartly *192*

*I wish to thank Rudi Krause for the preparation of this index in its novel tripartite form to facilitate student use.

Concept

Subject